A Behavioral Theory of Elections

A Behavioral Theory of Elections

Jonathan Bendor
Daniel Diermeier
David A. Siegel
Michael M. Ting

PRINCETON UNIVERSITY PRESS
PRINCETON AND OXFORD

Published by Princeton University Press,
41 William Street, Princeton, New Jersey 08540

In the United Kingdom: Princeton University Press,
6 Oxford Street, Woodstock, Oxfordshire OX20 1TW

press.princeton.edu

Library of Congress Cataloging-in-Publication Data

A behavioral theory of elections / Jonathan Bendor ... [et al.].
p. cm.
Includes bibliographical references and index.
ISBN 978-0-691-13506-9 (hardcover: alk. paper)
ISBN 978-0-691-13507-6 (pbk.: alk. paper)
1. Elections. 2. Voting–Psychological aspects.
3. Behaviorism (Political science). I. Bendor, Jonathan B.

JF1001.B414 2011
324.9001'9–dc22 2010048445

British Library Cataloging-in-Publication Data is available

This book has been composed in LucidaBright using TEX
Typeset by T&T Productions Ltd, London

Printed on acid-free paper. ∞

Printed in the United States of America

10 9 8 7 6 5 4 3 2 1

To Josh and Ben: boys when this project began; fine young men when it ended—JB

To Matan and Oran who hadn't been born when this project started—DD

To Mom, Dad, and Charlotte, for their constant support—DS

To Ella—MT

Contents

Acknowledgments

Our greatest thanks go to Dilip Mookherjee, Debraj Ray, and Sunil Kumar, who coauthored the work underlying chapters 3 and 5. We also owe a tremendous debt to our research assistants, Alex Hirsch, Carlo Prato, and Costel Andonie, for their patient and dedicated work.

Many colleagues and students have contributed to our discussions about the book. A partial list includes John Bullock, Alan Gerber, Bob Jackson, Sunil Kumar, David Laitin, Bob Luskin, Adam Meirowitz, Elijah Millgram, Neil Malhotra, Scott Page, Paul Pfleiderer, Ken Shotts, and Joel Sobel.

Over the years various parts of this project have benefited from conference presentations at the annual meetings of the Midwest Political Science Association and the American Political Science Association, the Agent2000 Workshop, the Stanford-Caltech Workshop, and the 7th Annual Wallis Conference. We have also received helpful feedback from seminars at UC Berkeley, Stanford, UC Irvine, UCLA, UNC Chapel Hill, MIT, Carnegie Mellon, the University of Chicago, and the Center for Advanced Study in the Behavioral Sciences.

A Behavioral Theory of Elections

CHAPTER ONE

Bounded Rationality and Elections

> *The capacity of the human mind for formulating and solving complex problems is very small compared with the size of the problems whose solution is required for objectively rational behavior in the real world—or even for a reasonable approximation to such objective rationality.*
>
> —Herbert Simon (1957, p. 198; original emphasis)

> One may speak of grand campaign strategy, rationally formulated and executed with precision, but a great deal of campaign management rests on the hunches that guide day-to-day decisions. The lore of politics includes rules of thumb that are supposed to embody the wisdom of political experience as guides to action.
>
> —V. O. Key (1964, p. 468)

AN INTELLECTUAL REVOLUTION has occurred in political science: the diffusion of rational choice theories. The study of elections has been one of the most receptive subfields. All of its major components—party competition (Downs 1957), turnout (e.g., Riker and Ordeshook 1968), and voters' choices (Downs's spatial-proximity theory; see Merrill and Grofman 1999)—have been strongly influenced by rational choice models.

We think this has been a salutary development for both the discipline in general and the study of elections in particular. The rational choice program has given political science a much-needed degree of intellectual coherence. This new-found coherence connects subfields both by causal claims—we can now more easily see the connections between foreign and domestic politics via, e.g., models of interest groups on trade policy (Grossman and Helpmann 1994)—and by giving us ideas that unify previously disconnected subfields—e.g., problems of credible commitment in governmental borrowing (North and Weingast 1989) and in fights over succession (Powell 2004). Rational choice theories have generated some predictions that have stood up rather well to empirical tests: delegation to congressional committees (Krehbiel 1991), macroeconomic effects of partisan elections (Alesina and Rosenthal 1995), bureaucratic independence (Huber and Shipan 2002), fiscal effects of constitutions (Persson and Tabellini 2003), and cabinet formation and stability in parliamentary democracies (Diermeier, Eraslan, and Merlo 2003; Ansolabehere et al. 2005). Some rational choice predictions, however, have been spectacularly falsified—famously so regarding turnout. Nevertheless, these theories have been wrong in interesting ways and so have stimulated much research.

Further, rational choice theorizing is now flourishing in subfields which once had been terra incognita to rigorous theories of decision making: e.g., the study of democratization (Acemoglu and Robinson 2006) and politics in violence-prone systems (Dal Bó, Dal Bó, and Di Tella 2006). All in all, no research program in political science has been more productive.

But nobody is perfect. Not even a research program.[1] The major weakness of the rational choice program is well known: virtually all models in this program assume that human beings are fully rational, and of course we are not. Some of our cognitive constraints are obvious. For example, our attention is sharply limited: we can consciously think about only one topic at a time. Some are more subtle: e.g., we are sometimes sensitive to small differences in how problems are described (framing effects). But their existence is indisputable.[2] And there is also considerable evidence (e.g., Rabin 1998; Gilovich, Griffin, and Kahneman 2002) that these constraints can significantly affect judgment and choice.

Rational choice theorists have tried a variety of responses to these criticisms of bounded rationality. For a long time they tended to be dismissive (famously, Friedman 1953), but as experimental evidence about cognitive constraints accumulated, a certain unease set in.[3] Most scholars working in the rational choice program know about the obvious cognitive constraints, and many have read the critiques of Simon and of Tversky and Kahneman and their coauthors. Indeed, today enough scholars in the home disciplines of the rational choice program, economics and game theory, take bounded

---

[1] We are using the term "research program" in Lakatos's sense (1970): roughly speaking, it is a sequence of theories united by a few core premises, e.g., about the rationality of decision makers. Thus, in Lakatos's view there is a hierarchy of symbolic formulations: a single research program contains multiple theories, and a single (often verbal) theory can generate multiple (often formal) models. Hence, competition between a specific rational choice and a specific bounded rationality model and competition between their parent research programs are not equivalent, though they are related.

[2] Psychologists even have accurate quantitative estimates of certain cognitive constraints: e.g., ordinary untrained working memory can only handle four to seven bits of information before getting overloaded (Miller 1956; Cowan 2000).

[3] See also Green and Shapiro (1994) for a critique of rational choice theories that is not confined to the cognitive foundations of the research program, and see Friedman (1996) for rebuttals.

rationality sufficiently seriously so that new subfields—behavioral economics (Camerer, Loewenstein, and Rabin 2004), behavioral game theory (Camerer 2003), and behavioral finance (Barberis and Thaler 2003)—are now flourishing.[4] (As evidence for this claim, one needs only to sample a few mainstream journals in economics and game theory and count the number of papers presenting behavioral models.) Things have heated up quite a bit in the home disciplines of rational choice theory—more so, it seems, than in political science. This is ironic, given that two of the most important behavioral theorists, Herbert Simon and James March, were trained in political science and, as indicated by the many disciplinary awards they have won, we still claim them as ours. As it is said, colonials can be more royalist than the king.

A change is overdue. The issues raised by the bounded rationality program—the impact of cognitive constraints on behavior—are as pertinent to politics as they are to markets, perhaps even more so. This is evident in the subfield of elections. Indeed, it is in this domain that the rational choice program has encountered one of its most spectacular anomalies: turnout. The problem is well known: as Fiorina put it, "Is turnout the paradox that ate rational choice theory?" (1990, p. 334). Canonical rational choice models of turnout, whether decision-theoretic or game-theoretic, predict very low turnout in equilibrium: if participation were intense, then the chance of being pivotal would be very small, so voting would be suboptimal for most people. Yet, of course, many citizens *do* vote: even in the largest electorates, participation rates are at least 50 percent in national elections. The difference between prediction and observation passes the ocular test: one needs only to eyeball the data to see the anomaly. Of course, as is often the case with anomalies, eminent scholars have tried to solve the problem. The best-known attempts

[4] Although it would be interesting to explore the relation between behavioral economics and bounded rationality, we have a tighter focus in this book: to develop a behavioral theory of elections. Thus, two short points must suffice. First, behavioral economics and bounded rationality are similar in significant ways. Both emphasize the cognitive foundations of social science theories; both rely on evidence and theories drawn from psychology. Second, they exhibit some subtle differences. Behavioral economics—especially work based on the heuristics-and-biases approach (Gilovich, Griffin, and Kahneman 2002)—often focuses on how decision makers make mistakes even in simple task environments. (See, however, Gilovich and Griffin (2002) and Griffin and Kahneman (2003) for a different perspective.) In contrast, work in the bounded rationality program is more likely to emphasize the adaptive qualities of human judgment and choice. This is especially true of the fast-and-frugal approach to the study of heuristics; see Gigerenzer and Goldstein (1996) and Gigerenzer (2004). For detailed discussions of these issues, see Samuels, Stich, and Bishop (2002), Samuels, Stich, and Faucher (2004), and Bendor (forthcoming).

(e.g., Riker and Ordeshook 1968) focus on voters' utility functions, positing that the costs of voting are negative either because of an internalized duty to vote or the pleasures of the process. Doubtless there is something to these claims. But as both rational choice modelers and their critics (e.g., Green and Shapiro 1994) have noted, one can "explain" virtually any behavior if one can freely make ad hoc assumptions about agents' utility functions. The victory—the purported solution to the anomaly—then seems hollow. Accordingly, there are craft norms that impose a high burden of proof against such approaches. Hence many scholars, rational choice theorists and others, are dissatisfied by such explanations and believe that a major anomaly persists regarding turnout.

The scientific situation is somewhat different for the two other components of elections. The study of party competition is probably in the best shape, empirically speaking, of the three components. Although the most famous prediction of rational choice models—that in two-party competition the unique equilibrium is for both parties to espouse the median voter's ideal point—has met with empirical difficulties (Levitt 1996; Stokes 1999; Ansolabehere, Snyder, and Stewart 2001), the gap between prediction and evidence is much smaller than it is in turnout. Moreover, the rational choice program has generated quite a few models in which the parties differ in equilibrium (Wittman 1983; Calvert 1985; Roemer 2001). Further, the Downsian tradition has been remarkably fruitful in the study of party competition. Even scholars (e.g., Wittman 1983) who develop models based on different premises[5] acknowledge the impact of Downs's formulation. The study of party competition clearly owes a great deal to *An Electoral Theory of Democracy* and other work in that tradition.

Rational choice models of voters' decision making are in between turnout and party competition. On the one hand, there's no 800-pound gorilla of an anomaly dominating the picture. But there is a sharp tension between the premises of most rational choice models of voting and the empirical findings of political psychologists. The former typically presume that voters have coherent ideologies in their heads and know a lot about politics: e.g., they know where

[5] Calvert-Wittman–type models presume that candidates are not merely seeking office but also have policy preferences, just as ordinary citizens do. Since one of Downs's central ideas is that parties compete in order to win office, this is a nontrivial departure. For a thorough analysis of the differences between models of opportunist versus ideological candidates, see Roemer (2001). See also the literature on citizen candidate models, e.g., Osborne and Slivinski (1996) and Besley and Coate (1997).

candidates stand in the (commonly constructed) ideological space[6] or at least have unbiased estimates of these positions[7]—claims that are vigorously disputed by scholars studying voter behavior (e.g., Delli Carpini and Keeter 1996; Kinder 1998).

Thus, rational choice theories of elections exhibit a mixed scientific picture: a big anomaly regarding turnout, a qualified success regarding party competition, and some serious issues about voters' decision making.

For the most part, political scientists have criticized rational choice electoral models only on empirical grounds. Although verisimilitude is tremendously important, the failure to construct alternative formulations has allowed rational choice scholars to use the defense "you can't beat something with nothing" (e.g., Shepsle 1996, p. 217). This defense has some merit: it describes a sociopsychological tendency of scholars and arguably makes sense as a normative decision rule. Our goal is to facilitate debate about theories by providing such an alternative formulation.

But because bounded rationality is a research program, it contains a set of alternative formulations, not a single theory or model. Indeed, the program now offers quite a few approaches that address a wide array of topics (Conlisk 1996; Rabin 1998; Mullainathan and Thaler 2000; Camerer 2003). To situate our approach in this collective endeavor, we briefly discuss two major topics: framing and heuristics (e.g., satisficing). As we will see, both topics are central to our theory.

1.1 Framing and Representations

A decision maker's *frame* is his or her mental representation of the choice problem he or she faces.[8] Tversky and Kahneman (1986) pioneered the study of framing in behavioral decision theory. In their work, framing has mainly been associated with just one approach:

[6] For an early pointed criticism of the Downsian assumption that voters in an electorate share the same mental model of campaigns and locate parties in this homogeneous cognitive construction, see Stokes (1963).

[7] And because processing probabilistic information is cognitively more difficult than processing deterministic data, models which assume that voters know party platforms only probabilistically trade greater realism in one respect (what voters know) in exchange for less realism in another (how they process information).

[8] In the cognitive sciences the term "representation" is much more common than the term "frame." This terminological difference may have inhibited theoretical unification—a pity, given the surprisingly weak connections between behavioral decision theory and cognitive psychology (Weber and Johnson 2009).

Prospect Theory. But cognitive psychologists use the notion of representation much more widely: "Virtually all theories about cognition are based on hypotheses that posit mental representations as carriers of information" (Markman and Dietrich 2000, p. 138–139; see also Stufflebeam 1999, p. 636–637). Indeed, in standard computational theories of mind, thinking is seen as operations performed on a sequence of representations (Billman 1999; Tversky 2005). In particular, a computational theory—as opposed to an "as if" formulation (Friedman 1953)—of optimal choice posits that a decision maker constructs a mental representation of her choice problem, which includes her feasible alternatives and their payoffs, and executes an operation of value maximization on this representation.[9]

Prospect Theory assumes that decision makers represent choice problems in a way that differs sharply from the representation implied by a computational version of classical decision theory. Whereas the latter assumes that alternatives and their payoffs are compared only to each other, the former posits that agents compare alternatives to a *reference point*—an agent's internal standard. (Most applications of Prospect Theory presume that the reference point is the decision maker's status quo endowment. However, a close reading of Kahneman and Tversky (1979) reveals that this is not part of the theory's axiomatic core; it is an auxiliary hypothesis.) This difference in hypothesized mental representations is fundamental: indeed, Prospect Theory's other two hypotheses about preferences—that people are risk-averse regarding gains and risk seeking regarding losses and that they are loss-averse—would not make sense without the first axiom and its central concept of a reference point.

More generally, one of Tversky and Kahneman's main findings, that people often violate the classical principle of *descriptive invariance*, follows almost immediately from the centrality of mental representations in most theories of information processing in cognitive psychology. It would be astonishing if agents covered by this class of theories satisfied descriptive invariance. These formulations (e.g.,

[9] It is no accident that classical utility theory posits (in effect) that alternatives are represented by a preference ordering. This representation makes the critical operation—select the optimal option—relatively easy. As cognitive psychologists have argued for a few decades, a specific type of representation facilitates certain operations while hindering others (Novick and Bassok 2005). And effects on mental operations can impact behavior. In particular, there is strong experimental evidence that the representation of options—whether "multiple options are presented simultaneously and evaluated comparatively, or ... options are presented in isolation and evaluated separately" (Hsee et al. 1999, p. 576)—significantly influences choice behavior. Because pure retrospective voting involves separate evaluation, whereas classical Downsian voting involves joint evaluations, this finding bears directly on the study of elections.

Simon 1999) usually presume that people solve problems by transforming one representation (e.g., the initial state) into another one (e.g., the goal state) by a sequence of operations. Although there are many computational theories of mind which allow for many different kinds of representations (Markman 1999; Markman and Dietrich 2000), this perspective is not vacuous: in particular, any theory in this class assumes that people perform operations on representations. Hence it follows, for example, that all else equal, the more operations that are required in order to solve a problem, the more time it takes to do the job (Tversky 2005). This point is familiar to us in our capacities as teachers: when we write up exam questions, we know that we can vary a problem's difficulty by describing it in different ways, so that solving it requires different numbers of operations.[10] Thus, such theories imply that for humans the representation of 492×137 is *not* cognitively equivalent to the representation of 67,404, even though the former implies the latter, and both of these are significantly different from the Latin numeral representation $\overline{\text{LXVII}}\text{CDIV}$.

In contrast, an agent who is logically omniscient (Stalnaker 1999) would immediately grasp *all* the information implied by a representation. Hence, such an entity would not be subject to framing effects. Of course, positing that any human is logically omniscient directly contradicts the principle of bounded rationality articulated in the Simon quote that began this chapter.

Prospect Theory is usually discussed as an alternative to rational choice modeling, but it is worthwhile pausing for a moment in order to note three ways in which Prospect Theory and classical decision theory overlap. First, both are forward-looking: e.g., in Prospect Theory, it is *anticipated* payoffs that are compared to the agent's reference point. Second, choices based on reference points involve value maximization. By now, however, this should cause no confusion. Maximization is an operation in the context of a representation. As framing experiments (Kahneman and Tversky 2000, passim) have repeatedly shown, if two decision makers use sufficiently different representations, their behavior will differ in some choice contexts even if they are using similar operations, i.e., both are maximizing some kind of objective function. Third, Prospect Theory assumes that the agent is following an *algorithm* that completely specifies

---

[10] The now-classic experiment by Shepard and Metzler (1971) beautifully demonstrated this property. It showed that the time it takes subjects to figure out whether a pair of three-dimensional objects, depicted by pictures, are equivalent is linear *in the degrees of angular rotation required to make the two pictures look the same.*

his or her behavior for the specified choice problem. This use of a complete plan is another feature shared by classical decision theory.

So, while the idea of framing is alien to the rational choice program, the concept of selecting complete plans of action by solving a forward-looking maximization problem is common, even though what is maximized, the objective function, differs between the approaches. In this sense Prospect Theory is quite similar to rational choice formulations. But not all behavioral theories presume that agents have complete action plans in their minds, especially when they confront complex problems. This takes us to the second topic: the notion of heuristics.

1.2 Heuristics

Although there is no unique agreed-upon definition in the cognitive sciences, a *heuristic* is generally presumed to have at least one of the following properties. (1) In general, heuristics are not complete plans: in all but the simplest problems they do not specify what to do under all possible contingencies.[11] (2) There is no guarantee that a heuristic will find a solution. Instead, heuristics promise only that they will increase the chance of discovering a solution (Pólya 1945). The two properties are related: if a plan is silent about what action to take if a certain contingency arises, then obviously it cannot guarantee optimality. (For example, the dramatic collapse of the economy in the middle of the 2008 presidential race made both parties improvise; John McCain's surprising move—reinjecting himself into the Senate's debate on bailouts—was widely seen as a blunder.) As we will see in chapter 2, however, incompleteness is only one cause of suboptimality.

More recently, it has been argued that heuristic reasoning is often rapid and automatic, per dual-process theories of mind (Stanovich and West 2000; see, however, Moshman 2000 and Evans 2008). This claim is now prominent in the heuristic-and-biases approach pioneered by Kahneman and Tversky (e.g., Kahneman and Frederick 2002). But automaticity is not universally regarded as a defining feature of heuristics. Some psychologists who study heuristics and biases argue that some rules of thumb can be deliberately used (Gilovich and Griffin 2002; Kahneman 2002). Scholars adhering to

[11] A *set* of heuristics may form a complete plan in somewhat complex situations. For example, in the repeated Prisoner's Dilemma the heuristics of niceness (don't defect first) and reciprocity (do today what your partner did yesterday) together are a complete strategy: tit for tat (Axelrod 1984).

the fast-and-frugal approach to heuristics not infrequently see adaptive rules as consciously deployed (Gigerenzer and Goldstein 1996, p. 666; Gigerenzer 2004). And when heuristics are socially transmitted, whether in professional communities, e.g., of mathematicians (Pólya 1945) or computer scientists (Silver 2004), or within lay communities, then these rules of thumb are obviously explicit. (For example, the common saying "If it ain't broke, don't fix it" is an explicit—and quite accurate—statement of satisficing.) Hence, in this volume we do not require heuristics to be implicit, though we do not exclude this possibility.

The most famous heuristic in political science is satisficing. In the original context of search problems (Simon 1955, 1956), satisficing was a stopping rule: terminate search once an acceptable solution is found. As is evident from the statement of the rule, the notion of an acceptable alternative is crucial. Simon's stipulation was straightforward: an option is acceptable if its payoff is at least as good as the agent's *aspiration level* (Lewin et al., 1944). In turn, an aspiration level is a quality threshold or cutoff which partitions options into two mutually exclusive subsets: satisfactory versus unsatisfactory alternatives. Thus, it is evident that the satisficing heuristic shares an important aspect of Prospect Theory's premise about the representation of choice problems: each posits quality or payoff thresholds that partition options into two subsets—essentially, good ones and bad ones.[12] The similarity is so strong that the terms "aspiration level" and "reference point" appear to be synonyms (Bendor, forthcoming). The only significant difference arises from their original use in different kinds of choice contexts: static for Prospect Theory and dynamic for satisficing.

In general, satisficing is not a complete plan. The reason is simple. Although the heuristic pins down what to do if the solution in hand is satisfactory (keep it), it says little about what to do if the option in hand isn't okay, beyond "look for new ones." This injunction may suffice for simple problems—e.g., new options are tickets in an urn and search simply involves randomly drawing from the urn—but in realistically complicated choice contexts "look for new ones" is merely the start of a complex process of policy design (Kingdon 1984).

There is one important class of problems for which satisficing constitutes a complete plan: the agent has only two options. In such situations, dissatisfaction with the current option can lead in only one direction: the decision maker must take up the other alternative.

---

[12] Note, however, that under satisficing, agents do not solve maximization problems, unlike Prospect Theory.

Because these problems—now called two-armed bandits—are simple enough to help us gain valuable intuition about satisficing and related forms of imperfectly rational adaptation, we will use them as a running example throughout the book.

Outside of this class, however, positing that a decision maker satisfices typically does not yield precise predictions when outcomes are unsatisfactory. Obviously, this is methodologically undesirable. Hence, in order to make our predictions more precise, in models in which agents have more than two options, we usually add auxiliary assumptions about how a dissatisfied agent searches.

In sum, satisficing is an often incomplete heuristic that encodes two key properties: (1) a choice representation in which an aspiration level is central; (2) an operation or decision rule—keep (or keep doing) satisfactory alternatives—that follows naturally from the representation. By generalizing property (2), we construct the class of heuristics that form the core of all the models in this book. The generalization is based on the observation that in the context of repeated choices, satisficing is simply the extreme case of psychological learning theory's *Law of Effect* (Thorndike 1898). This law—probably "the most important principle in learning theory" (Hilgard and Bower 1966, p. 481)—states that organisms tend to become more disposed to try alternatives that generate positive feedback and less likely to try those associated with negative feedback.[13]

The satisficing heuristic is a special case, as it assumes that the reaction to positive feedback is deterministic: if one tries an option today and finds it satisfactory, then one will try it again tomorrow

[13] Originally, many learning theorists in psychology thought that reinforcements could be identified objectively; observers would not need to make claims about subjects' mental states. This view was important to early learning theorists because it was integral to behaviorism, the dominant methodological posture of the time. But the search for objectively defined reinforcers failed: too much evidence conflicted with the idea (Flaherty 1996, pp. 11–16). Hilgard and Bower explain how the thinking of learning theorists evolved: "... in studies of learned performance, a given reward for a response may have either an incremental or decremental effect upon performance depending on what reward the subject expects or on the range of alternative rewards the subject has been receiving in similar contexts. If a person is expecting a one cent payoff, getting ten cents is going to be positively rewarding; if he is expecting a dollar payoff, the ten cents is frustrating and may have the effect of a punishment. Effects such as these have been observed with animals as well as men.... They can all be interpreted in terms of Helson's concept of adaptation level. The rewards obtained over the past trials in a given context determine, by some averaging process, an internal standard or norm called the adaptation level. *Each new reward is evaluated in relation to this adaptation level, having a positive influence on behavior if it is above the norm, a negative influence if it is below*" (1966, p. 486; emphasis added).

with certainty. Since relaxing an assumption is an armchair method of increasing the empirical plausibility of a theory, whenever possible we use the more general assumption described by the Law of Effect. (Sometimes we fall back on the specific case of satisficing in order to make a model more tractable.)

Note also how satisficing and related types of adaptation relate to the literature on framing and mental representations. We take from this literature the importance of two points: one general; the other, specific. The general point is that our theories of choice should take decision makers' problem representations into account; the specific, that reference points are often a significant part of these representations. Thus, because the notion of reference point is central to Prospect Theory, there are important similarities between that approach and formulations based on satisficing. However, we must remember that there are also significant differences: in particular, in contrast to Prospect Theory, agents in satisficing theories do not solve maximization problems; they adapt their behavior according the Law of Effect. Moreover, although their adjustment is shaped by reference points, these internal standards themselves adapt to experience in ways that are closer in spirit to Simon's original formulation than they are to canonical Prospect Theory. It is now time to examine this family of adaptive rules more closely.

1.2.1 Aspiration-based Adaptation

As we define them, *aspiration-based adaptive rules* (ABARs) have two key components: a representational property and an operation linked closely to that mental representation. The representational feature is a threshold, variously called an aspiration level or a reference point, that partitions all possible payoffs into two subsets: good and bad. Since we are examining mental representations, an agent's threshold is not directly observable. Instead, we infer its existence based on observed behavior: e.g., preference reversals (Slovic and Lichtenstein 1983; Hsee et al. 1999).[14]

The procedural property, which is probabilistic, is based on the Law of Effect: the organism compares payoffs to its reference

[14] That aspiration levels are not directly observable would be regarded as a methodological defect by behaviorists, who thought that theoretical concepts were unscientific. Today, however, virtually all social and cognitive scientists freely use beliefs, preferences, attitudes, and other unobservable mentalistic constructs in their theories.

point and becomes more inclined to try alternatives associated with good payoffs and less likely to try those associated with bad ones. Together, these properties identify a form of trial-and-error learning.[15]

Chapter 2 gives a precise mathematical definition of these properties and the corresponding class of adaptive rules. For now the main point to keep in mind is that both properties identify *classes* of representations and operations, respectively. Hence, our subsequent results about ABARs include many adaptive rules in addition to satisficing. Many of these rules are considered by cognitive scientists to be general heuristics that can be deployed in a wide array of situations—including, importantly, ill-defined problems. However, domain-general heuristics tend to be weak procedures (Newell 1969) that can often fall well short of optimality, even when they constitute complete plans.[16]

For the most part we focus on pure ABARs, i.e., those in which decision makers compare the payoffs of alternatives only to their reference points. It is possible to construct coherent hybrid rules, which compare alternatives to each other as well to aspirations. Indeed, one such rule already exists: Prospect Theory's value maximization procedure, which operates on a representation built on a reference point, makes it a hybrid. In a few places we show that our results are robust, i.e., hold for hybrid rules.

1.3 Aspiration-based Adaptation and Bounded Rationality

ABARs do not exhaust the set of bounded rationality theories. They are just one family of theories in the broader research program.[17] Needless to say, we believe that it is a particularly important class of theories.

That said, to ensure that readers grasp the difference between ABARs and the larger research program, we now spell out what we see as the heart of the latter, and how this programmatic core relates to ABARs. Our starting point is the sentence from Simon's *Mod-*

[15] We use the terms "adaptation" and "learning" interchangeably throughout this book.

[16] For an in-depth examination of the performance profile of the satisficing heuristic, see Bendor, Kumar, and Siegel (2009).

[17] An even more egregious error is to conflate *one* member of this family, satisficing, with the entire bounded rationality program. This is, unfortunately, a common mistake.

els of Man that opened this chapter. We unpack his statement into three claims or programmatic premises (Bendor 2001). First, humans are cognitively constrained in many ways, e.g., there are limits on short-term memory and on attention. Second, these mental properties significantly affect decision making. Third, the impact of these information-processing constraints increases with the difficulty of the choice problem that a person faces.

These premises can help us understand the relation between the research programs of bounded rationality and rational choice. To use Simon's metaphor, together "the structure of task environments and the computational capabilities of the actor" act as "a scissors [with] two blades" (1990, p. 7): theories of bounded rationality have cutting power, compared to theories of complete rationality, only when both blades operate (Bendor 2003, p. 435). Cognitive constraints "show through" only when a problem is sufficiently difficult (Simon 1996). If a problem is simple enough so that a person can easily maximize expected utility, then we expect this to happen. Consider, for example, a wealthy citizen repeatedly facing a choice between two parties in a general election. Suppose further that the citizen cares only about which party offers him the lower top tax rate, nothing else. In this case voting is easy and citizens are very likely to vote optimally given their objectives.

If a reader thinks that even such problems might be too difficult for some citizens, consider the proverbial $20 bill lying on the sidewalk right in front of a pedestrian. The natural problem representation and the corresponding operation—"There is $20 on the sidewalk. Either I bend over and pick it up or I don't bother"—together imply that the pedestrian will maximize expected utility.

Thus, the claim that people will optimize when the choice problem is sufficiently easy is very plausible. We might disagree about what *is* sufficiently easy, just as might a group of teachers who are designing a test that should contain problems simple enough for even weak students to solve. [Hence, figuring out what makes certain problems hard for most humans (e.g., Kotovsky, Hayes, and Simon 1985) is an important topic in the research program of bounded rationality.] But the general point is clear.

Since theories of aspiration-based adaptation belong to the bounded rationality research program, it follows that the same point holds for ABARs: when choice problems are sufficiently easy, we do not expect people to use these rules or their associated mental representations. Indeed, thinking about cognitive constraints can help us generate hypotheses about situations in which aspirations will *not* be part of an agent's activated problem representation.[18] Because constructing new representations is effortful and because relevant cognitive resources are constrained, people sometimes accept problem representations offered by others: politicians, advertisers, experimenters, and the like.

How one person influences another person's choice representation might be viewed as manipulation—some critics of framing studies adopt this perspective—but some choice representations may be offered to decision makers quite innocuously yet can still have an impact. Further, that impact may vary based on the context of the choice problem. Consider a diner who enters a restaurant. A typical diner perusing a long menu in a fancy restaurant might entertain a wide variety of options and might consider issues of nutrition, taste, recent dining history, and so on. This is a hard decision; hence all diners often use heuristics (I'll have the usual, I'll have what she's having, I always order seafood in a restaurant on the coast, etc.) to deal with this problem. A waiter recommending both the New York steak and the sole Florentine provides useful information that may inform the diner's heuristics but likely nothing more. For example, a diner that uses some version of an ABAR may usually select the same dish as long as it is prepared to his satisfaction but may occasionally experiment with a new dish.

Now consider a diner who needs to make a theater performance an hour later. For that diner the choice problem is much simpler: appeasing her hunger as quickly as possible is her overriding goal; all other considerations are secondary. When the waiter tells her about, say, the steak and the sole—the only two dishes which can be prepared within her time frame—this diner is perfectly willing to act on the waiter's recommendations, as doing so simplifies her choice problem: she no longer needs to create a problem representation—one is provided by the waiter—and most options have been eliminated to boot! For this much-simplified problem, heuristics are

[18] If aspirations are not part of an evoked representation, it does not follow that the activated representation will lend itself naturally to an operation of value maximization. However, scholars who study problem solving do offer a related (ordinal) hypothesis. As noted, many aspiration-based heuristics are general—hence weak—rules. Newell (1969) and Simon (1999) have argued that people use such heuristics when they lack more powerful domain-specific knowledge and problem-solving methods or when they do not recognize the problem as belonging to such a domain. But if a decision maker is an expert in the given domain, she or he may have recourse to a domain-specific heuristic that is more powerful than a domain-general ABAR. Nevertheless, if the problem is of chess like complexity, it may not be known whether the powerful domain-specific heuristic is optimal (Silver 2008), and its associated representation may not be the canonical one of classical decision theory.

unnecessary. She can easily maximize her utility by explicitly comparing steak versus fish. Note that, given this problem representation, our diner will probably be able to rank-order the steak versus the sole in terms of her preferences (suppose she prefers a lighter dish before attending the theater)—exactly the procedure mandated by classical decision theory.[19] Once again we see Simon's scissors at work: the cutting power of theories of bounded rationality depend on the relation between the difficulty of the choice problem and the decision maker's cognitive capacities.[20]

Note, however, that this dinner example involves *myopic* utility maximization. As represented, the problem turns on an immediate choice between two entrees; implicitly, the consequences are limited to the immediate future, ignoring considerations such as the long-term health effects of diet. If the future were seriously engaged, as in the choice of a mate or a career or whether to challenge a well-entrenched incumbent, the problem would be much harder.

In sum, people can represent complex problems in simple ways. This process, called "editing" by March (1994), is a major way of cutting a complicated situation down to cognitively manageable proportions. Because this point is both important and somewhat subtle, it is worthwhile examining it carefully in contexts that are substantively relevant to this book. We will look at voters first and politicians second.

---

[19] Whether this is analogous to a voter's choice between two candidates is an interesting but open question. But Sniderman (2000) is surely right in asserting that choice in a two-party system is cognitively simpler than it is in a multiparty one.

[20] For this reason some behavioral decision theorists (e.g., Bettman, Luce, and Payne 1998, p. 191) have argued that people facing a complex choice might initially screen alternatives by testing them against a set of independent constraints. This process is brutal and swift partly because it is *noncompensatory*: if an alternative does not satisfy a constraint (e.g., does the job candidate have a master's degree in statistics?), then reject it out of hand. Trade-offs are not considered at this point. Having winnowed the number of options down to a manageable number, the decision makers would then engage in the more challenging task of comparing alternatives against each other, weighing their pluses and minuses. This involves *compensatory* decision rules, including classical ones such as maximizing utility in multiattribute choice problems. Hence, behavioral decision theorists are arguing that the same person, in the same (extended) choice process, may in one phase compare alternatives to an aspiration level and later compare them directly to each other. Although this book focuses on the former process, we believe that most of our results would continue to hold if our agents used both choice modes, i.e., compared options both to an aspiration point and directly to each other. (To buttress this claim, we show that two propositions—2.3 and 5.7—are robust in exactly this sense.)

1.3.1 Voters and Turnout

Scholarly debates on the choice-theoretic foundations of turnout often focus on whether voters are rational. This, in turn, typically turns into a discussion of whether they are optimizing in light of anticipated consequences of their actions. This, however, overlooks a key difference *within* the rational choice program between decision-theoretic (e.g., Riker and Ordeshook 1968) and game-theoretic formulations (e.g., Feddersen and Pesendorfer 1996). Under both types of theories citizens maximize utility, but they make significantly different assumptions about people's mental representations.

In standard decision theories (of two-party races) such as Riker and Ordeshook's, a focal citizen estimates a probability of being pivotal and votes if and only if that probability times the value of his or her preferred party winning exceeds his or her private cost of voting. This is not a very difficult problem, and we suspect that it is within the cognitive capacities of most adults. Perhaps the most difficult part is estimating the probability of being pivotal, but in the United States and many other affluent democracies, polls usually provide a reasonable approximation. And once a citizen has estimates of the three parameters, applying the optimization rule itself is straightforward, involving only one multiplication and then a comparison of two magnitudes.

The cognitive operations are easy because the initial representation has a crucial feature: *the probability of being pivotal is treated as an exogenously fixed parameter.* But as game theorists have recognized for some time, if citizens were fully rational and this was common knowledge,[21] then pivot probabilities would be endogenously determined, i.e., in equilibrium (e.g., Palfrey and Rosenthal 1983, 1985). Hence in order to implement the internal logic of the rational choice research program, most scholars working inside this program have turned to game-theoretic models (Feddersen 2004).

The significance of this shift, ignored by most critics of rational choice theories of voting, is huge. As noted, decision-theoretic models assume that voters use a mental representation that imposes quite modest cognitive demands. In contrast, in a game-theoretic model a focal citizen represents the situation as involving thousands or even millions of rational peers who are simultaneously making participation decisions. Hence, here optimization entails the choice of an alternative that is only conditionally best: it depends on the actions of other agents who are simultaneously trying to solve

[21] In a two-person game, a property of player A is common knowledge if player B knows it, A knows B knows it, and so on ad infinitum.

the same complicated problem. To paraphrase Converse, the game-theoretic representation is "orders of magnitudes of orders of magnitudes" (Converse 1990, p. 373) harder than the decision-theoretic one. Indeed, the variation in the difficulty of these problem representations probably swamps the variation in voters' sophistication: we believe that almost no one, apart from a handful of brilliant game theorists, can use the game-theoretic representation to think about the situation; still less can they use it as a basis for optimization.[22] Note that, from the perspective of the rational choice program, the game-theoretic representation is "correct"; it is necessitated by that program's premises. But, outside the rational choice framework, one may very well want to posit that the actual representation in voters' minds may be closer to the simple decision-theoretic frame which would simplify the decision-making problem significantly. Which representation to use would then be an empirical question.

Similar issues occur in the debate over voters' motivations. This is normally discussed in terms of whether citizens are purely egoistic or partly altruistic. Although this issue is obviously important, it is orthogonal to the competition between the research programs of rational choice and bounded rationality. As in the case of purely self-interested voters, moral motivations can be represented in very different ways, some much more cognitively demanding than others. As some moral philosophers (e.g., Braybrooke 2004) have pointed out, utilitarianism is mentally demanding, a claim that has been supported experimentally (Greene et al. 2008). In contrast, certain kinds of nonconsequentialist moral considerations can greatly simplify the choice problem. For example, if voters simply follow a strict moral norm of participating in elections, perhaps out of a sense of duty, then one needn't worry about the chance that one will be pivotal.[23] Similarly, the cognitively simple decision-theoretic framework presented by Riker and Ordeshook can

[22] Indeed, many rational choice theorists (see the contributions in Friedman 1996) argue that game-theoretic models make no claims about how agents optimize. They are to be interpreted "as if" and judged only by their empirical implications. A key problem for this approach is that many of these empirical implications are not well supported by the data, whether at the aggregate level of, e.g., turnout levels or in laboratory studies, e.g., in the context of framing effects or the inability of the subject to reason probabilistically. (A second issue concerns the explanatory power of theories given an "as if" interpretation. This, however, involves an unsettled debate—between instrumentalist and realist philosophies of science—that we cannot examine here.)

[23] Students of modernization have long understood that obeying unconditional religious rules because they are prescribed by a sacred text is cognitively simple. Indeed, the critique of "the oversocialized conception of man" (Wrong 1961) was partly a rejection of the Parsonian view of people as rule-following automata.

be easily extended by adding the (in)famous "d-term" representing the utility component of doing one's duty. Feddersen and Sandroni (2006), on the other hand, provide a (nonstandard) game-theoretic treatment of the duty to vote derived from a rule-utilitarian framework. Their analysis reveals that if citizens were game-theoretically rational, doing one's civic duty involves significant complexities.[24] More generally, whether a person's mental representation of turnout is morally charged has no direct bearing on the fundamental differences between the two big research programs considered here. Both moral and selfish motivations are consistent with both simple and complex representations.

Thus, the main claim of the bounded rationality program is not that people satisfice instead of optimize. Rather, it is that cognitive constraints will bind *somewhere* in choice processes when tasks are sufficiently complex—in mental representations if not in operations on those representations (Simon 1979a, p. 498; Bendor 2003).

1.3.2 Voters Okay, but Politicians...?

Because most voters are political amateurs, hypothesizing that they use adaptive heuristics such as satisficing is quite plausible. Candidates and their staffs, on the other hand, are professionals. Many have been politically active for decades. And whereas amateurs may satisfice, professionals optimize. Or so it is believed.[25]

But the slogan "Amateurs satisfice; professionals optimize" reflects the same serious misunderstanding of the core notion of bounded rationality discussed above.[26] We follow Simon in stressing that bounded rationality is a *relation* between a decision maker's mental abilities and the complexity of the problem she or he faces. It is *not* a claim about the brilliance or stupidity of human beings, independent of their task environments. It is common to miss this central

---

[24] In particular, Feddersen and Sandroni observe that, if going to the polls involves any costs—e.g., driving or lost time—a duty to vote has a strange property: it is inefficient and a fortiori inconsistent with utilitarian criteria. This holds because any election outcome can be reached by either exactly one citizen voting (producing a winning candidate) or exactly two doing so (one from each faction, generating a tie). Hence, mass turnout wastes effort.

[25] This is not just casual hallway talk. It is a standard claim made in economics: see, e.g., Rabin's description of the conventional wisdom (1998, p. 31). Sometimes the claim, appropriately and carefully stated, has been supported by data (Feng and Seasholes 2005); sometimes not. [See Barberis and Thaler (2003) for a review of the findings in financial economics.] Presently this is an open question and fundamentally an empirical one. To our knowledge it hasn't been subjected to the kind of careful empirical scrutiny applied to equivalent behavior of, say, investors.

[26] The rest of this paragraph is from Bendor (2003).

point and to reify the notion of bounded rationality into an assertion about the absolute capacities of human beings, whether novices or experts. The fundamental notion is cognitive limits, and as is true of any constraint, cognitive constraints matter—affect behavior—only if they bind. *And per Simon's scissors, whether they bind depends vitally on the demands placed on decision makers by the problem at hand.* Thus, any analysis that purports to fall into this research program yet focuses only on the agent's properties is incomplete.

Hence, whether a specialist optimizes—more precisely, whether cognitive constraints bind—depends vitally on the difficulty of the task at hand. Of course, all else equal, we expect a specialist to outperform an amateur. (If that usually didn't happen, then we would suspect that the profession in question was bogus.) But "all else equal" includes problem difficulty. If the task facing a professional is much harder than that facing an amateur, the former might be just as cognitively constrained as the latter. In other words, while children quickly learn to play tic-tac-toe optimally, even grandmasters do not play chess optimally (Simon and Schaeffer 1992).

Running effective campaigns in large jurisdictions is a hard problem. It is not merely a one-shot selection of a point (i.e., a platform) in a low-dimensional space, as Key's description makes clear.

> A presidential campaign ... may be conducted in accord with a broad strategy or plan of action. That general plan may fix the principal propaganda themes to be emphasized in the campaign, define the chief targets within the electorate, schedule the peak output of effort, and set other broad features of the campaign. The strategic scheme then provides a framework to guide the detailed work of the party propagandists, the labors of the speech writers, the decisions of those who parcel out the campaign funds, the schedulers of the itineraries of the principal orators, and the day-to-day endeavors of all the subordinate units of campaign organization.
>
> *Often the outlines of a campaign strategy are scarcely visible amidst the confusion of the campaign* and, indeed, campaigns often rest on only the sketchiest of plans. The preparation of a reasoned and comprehensive strategy requires more of a disposition to think through the campaign in its broad outlines than often exists around a national headquarters. Once the plan is made, its execution requires organization sufficiently articulated to respond to general direction in accord with the plan, a requisite that is not always met. And even when a campaign is blueprinted in advance, *a flexibility must be built into it to take advantage of the breaks and to meet unexpected moves by the opposition.*
>
> (Key 1964, pp. 462–463; emphasis added)

Key was arguing that complete plans of actions—strategies, in the game-theoretic sense—*do not exist in major campaigns.* The task is far too complex and filled with too many uncertainties.[27] Campaigns are of chess like complexity—worse, probably: instead of a fixed board, campaigns are fought out on stages that can change over time, and new players can enter the game.[28] Hence, cognitive constraints (e.g., the inability to look far down the decision tree, to anticipate your opponent's response to your response to their response to your new ad) inevitably matter. Professionals are not immune to Simon's scissors.[29]

Thus, political campaigns, like military ones, are filled with trial and error. A theme is tried, goes badly (or seems to), and is dropped. The staff hurries to find a new one, which seems to work initially and then weakens. A third is tried, then a fourth. (Recall, for example, the many themes in Robert Dole's 1996 presidential race.) In short, there are good reasons for believing that the basic properties of experiential learning—becoming more likely to use something that has worked in the past and less likely to repeat something that failed—hold in political campaigns.[30]

In sum, we have much stronger theoretical commitments to the claim that cognitive constraints are causally important in many significant political situations than we do to the hypothesis that people adjust via aspiration-based adaptation. The first claim is a fundamental premise in the bounded rationality research program. The latter, though an important theoretical position in this program, is

---

[27] Key's point applies to some relatively well-bounded events that are only a part of campaigns, such as nomination battles. It is unlikely, for example, that many strategists at the Democratic convention of 1924 thought about what they should do if the 102nd ballot were reached without picking a winner. (John Davis was selected on the 103rd.) Nobody thinks that far ahead: not in 1924; not now.

[28] For example, in the 1996 Israeli elections, four suicide bombings at a crucial point in the campaign pushed Benjamin Netanyahu past the incumbent, Shimon Peres.

[29] Indeed, if institutions sort problems sensibly, giving the hardest ones to the top specialists, then the raw performance scores of the best professionals or organizations may be worse than those of less skilled agents or organizations. (For an example of this problem regarding the evaluation of hospitals, see Dranove et al. 2003).

[30] In our formal model of party competition (chapter 3), we make the conventional assumption that a campaign strategy is simply a platform: no more, no less. But *everything* is scaled down in these models: both the cognitive sophistication of the decision makers as well as the complexity of their problems. From the perspective of the bounded rationality program, a key question regarding a model's plausibility is whether the *relation* between the agents' mental capacities and the difficulty of the problems they face is reasonable. The absolute level of either parameter is less important (Bendor 2003).

not one of its fundamental premises. As the Simon-March point on problem-editing makes clear, what is central to the program is a claim that humans use *some* method of reducing a complex problem to a cognitively manageable one. Aspiration-based choice is one way of doing this; it is not the only way. In this book, of course, we are betting that this particular family of theories is a fruitful way to go.

1.4 Plan of This Book

Chapter 2 will discuss aspiration-based theories of adaptation in some detail. It will provide some general properties of ABARs that will be useful for specific models of voting and elections. Chapters 3–7, the heart of the book, present models of elections. The approach is modular: first we present partial models that focus intensely on specific topics. This one-at-a-time approach also enables us to generate some analytical solutions to the models, which helps us to understand the guts of aspiration-based adaptation in the context at hand.

The first partial model, in chapter 3, takes up the classic issue of Downsian party competition. In this model, incumbents do not change policy positions; only challengers search for alternatives. We find conditions under which sets of policies are ruled out by this process but also that platform convergence can only occur under some special circumstances. The second model, in chapter 4, deals with voter participation. Now campaign platforms are fixed and everything turns on electoral participation: whichever side mobilizes more voters wins the election. Contrary to the well-known "paradox of turnout" raised by game-theoretic models of turnout, our model consistently generates realistically high levels of turnout. Moreover, this model produces comparative statics that are intuitive, consistent with those of game-theoretic models, and empirically supported. Finally, chapter 5 brackets both party platform locations and turnout and considers the voter's choice between candidates. We find here, inter alia, that using simple retrospective voting rules, citizens can generate endogenous partisan affiliations. This creates ideological polarization when aggregated over the entire population.

Chapter 6 then assembles these modules into one large model of elections. This synthesizes the constituent models into one complex formulation in which everything is at play: citizens must decide whether to turn out, and if they do, whom to vote for, while parties figure out what platforms to espouse. The complexity of this synthetic model obliges us to turn to computation as the main way to generate results (predictions). We do this exclusively for pragmatic reasons: if a model is too complicated to solve by hand, computing is better than giving up. This integrated model yields a "general equilibrium" of the election game. Many of the elements of the partial models appear here: winning parties adopt relatively centrist platforms, and citizens vote in significant numbers. One consequence of the constantly shifting party platforms is that voters choose the ideologically more distant party with surprising frequency.

All of the above is confined to two-party races. Starting there is sensible, but ending there would not be; there are too many multiparty systems to do that. Thus, chapter 7 extends the model to multiparty democracies. This raises a host of interesting questions that do not arise in two-party races, such as the need for voters to coordinate on a preferred candidate. Voters in this environment often face the problem of coordinating their behavior in order to prevent their least-preferred candidate from winning. This has given rise to an extensive literature on Duverger's Law. We show that the model leads to the selection of Condorcet winners yet allows significant vote shares for all candidates. We also find that our model does a good job of accounting for the partial coordination seen in election data from the United Kingdom.

Chapter 8 summarizes our major findings and provides some concluding thoughts.

CHAPTER TWO

Aspiration-based Adaptive Rules

IN THIS CHAPTER we discuss general ideas that will be used in all our models. In particular, we introduce the central notion, *aspiration-based adaptive rules* (ABARs), examine some basic properties of ABARs, and at the chapter's end turn briefly to some evidence regarding aspirations.[1]

2.1 ABARs DEFINED

2.1.1 Propensity and Aspiration Adjustment

We typically assume that n (finite) decision makers adapt by a form of trial-and-error learning: if an action seems to work, then the agent becomes more likely to use it in the future; if it doesn't work, then the agent is less likely to use it again. An action works if it is subjectively satisfactory, i.e., if the agent's payoffs meet or exceed her aspiration level. An action doesn't work if the payoffs are below the agent's aspiration level.

We can state this precisely with the help of some notation.

1. Actions: agent i has a set of actions $A_i = \{\alpha_{i,1}, \ldots, \alpha_{i,m_i}\}$. When the meaning is clear, we will occasionally simply use α or α_i to refer to generic actions or an action taken by agent i, respectively.
2. Aspirations: $a_{i,t}$, a number on the real line, is i's aspiration in date t. If aspirations are exogenously fixed, then agent i's aspiration is denoted by a_i, which is independent of time.
3. Payoffs: $\pi_{i,t}$ is i's payoff in date t. If payoff distributions have compact (bounded and closed) supports, then the minimal payoff of player i is denoted by $\underline{\pi}_i$ and $\overline{\pi}_i$ is her maximal payoff.
4. Action propensities: $p_{i,t}(\alpha)$ is the probability that i will use action α in date t.

[1] For an insightful early analysis of ABARs along these lines, see Cross (1983).

We can now define ABARs, via (A2.1) and (A2.2). Put informally, these axioms represent three premises: agents have aspirations, they compare payoffs to aspirations, and these comparisons determine the key qualitative properties of how agents adjust their action propensities.

(A2.1) Positive Feedback: For all i and t, if $\pi_{i,t} \geqslant a_{i,t}$ and i used α in t, then $p_{i,t+1}(\alpha) \geqslant p_{i,t}(\alpha)$. If in addition $\pi_{i,t} > a_{i,t}$ and $p_{i,t}(\alpha) < 1$, then $p_{i,t+1}(\alpha) > p_{i,t}(\alpha)$.

(A2.2) Negative Feedback: For all i and t, if $\pi_{i,t} < a_{i,t}$ and i used α in t, then $p_{i,t+1}(\alpha) < p_{i,t}(\alpha)$.[2]

An ABAR is any aspiration-based adaptive rule that satisfies (A2.1) and (A2.2). Note that the axioms make only directional assumptions about the effect of comparing payoffs to aspirations: magnitudes—how much propensities adjust—are not specified. Further, adjustment needn't be deterministic: given feedback in t, a *set* of new possible propensities might arise in $t + 1$.

An example will give readers a sense of what kinds of adaptive rules are included in the ABAR family. Consider a standard idea from psychological learning theory, the Bush-Mosteller rule. For simplicity let's examine a single person playing a two-armed bandit with a left arm (L) and a right arm (R). Let $p_t(L)$ denote the probability the agent chooses L at t. Suppose she tries L today and it is a success: the payoff is at least as high as her aspiration level. Then $p_{t+1}(L) = p_t(L)+\lambda(1-p_t(L))$, where $\lambda \in (0, 1]$ is the speed of learning. Thus, given positive feedback, $p_{t+1}(L)$ must exceed $p_t(L)$ [unless $p_t(L)$ already equals 1]. Unlike satisficing, however, positive feedback need not drive the propensity to use L all the way to 1; instead, how much it increases depends on a parameter—the speed of adjustment, λ. Similarly, if the agent tries L today and it fails, then $p_{t+1}(L) = p_t(L) - \lambda p_t(L)$. Thus, given negative feedback, $p_{t+1}(L)$ must be less than $p_t(L)$. Similar equations describe the adjustments that follow the use of R.

Note that if λ, the speed of adjustment, equals 1, then in effect we get an extreme form of satisficing: the agent will with certainty repeat the use of a currently satisfactory action; if dissatisfied, she will switch to the other action with probability 1. This is possibly the simplest ABAR.

---

[2] Axioms (A2.1) and (A2.2) presume that propensity adjustment occurs with certainty. This excludes some well-known rules: e.g., most satisficing rules allow for search (hence propensity adjustment) to occur with a probability of less than 1. This feature could be relaxed without affecting our major results, but the gain in insight is small and is not worth the increase in the models' complexity.

However, many intuitive decision rules are *not* ABARs. For example, any rule that places positive weight on a prospective evaluation of expected payoffs would violate (A2.1) and (A2.2). An agent who chooses actions by "looking down a game tree" therefore cannot be using an ABAR. Furthermore, retrospective rules for which the direction of propensity of adjustment is based on periods prior to the immediately preceding period also are not ABARs. For example, suppose that an agent chose some action α in periods $t-2$, $t-1$, and t. If her payoff weakly exceeded her aspiration in the first two periods but not in the last, then any adjustment rule that can strictly increase her propensity to choose α in period $t+1$ cannot be an ABAR.[3]

(A2.1) and (A2.2) suffice as general axioms when an agent has only two alternatives. If she has more than two, then additional structure is needed. To see why, suppose that player i with options $\{\alpha_{i,1}, \alpha_{i,2}, \alpha_{i,3}\}$ tries $\alpha_{i,1}$ in t and gets negative feedback. (A2.2) tells us that i's propensity on $\alpha_{i,1}$ will fall. This implies that her probability of trying $\alpha_{i,2}$ or $\alpha_{i,3}$ in $t+1$ must rise, but it doesn't stipulate whether exactly one increases (and if so, which) or both, and if the latter, how $\alpha_{i,1}$'s probability decrement is allocated. The following axiom addresses this issue.

(A2.3) Negative Feedback—Indirect Effect: If i used action $\alpha_{i,r}$ in t and if $\pi_{i,t} < a_{i,t}$, then for every other action $\alpha_{i,s}$ (where $s \neq r$), with strictly positive probability i moves to some new propensity vector in $t+1$ in which $\alpha_{i,s}$ has positive weight.

Assumption (A2.3) implies that if an action fails today, then there is some chance of trying any other action tomorrow.

A straightforward extension of our basic propensity adjustment rules is to let an action that was *not* chosen determine which actions are encouraged or inhibited. To see why this might be useful, observe that in some circumstances an agent may want a certain alternative to be selected, but for reasons beyond her control some other action is implemented. In one respect this is the norm in collective choice processes: for example, although a voter can pull whichever lever she chooses, the electoral winner is almost always selected by larger forces—the choices of numerous other citizens. In such contexts it makes sense for an agent to assess the performance of the alternative that was chosen by these larger forces: e.g., a voter should assess

[3] As noted in chapter 1, there are coherent mental representations which allow alternatives both to be compared to an aspiration level, per (A2.1) and (A2.2), and also to be compared prospectively to each other. Examples of coherent hybrid decision rules will be given at the end of this chapter and also in chapter 5, with corresponding results.

the performance of the party that won the election.[4] (We will see in chapter 5 that this is a natural way to formalize Key's verbal theory of retrospective voting.)

(A2.1) and (A2.2) allow ABARs to take as inputs either exogenously fixed or endogenously adjusting aspirations. If aspirations are endogenous, then we follow Cross (1983, p. 34) in stipulating that the following property governs adjustment.

(A2.4) Aspiration Adjustment: For all agents i and periods t:

1. If $\pi_{i,t} > a_{i,t}$, then $a_{i,t+1} \in (a_{i,t}, \pi_{i,t}]$.
2. If $\pi_{i,t} = a_{i,t}$, then $a_{i,t+1} = a_{i,t}$.
3. If $\pi_{i,t} < a_{i,t}$, then $a_{i,t+1} \in [\pi_{i,t}, a_{i,t})$.

(A2.4) defines a large class of aspiration-adjustment rules. Note that the conventional weighted-average rule,

$$a_{i,t+1} = \lambda a_{i,t} + (1 - \lambda)\pi_{i,t},$$

belongs to this class if λ is in $(0, 1)$.[5] But this rule is linear, deterministic, Markovian, and stationary, whereas many rules that satisfy (A2.4) have none of these properties.

For simplicity, however, we assume throughout this book that propensity and aspiration adjustment are deterministic in the following special sense: given a realized payoff, a current aspiration level, and a current propensity vector over the feasible actions, the agent acquires a unique updated aspiration level, consistent with (A2.4), and a unique new set of action propensities, consistent with (A2.1) and (A2.2). We believe that most of our findings continue to hold for nondeterministic rules, but we suspect that little insight would be gained by this generalization and that the cost in added complexity would be considerable.

In much of this book, we assume that each agent has finitely many possible propensity values (e.g., she could take up action α with

---

[4] To see this in the general context of adaptive behavior, suppose an agent is choosing between two options, $\alpha_{i,1}$ and $\alpha_{i,2}$. The agent knows that if he pulls the lever for $\alpha_{i,1}$ then that action will usually—but not always—be implemented, and similarly for $\alpha_{i,2}$. If the agent always finds out which action was implemented, then he is getting negative or positive feedback about *that* action, not the one that he chose. Hence, it follows that psychological reinforcement should be associated with the implemented action. In the standard models of adaptive learning, the implemented action is always the one chosen by the agent; in that special case no distinction is necessary.

[5] The weighted-average rule has often been used in models of endogenous aspirations: see, e.g., Cyert and March (1963) and Karandikar et al. (1998).

probability 1 or 0.999 or 0.998 or ...) and finitely many possible aspiration levels. We also sometimes assume that the agents' payoff distributions have finite support. For the most part, these assumptions are not necessary for the presented results, but they greatly simplify the analysis.

Most of these assumptions are technically useful and substantively innocuous. For example, for current measurement technologies, there is no empirical difference between assuming a huge but finite number of propensity values and infinitely many. However, some of our results also presume that payoffs are unidimensional, and this premise has real substantive bite. Behavioral decision theorists increasingly regard the resolution of trade-offs as an impressive mental accomplishment that should not be taken for granted.[6] Hence some justification is in order.

First, it is important to note that ABARs, as defined by (A2.1) and (A2.2), do *not* require that a decision maker have a complete and consistent preference ordering over all alternatives—i.e., they needn't be equipped with a classical utility function.[7] Instead, these rules can operate on mental representations with multiple payoff dimensions, with conflicts unresolved. For example, Simon offered the following quite natural stipulation of satisficing with multiple goals: "an alternative satisfices if it meets aspirations along all dimensions" (1996, p. 30).

Second, at this point in the construction of formal behavioral models of elections, a prudent research strategy is to assume unidimensional payoffs whenever possible. We usually follow this rule of thumb in the present work, and we do so for a purely practical reason: modeling tractability. We believe that the basic thrust of our findings will stand up if agents have multidimensional payoff representations, but we recognize that this is presently an open question. Fortunately, building models that can investigate this issue can be done with the basic axiomatic structure of ABARs left intact.

2.1.2 A Stochastic Process Interpretation

The ABAR models developed throughout this book are instances of stochastic processes. Since we will use the concepts behind stochastic processes frequently, we briefly (and informally) introduce some

---

[6] For evidence that resolving trade-offs is often difficult for many people, see Slovic (1995) and Bettman, Luce, and Payne (1998).

[7] Simon believed that this was one of the most important properties of the satisficing ABAR (see, e.g., 1957, p. 205, and 1979b, pp. 500–501).

of them here.[8] *Stochastic processes* describe the dynamics of a system over a set of states. A *state* is a specification of the system in question at a given time. For example, under the assumptions of the preceding subsection, states are action propensities, if aspirations are exogenous, or action propensities and aspirations if the latter are endogenous. There is usually more than one way to define states in a given system; how to define them is an important modeling decision. The set of states of a specific stochastic process is often called its *state space*, and a *state vector* is a probability distribution over the state space at a given time.

All the stochastic processes that we discuss are *discrete state*, which means that the state space is finite or countably infinite. We also consider only *discrete time* processes, which define states only at discrete times, i.e., $t = 0, 1, 2, \ldots$.

At each period a discrete time stochastic process transitions from one state to the next based on some rule and the outcome of some random variable. *Markov chains* are a common class of processes whereby the state vector in period $t + 1$ depends only on the state at period t and the system's transition rules. It does not depend on the system's state prior to t. Thus, Markov chains embody the simplest form of history dependence. Many of the extant models of adaptive behavior are discrete time Markov chains with finitely many states.[9]

Broadly speaking, discrete time stochastic processes may be used to characterize an election as follows. ABARs can describe the evolution of each voter's state—her voting propensities and her aspiration level—based on the payoffs derived from a random election outcome. As long as axioms (A2.1)–(A2.4) depend only on the immediately preceding payoffs and state values, the model is also a Markov chain.

The probability of transitioning from one state to another is often represented by a *probability transition matrix*. A matrix that is constant over time is called *stationary*. Stationary Markov chains are much more tractable than nonstationary ones; hence the mathematical theory of stationary Markov chains is more highly developed.

Transition probabilities can also be represented by a set of equations or by a diagram depicting states (circles) and their transitions (arrows), as in figure 2.1. This figure illustrates a two-state stationary

[8] For an introduction to stochastic processes, see Kemeny and Snell (1960) or Karlin and Taylor (1975, 1998).

[9] Indeed, as Epstein and O'Halloran (2005) have pointed out, in political science many Markov models are restricted to just two states. In light of this pattern, it is worth noting that here "finite" does not mean "a few." In this book, results regarding finite Markov chains hold for any (finite) number of states.

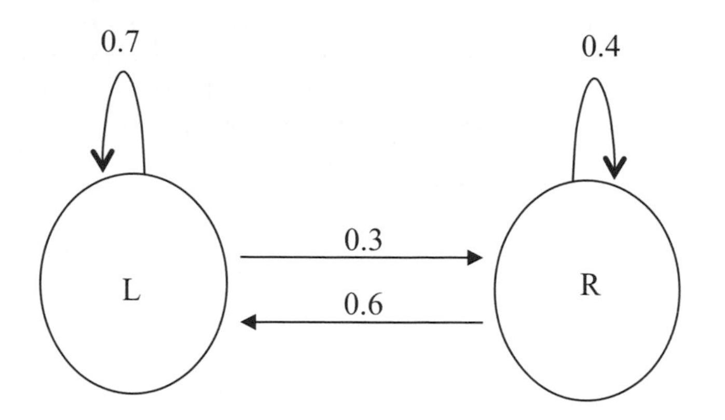

Figure 2.1. Markov chain example.

Markov chain, with state L transitioning to state R with probability 0.3 and remaining at state L otherwise, and with state R transitioning to state L with probability 0.6 and remaining at state R otherwise. Note that these rules are stationary because they apply consistently to all periods. They are also Markovian since the future path, given the current state, does not depend on what happened prior to arriving at the current state.

The transition probabilities of a Markov chain can induce numerous properties for each state. State s' is *accessible* from state s'' if it is possible to go from s' to s'' in finitely many steps, i.e., if the transition between them occurs in a finite number of steps with (strictly) positive probability. States s' and s'' *communicate* if each is accessible from the other. A state is *transient* if the system must eventually leave it and never return. Such states may be ignored if one cares only about long-run properties. A state is *recurring* if it is not transient. Finally, a recurring state is *absorbing* if, once reached, the system stays there forever. In the Markov chain depicted in figure 2.1, both states communicate and are recurring but not absorbing.

The pattern of state recurrence is a useful way of classifying Markov chains. A state s' has *period* k if, starting from s', k is the greatest common divisor of the set $\{\tau \mid s'$ reoccurs with positive probability after τ periods$\}$. A Markov chain is *periodic* if each state has a period greater than 1, and *aperiodic* if each state has a period of 1. Along with the one illustrated in figure 2.1, most Markov chains studied in social science models are aperiodic. (Periodic Markov chains have an orderly "clockwork" temporal pattern that is rarely seen outside tightly scheduled processes.)

A key concept for our purposes is that of a *limiting* or *invariant* distribution. This is a stable state vector, i.e., one that does not change when operated on by its probability transition matrix. Thus, an invariant distribution is a probability distribution over states that reproduces itself under the rules of the Markov chain. In the example in figure 2.1, the invariant distribution is state L with probability $\frac{2}{3}$, and state R with probability $\frac{1}{3}$. To see why this distribution self-replicates, note that it implies that with probability $\frac{2}{3}$ (i.e., starting from state L), the next period state is L is probability 0.7, and with probability $\frac{1}{3}$ (i.e., starting from state R), the next period state is L with probability 0.6. Thus, the overall probability of being in state L next period is $\frac{2}{3}(0.7) + \frac{1}{3}(0.6) = \frac{2}{3}$. Obviously, then, the probability of being in state R is $\frac{1}{3}$. The notion of a limiting distribution serves as the main explanatory concept in our theory. Its role is analogous to a Nash equilibrium in noncooperative game theory.

There are two types of invariant distributions. In a *degenerate* distribution, all the probability mass is on one state. A *nondegenerate* distribution puts probability on more than one state. Not all Markov chains have limiting distributions, but all finite-state, discrete-time stationary Markov chains must have at least one such distribution. A system with multiple absorbing states does not have a unique limiting distribution. Such systems generally exhibit more history and path dependence than do those with a unique invariant distribution.

Limiting distributions are one of the main ways in which modelers derive comparative statics predictions from Markov chain models. The long-run, stable behavior that they imply yields perhaps the closest comparison to equilibrium solutions of rational choice models. A second approach to deriving empirical predictions is to examine *sample paths*, or particular, period-by-period realizations of a Markov chain. A *pathwise* or *dynamic* property is something that is true not just in the long run but along all sample paths that the system may take. Thus, it is informative of what happens "along the way" to a limiting distribution. Such a property is of course stronger (and often more difficult to derive) than an equivalent one that holds only in the limit.

Our ABAR-based models inherit the relevant properties of stochastic processes, and throughout this book we will frequently make use of these connections. The most important property, ergodicity, captures the idea of long-run history independence. It is defined as follows.

Definition 2.1. A Markov chain is *ergodic* if the following two conditions hold:

(i) It has a unique invariant distribution.

(ii) It converges to that distribution from all initial state vectors.

The following result provides necessary and sufficient conditions for ergodicity. Satisfying these conditions ensures that the long-run observed behavior of a Markov chain will be insensitive to its initial state (though it may be affected by exogenous parameters). The result is standard and is therefore stated without proof.

Theorem 2.1. *A finite stationary Markov chain is ergodic if and only if it is aperiodic and all recurrent states communicate.*

Ergodicity is a very powerful property. It ensures not only that a model's predictions are unique (unique *distributions* to be sure) but also that the process will converge to these unique patterns from any initial state. No multiplicity of equilibria here, nor any mystery about how players coordinate on equilibrium play—two problems typical of Nash equilibrium. Thus, as we will discuss shortly, ABARs with Markovian adjustments are especially appealing. Note, however, that (A2.1) and (A2.2) do not presume that adjustment is Markovian or stationary.[10] And although many of our results are based on ABARs that are both Markovian and stationary, not all are: the model in chapter 3 uses neither assumption, and most of the results in chapter 5 allow for nonstationary adjustment.

2.1.3 Some Useful Types of ABARs

Throughout the book, we will often be interested in seeing which features of an ABAR are important for a result to hold. We therefore identify three properties of ABARs, defined formally below. The following notation is useful. Let

$$\delta^+_{i,t}(\alpha, p_{i,t}(\alpha)) := E[p_{i,t+1}(\alpha) \mid \alpha \text{ succeeds}] - p_{i,t}(\alpha),$$
$$\delta^-_{i,t}(\alpha, p_{i,t}(\alpha)) := p_{i,t}(\alpha) - E[p_{i,t+1}(\alpha) \mid \alpha \text{ fails}]$$

represent the expected increment and decrement in propensities for success and failure, respectively.

[10]The Bush-Mosteller rule is both deterministic and Markovian and typically stationary as well. In short, the Bush-Mosteller rule is an ABAR, but not all ABARs are deterministic or Markovian or stationary.

Definition 2.2.

(i) Suppose that $p'_{i,t}(\alpha) > p_{i,t}(\alpha)$ for some action α. An ABAR is *weakly monotonic* (with respect to α) if $\delta^+_{i,t}(\alpha, p'_{i,t}(\alpha)) \leqslant \delta^+_{i,t}(\alpha, p_{i,t}(\alpha))$ and $\delta^-_{i,t}(\alpha, p'_{i,t}(\alpha)) \geqslant \delta^-_{i,t}(\alpha, p_{i,t}(\alpha))$.

(ii) Suppose that $p'_{i,t}(\alpha) = 1 - p_{i,t}(\alpha)$ for some action α. An ABAR is *symmetric* (with respect to α) if $\delta^+_{i,t}(\alpha, p_{i,t}(\alpha)) = \delta^-_{i,t}(\alpha, p'_{i,t}(\alpha))$.

(iii) Suppose that $p_{i,t}(\alpha) = p'_{i,t}(\alpha')$ for all actions α, α'. An ABAR is *action-invariant* if $\delta^-_{i,t}(\alpha, p_{i,t}(\alpha)) = \delta^-_{i,t}(\alpha', p'_{i,t}(\alpha'))$ and $\delta^+_{i,t}(\alpha, p_{i,t}(\alpha)) = \delta^+_{i,t}(\alpha', p'_{i,t}(\alpha'))$.

The first property implies that the expected increase in the propensity to take an action, if that action was tried successfully, is weakly decreasing in the current propensity to take the action.

The second property specifies that given the same amount of adjustment room, the ABAR adjusts identically in response to failure and to success (say, upward adjustment from 0.65 and downward adjustment from 0.35). Any ABAR that is both (strictly) monotonic and symmetric must display ceiling effects.[11] Under such an ABAR, when the propensity to choose an action is high, then the tendency to choose it cannot rise by much, whereas feedback that is favorable to choosing other actions can lead to big changes. We do not require symmetry throughout; therefore, when symmetry is needed in a particular result, it will be stated explicitly.

The third property asserts a symmetry across actions rather than propensity levels. Although nothing in the definition of ABARs requires such rules to treat different actions identically, we do not want to complicate the analysis by allowing rules to have this type of flexibility. (In some contexts, such as the analysis of party choice in chapter 5, we want to ensure that the ABARs we study are neutral with respect to citizens' choices: the adaptive rule should not hardwire in a bias toward Democrats, for example.) Hence, all the ABARs that we study in this book are action-invariant. Intuitively, an adaptive rule is action-invariant if the propensities to select different actions are adjusted identically, given the same initial propensity and the same feedback.

---

[11] More generally, since learning rules pertain to choice probabilities—which must be bounded by zero and one—*all* such rules exhibit ceiling effects for increases (decreases) to very high (low) propensities.

Finally, it is worth noting that throughout this volume we presume *magnitude-insensitive* adaptive rules. Such ABARs are insensitive to the size of the discrepancy between payoffs and aspirations. For example, satisficing responds to payoffs dichotomously: in Simon's search context the agent continues to search until she encounters a satisfactory option, which she adopts. For a given aspiration level, all satisfactory alternatives are equivalent: they produce the same behavior. Similarly, all unsatisfactory ones are equivalent to each other. However, axioms (A2.1)–(A2.3) allow propensity adjustment to be sensitive to quantitative differences between payoffs and aspirations. This is plausible: big surprises—payoffs very different from aspirations—probably induce larger propensity adjustments than small ones, all else being equal.[12] But because models with magnitude-insensitive rules are generally more tractable, we stick with this subset of ABARs throughout the book.

2.2 Some Important Properties of ABARs

Given the lack of familiarity with aspiration-based models of adaptation, it is useful to understand some general features of ABARs.

The properties described below hold for the class of ABARs used almost everywhere in this book: deterministic adjustment and finitely many propensity values and aspiration levels. (Proofs of propositions 2.1 and 2.3 and of theorem 2.3 can be found in appendix A. Proposition 2.2 and theorem 2.2 were established elsewhere; see the cited references for their proofs.)

2.2.1 ABARs Emphasize an Agent's Own Experience—Sometimes Suboptimally So

The positive and negative feedback axioms (A2.1) and (A2.2) seem so sweetly reasonable that at first glance it is hard to see how they could lead a decision maker astray, i.e., how they could be inconsistent with optimal behavior. But they can be.

Consider a small band of humans foraging for food. Suppose further that this is not a game—payoffs depend only on one's own actions—but everyone faces the same choice problem and everybody

[12] See Cross (1983, pp. 19–21) for a useful discussion of possible assumptions (e.g., monotonicity and continuity) regarding the magnitude of propensity adjustment. Note that if one adopts his suggestion that the amount of propensity adjustment be a continuous function of $\pi_{i,t}$, then it will follow that an actor won't adjust propensities after getting a payoff that exactly equals her current aspiration level. This seems reasonable.

knows this. Hence, one could learn from the actions or payoffs of others. Suppose that realized payoffs are known to all players. Player 1 tries food A and likes it. But four people try B and like that. Then the next time it is player 1's turn, it would be rational for her to imitate the rest of her group and try B. Doing so violates (A2.1).

Imitation in general and rational herding in particular (Bikhchandani, Hirshleifer, and Welch 1992, 1998) can require, in certain informational environments, that one ignore one's own experience and rely instead on the experience of others. Thus, it can produce violations of (A2.1) and (A2.2).[13]

Of course, (A2.1) and (A2.2) also preclude many kinds of irrational herding, such as blind conformity.

2.2.2 Even in Decision-Theoretic Contexts ABARs Are Not Necessarily Optimal, Even in the Long Run

Putting insufficient weight on the experience of others is not the only way that ABARs can fall short of optimality: they can be suboptimal even in decision-theoretic contexts, where imitation is impossible. The next result illustrates this.

Proposition 2.1. *Suppose* $n = 1$, *and the agent uses a finite, stationary, Markovian ABAR. Aspirations adjust via (A2.4). If payoffs are stochastic with stationary probabilities and there is a uniquely optimal action, then with probability* 1 *the agent plays suboptimal actions infinitely often.*

Proposition 2.1 says that in a large class of decision-theoretic situations—e.g., those in which payoffs are stochastic—many ABARs cannot settle down on the optimal action. Indeed, no Markovian ABAR with stationary transition probabilities can do so, and it is precisely this class that is best understood.

To understand what's going wrong, consider one of the simplest ABARs, satisficing: keep the present action if and only if it is satisfactory.[14] The agent uses this rule when choosing between two actions with unknown payoff probabilities. (If they were known, then the problem would be easy enough to allow the agent to eschew ABARs

---

[13] For an analysis of rational herding among voters, see Ali and Kartik (2008).

[14] It is probably consistent with Simon's verbal theory (1955) to regard satisficing as denoting a class of rules that have two properties: (1) keep the current action if current payoffs are satisfactory; (2) otherwise, search for a new action with some probability greater than zero (Bendor, Kumar, and Siegel 2009). The rule described in the text fixes the search probability at 1. (This rule is an ABAR; technically, the others are not because they violate (A2.2), which requires that the propensity to use an unsatisfactory action falls with certainty.)

altogether and instead, per Simon's scissors, maximize expected utility by choosing the optimal arm.) For example, consider a two-armed bandit problem in which each action produces either a high payoff (h) or a low one (l). Suppose the left arm (L) is best. However, even optimal alternatives are rarely perfect: i.e., they do not invariably deliver the maximal payoff. Hence, we assume here that $\Pr(\pi = h) < 1$ even for L. Since aspirations are endogenous, they respond to experienced payoffs, so sometimes aspirations will exceed l (see proposition 2.2 below). Hence, eventually the agent will get the low payoff from L and find it disappointing. Since she uses the simple satisficing rule, in the next period she will switch to R for sure. This is suboptimal.[15] Satisficing is too reactive, partly because its memory is too short. Optimality here requires that the agent keep track of statistics that summarize her *entire* experience: the fraction of the time that L paid off versus the fraction that R did. In contrast, satisficing's response is based only on current experience. To be sure, this guarantees that the agent will never get stuck on the wrong arm: satisficing produces sufficient exploration. But it does so at the expense of generating suboptimal exploitation. When payoff probabilities are unknown and all actions are imperfect—as is typically the case—then finding a good trade-off between exploration and exploitation (March 1991) may not be easy; finding the *optimal* trade-off can be difficult indeed. Garden-variety ABARs such as satisficing fail this test (Bendor, Kumar, and Siegel 2009).

Political scientists usually study strategic contexts—those with more than one decision maker—and proposition 2.1 is silent about such situations. But the logic of the result clearly extends to strategic settings. As the simulations of Bendor, Diermeier, and Ting (2003a) suggest, agents in n-person games who use ABARs covered by proposition 2.1 cannot settle down on pure Nash equilibria when payoffs are stochastic. (When payoffs are deterministic, other issues arise. We take these up shortly.) We can illustrate this via a 2×2 game: the Stag Hunt. This game has two pure Nash equilibria (figure 2.2). (Note that the entries in the payoff matrix refer to *expected* payoffs.)

The (C,C) equilibrium Pareto-dominates the (D,D) equilibrium, so we focus on the former. Suppose that mutual cooperation yields either $2 - \epsilon$ or $2 + \epsilon$, each with some fixed probability in $(0, 1)$. Now

[15] More precisely, optimal play implies that the decision maker settle down on one of the alternatives with probability 1 (Whittle 1983). (Typically he will select the optimal arm, but occasionally the inferior action will generate so many high payoffs that the agent will mistakenly settle down on that arm. In either case, however, perpetual restlessness is suboptimal.)

	C	D
C	2,2	0,1
D	1,0	1,1

Figure 2.2. Expected payoffs in Stag Hunt game.

imagine that the players *could* settle down on (C,C). Then aspirations must eventually enter the $(2 - \epsilon, 2 + \epsilon)$ interval and stay there. But this means that eventually they will experience the $2 - \epsilon$ payoff as dissatisfying and with positive probability will experiment with defecting. So our assumption that the players could settle down on (C,C) must be wrong. Hence, even the Pareto-optimal Nash equilibrium is not absorbing. The same logic holds for the Pareto-deficient equilibrium.

Thus, we shouldn't be surprised when, in models in the rest of the book, agents who use ABARs typically don't converge to Nash equilibria. Only quite special adaptive rules succeed in doing that (cf. Kiefer and Wolfowitz 1952).[16]

2.2.3 Yet ABARs Are Sensible

Herbert Simon frequently argued that satisficing may not be optimal but is sensible. This conjecture extends, we believe, to many adaptive rules used by humans. Indeed, given genetic and cultural evolution and individual learning, it would be surprising if common and fundamental heuristics weren't adaptive in important ways. To be sure, the products of natural selection may be ill-prepared for new environments. But with our big brains and capacity for vicarious learning (Bandura 1986; Richerson and Boyd 2005), humans can adjust their behavior in response to environmental shifts, sometimes quite swiftly. So the "adaptive toolboxes" (Gigerenzer and Selten 2001) of viable cultures are probably well-stocked with sensible decision rules.

[16] Economists and game theorists often respond to a finding that a type of adaptive rule doesn't converge to optimal in the long run by concluding that there is something wrong with the rule (e.g., Feinberg 2004). This is justifiable if one is constructing normative theories of choice. In this book we focus on descriptive theories. A finding of persistent suboptimality—even if playing dominated strategies (e.g., Karandikar et al. 1998)—is not grounds for rejecting such formulations. Doing so would beg an important question: it would presume that humans optimize in the environments at hand. Whether we do so is an empirical question; it cannot be settled by theoretical fiat.

Because the terms "sensible," "reasonable," "adequate," and "good" can be thrown around too casually in these discussions, we want to give some content to these important yet vague notions. We do so by providing a formal result about the performance of perhaps the most famous ABAR, satisficing, in the context of a two-armed bandit. For simplicity we suppress aspirations in the following result, presuming instead that feedback operates directly on payoffs: the high payoff is satisfactory; the low one is not.

Proposition 2.2 (Bendor, Kumar, and Siegel 2009). *Consider an agent with alternatives L and R, with payoffs* $\{l, h\}$. *Action L is optimal:* $\Pr(\pi_L = h) > \Pr(\pi_R = h)$. *If the start is neutral—she is equally likely to use L or R—and the agent satisfices, then* $p_{L,t} > p_{R,t}$ *for all* $t > 0$.

So satisficing leads the decision maker to use the better action more often, at all dates.[17] This is not optimal performance, but it is something.

2.2.4 Realistic Aspirations

Citizens may not know what payoffs are feasible; their aspirations may be unrealistic, i.e., outside the set of feasible payoffs. (More subtly, their aspirations may be unrealistic even when there is good reason to believe that they cannot be achieved: the question "why should I vote for the lesser of two evils?" comes to mind. We will return to this question in the chapter on voting choice.) However, if agent i responds to experience by adjusting her aspirations in accord with (A2.3), then she will move steadily toward her set of feasible payoffs, $[\underline{\pi}_i, \overline{\pi}_i]$, if her initial aspiration level is unrealistic. Moreover, if she starts off with realistic aspirations, then adjusting via (A2.4) ensures that she never becomes unrealistic. (A stronger convergence result, which requires an assumption somewhat stronger than (A2.4), is stated formally in chapter 5.) Thus, under (A2.4) a person's set of feasible payoffs is a black hole for aspirations: it is both globally attractive and retentive.

Although ergodicity implies that the values of initial aspiration levels are not important in the long run, realistic aspirations are a natural starting point for models of political behavior. For example,

[17] Computational investigations indicate that proposition 2.2 holds if the agent uses either the (symmetric) Bush-Mosteller rule or the equal-increments rule (i.e., propensities move up and down on an equally spaced grid, such as $\{0, 0.01, 0.02, \ldots, 0.99, 1\}$, one value at a time). See http://press.princeton.edu/titles/9352.html for links to these results. We suspect that it holds for a large class of ABARs.

in stable political systems in which children's aspirations are influenced by their parents' experiences, aspirations tend to be realistic.[18] We will exploit this useful fact in setting up some of our models. (We will also, however, take a close look at some interesting short-run dynamics produced by unrealistic aspirations in section 4.2.)

2.2.5 ABARs and Dominance

The behavior and performance of ABARs is tightly connected to the existence of relations of *Pareto dominance* among alternatives.[19] The following property illustrates this link. Consider two alternatives that face the same group of decision makers. Option 1 generates a payoff vector of $(\pi_1, \ldots, \pi_n)$; option 2 yields $(\pi'_1, \ldots, \pi'_n)$. If the latter strictly Pareto-dominates the former, then the following hold for all i for *any* mix of ABARs: (1) if agent i's propensity to retry the current action rises under payoff vector 1, then it will rise given vector 2; (2) if agent i's propensity would fall given vector 2, then it must also fall given vector 1.[20]

Pareto dominance is less important for rational choice solution concepts, especially strategic (i.e., game-theoretic) ones. The central solution concept of noncooperative game theory is Nash equilibrium. As the Prisoner's Dilemma famously illustrates, an outcome (mutual defection) may be a Nash equilibrium even though an outcome that Pareto-dominates it (mutual cooperation) is not. In contrast, if aspiration-driven decision makers would be satisfied by mutual defection, then they would also be satisfied by mutual cooperation. The explanation for the difference is subtle and important.[21] A game-theoretically rational player assesses an outcome via a counterfactual: she compares it to payoffs that she *could* get if she selected another action and all her partners continued using the same actions. Hence, although cooperation Pareto-dominates the Nash equilibrium outcome of defection, the former is not Nash because an agent in a cooperative outcome could do still better by unilaterally cheating. In contrast, ABAR-driven assessments are not based on counterfactual

---

[18] However, if their income aspirations are influenced by the experiences of socioeconomic outliers—e.g., entertainers or sports stars—then they could remain unrealistic for a long time.

[19] These two paragraphs are from Bendor (forthcoming).

[20] This property need not hold over time. Suppose that the group first encounters option 1, which they adopt. They then stumble onto alternative 3, which gives some people payoffs that exceed anything they could get from option 1 or 2. If aspirations adjust sufficiently quickly—and there is some evidence that good times rapidly boost aspirations (Kahneman, Knetsch, and Thaler 1991)—then these persons will regard the payoffs they later get from option 2 as disappointing.

[21] This is based on Bendor, Kumar, and Siegel (2009).

reasoning: they turn on direct comparisons between an alternative and the agent's evaluation threshold, which are mentally easier than counterfactuals. This is a fundamental cognitive difference between game-theoretic and aspiration-based reasoning.

2.2.6 The Empirical Content of ABAR-Driven Models

Obviously, aspirations are a key component of ABARs. For example, different levels of aspirations can produce strikingly different behavior in the short run. Suppose, e.g., that two people are playing the standard binary choice Prisoner's Dilemma. (We use the standard notation: T is the temptation payoff earned by cheating someone who cooperates, R is the reward for mutual cooperation, P is the punishment for mutual defection, and S is the sucker's payoff, with $T > R > P > S$.) If both people start with aspirations in (S, P), then they can immediately stabilize on either mutual defection or mutual cooperation; but if both players are initially satisfied only by the game's maximal payoff (T), then no outcome is stable at the start of their relationship.

This dependence on initial conditions is methodologically worrisome: if anything can happen, the theory is vacuous. (This is similar to the folk theorem problems in noncooperative game theory.) Our next result, established in Bendor, Diermeier, and Ting (2007), shows that there is indeed cause for concern.

In the next result, we say that an outcome is *stable* if it is an absorbing state of the corresponding stochastic process. In such a state, the players' action propensities and aspirations form what Macy and Flache (2002) aptly call a self-reinforcing equilibrium: the actions produce payoffs that reinforce the underlying propensities that generated those actions in the first place, and they also maintain the same aspiration levels. Formally, we define a self-reinforcing equilibrium as follows.

Definition 2.3. A *self-reinforcing equilibrium* is a vector of propensities $(p_{i,t})_i$ and a compact set of aspirations $\mathcal{A}_i$ satisfying $a_{i,t} \in \mathcal{A}_i$ for each i, where for all i, α_i, and $t' > t$,

(i) $p_{i,t'}(\alpha_i) = p_{i,t}(\alpha_i)$,

(ii) $a_{i,t'} \in \mathcal{A}_i$.

Under this definition, which generalizes Macy and Flache's notion of a self-reinforcing equilibrium, the propensities must be self-replicating, but specific aspiration values need not be. Instead, we require only that there exists a *set* of aspirations that (1) is absorbing—once aspirations enter the set they never leave it—and

(2) as long as aspirations stay in that set, then propensities replicate the required specific values. (Of course, a singleton set can satisfy these properties.)

Using this definition, the next result can be established.

Theorem 2.2 (Bendor, Diermeier, and Ting 2007). *Consider any* n*-person choice situation* ($n \geqslant 1$) *in which everyone adapts their action propensities by any arbitrary mix of ABARs. Any outcome of the stage game can be sustained as a stable outcome by some self-reinforcing equilibrium if either of the following conditions holds:*

(i) *Aspirations are exogenously fixed and* $\underline{\pi}_i$ *exists for all* i.

(ii) *Aspirations adjust via any arbitrary mix of rules that satisfy (A2.4) and payoffs are deterministic and stationary.*

Theorem 2.2 covers a great many situations. The game could last indefinitely, or it could end after a fixed number of periods. It holds for any number of players—from small electorates to gargantuan ones—who can have any number of actions. Further, the game need not be symmetric: players may have different action sets. And a person could switch to different ways of adapting over time, provided only that new methods continue to satisfy the relevant axioms.

This result warns us that the methodological problem confronting models of adaptive learning are in some ways more dire than the folk theorems of repeated game theory. The latter do leave *some* empirical content to game theory: outcomes that are not individually rational (e.g., the sucker's payoff in the Prisoner's Dilemma) cannot be supported by any Nash equilibrium no matter how important the future is. (A rational player will not tolerate the sucker's payoff in equilibrium since she can unilaterally do better by defecting.) But in the former, *any* outcome of a stage game can be sustained by some self-reinforcing equilibrium, even those with payoffs below the maximin level.

Part (ii) hints at a solution to the problem. When everyone has deterministic payoffs, people can lock onto any pattern of behavior because each person's experience can be self-confirming. For example, suppose in the two-person Prisoner's Dilemma that Row initially is fully disposed to cooperate while Column is completely inclined to defect. Further, suppose that Row's initial aspirations are very low—below S—while Column's are realistic, i.e., in (S, T). Then Row will always get S, Column will always get T, and both will be content. Moreover, their aspirations will climb steadily toward their respective payoffs. All is, if not well, stable. But now consider situations in which payoffs are stochastic: they equal the standard Prisoner's Dilemma payoffs plus a random shock. Now Row will sometimes experience a better than ordinary payoff, even though he cooperated while his vile partner defected. This will push up his aspirations, so when he returns to the usual payoff neighborhood around S, he might be discontented: *he has experienced something better and found it good.* This will eventually destabilize the outcome in which one person is exploited by another.

Hence, the ongoing possibility of disappointment implies that the process cannot lock onto any particular state or pattern of behavior. Since locking onto arbitrary states was the heart of the adaptive folk theorem, this instability is good news, methodologically speaking: it helps restore empirical content to adaptive models. When disappointment is inevitable, such models do make predictions. To get a feel for the kind of predictions they give, we turn to a simple decision-theoretic example.

Consider a satisficer playing a two-armed bandit. Alternatives L and R have binary payoffs, with $\Pr(\pi_L = h) = 0.7$ and $\Pr(\pi_R = h) = 0.4$. To keep the example simple, assume that the agent's aspiration is exogenously fixed between l and h. Hence, he always regards the low payoff as disappointing and always considers h to be satisfactory. (We will see in chapters 3 and 5 that this approach makes models of aspiration-based adaptation very tractable.) The corresponding Markov chain is represented by figure 2.1.

Suppose that he starts off equally disposed toward L and R: $p_1(L) = p_1(R) = \frac{1}{2}$. If he picks L in the first period, then he will be discontent with a probability of 0.3 and so will switch to R in $t = 2$ with that probability. Similarly, if he starts off with R, he'll switch to L in $t = 2$ with probability 0.6.

What, then, is the probability that the agent will try L in period 2? There are two paths to consider. He might start with L and be satisfied, or he might try R and be dissatisfied. So $p_2(L) = (0.5)(0.7) + (0.5)(0.6) = 0.65$. The chance of trying L in the second period exceeds the neutral start because the right arm is more likely to fail than is the left one.

Similarly, we can compute $p_3(L)$. This probability is simply the chance that he tries L in the second period and gets the high payoff plus the chance that he tries R and gets the low one: $(0.65)(0.7) + (0.35)(0.6) = 0.665$. Continuing this, we get $p_4(L) = 0.6665$, $p_5(L) = 0.66665$, and so on.

The probability of picking L seems to be converging to something. This is indeed so: it is converging to $\frac{2}{3}$. Why? The reason is that this probability, and *only* this one, has a self-replicating property: if in some t the agent's chance of picking L is $\frac{2}{3}$, then the probability of trying L in $t+1$ would again equal $\frac{2}{3}$. (To see this, consult the limiting distribution example following figure 2.1.) So $(\frac{2}{3}, \frac{1}{3})$ is an invariant (self-replicating) distribution: if the Markov process ever gets there, it will stay there forever.[22]

By theorem 2.1, the Markov chain in figure 2.1 has exactly one invariant distribution. If we can actually calculate the limiting probabilities, we have a model with empirical content: in the case of figure 2.1, the prediction is that the agent will settle down to choosing L two-thirds of the time. Thus, *a unique invariant distribution is the heart of our solution concept for ABAR-driven processes.* A well-constructed (falsifiable) model in this class has a unique stochastic limit, and the properties of that limit are what we expect to happen.

We are not quite done, however. A unique invariant distribution is the fixed point of a stochastic process. But to make predictions we also need to know something about dynamics: will the system always move toward this fixed point? If the answer is yes—if the process converges to the unique invariant distribution from any initial probability vector over the system's states—then the limiting distribution is the unique global attractor of the process. In that case, we have a clear, strong prediction: eventually the endogenous variables will have values that are close to those of the properties of the invariant distribution. We needn't condition that prediction on the system's initial conditions; they will not endure. It is therefore critical to know whether the process is ergodic.

Not all Markov chains with unique limiting distributions are ergodic. For example, consider the chain depicted in figure 2.3(a). Although this process has a unique invariant distribution—$(0.5, 0.5)$—it will never reach that stochastic equilibrium from any other probability distribution over L and R. (For example, if the initial probability vector is $(0.7, 0.3)$, then the process will alternate between this vector and $(0.3, 0.7)$ forever.) It does not converge to its limit because it deterministically flip-flops between states: if the process is currently in L, then it will go to R with certainty in the next period, and vice versa. This is a periodic chain, where all states have period 2.

Fortunately, most stochastic models of social phenomena are aperiodic. The clockwork rigidity of the process in figure 2.3(a) is extremely fragile: it would be destroyed by even the slightest possibility that the system will stay put from one period to the

[22] This statement does *not* imply that the *realizations* of the process—its sample paths—ever settle down. Because neither action is perfect, the agent never settles down on either one. Rather, it is his *probability* of choosing L or R that settles down. See Feller (1950, pp. 78–88) for an enlightening discussion of this crucial point.

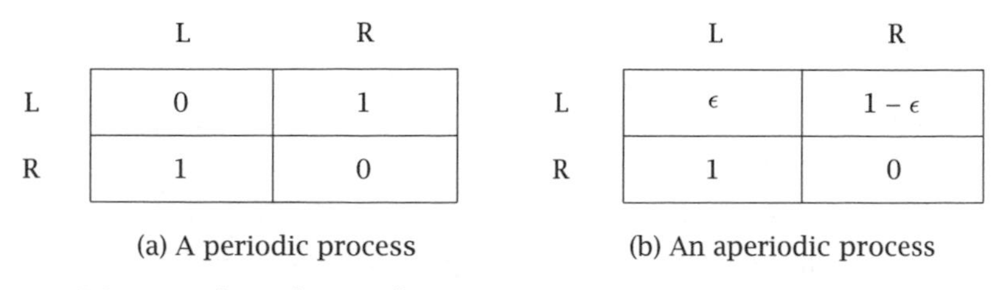

	L	R
L	0	1
R	1	0

(a) A periodic process

	L	R
L	ϵ	$1-\epsilon$
R	1	0

(b) An aperiodic process

Figure 2.3. Periodic and aperiodic processes.

next. Consider, for example, figure 2.3(b). This slightly perturbs figure 2.3(a) by allowing (with arbitrarily small probability) the process to stay in state L. To see the effect of this perturbation, start the process in L for sure. Calculations show that the probabilities of being in L thereafter still flip-flop, but because of the tiny possibility of staying in that state, they do not cycle between zero and one. Instead, they converge toward each other, toward the unique invariant distribution of

$$\left(\frac{1}{2-\epsilon}, \frac{1-\epsilon}{2-\epsilon}\right).$$

Thus, the process in figure 2.3(b) is ergodic.

Periodicity is fragile not only in the above mathematical sense; it is also substantively dubious in models of aspiration-based adjustment. Although such models capture important adaptive properties—the responsiveness of action propensities and aspirations to experience—a boundedly rational actor may not always attend to feedback. Attention is a limited mental resource (Lavie 1995); a particular voter, for example, may expend it on something other than elections. Hence, we assume throughout this book that each agent may be inertial with respect to aspiration adjustment or to propensity adjustment, each with probability $\varepsilon \in (0, 1)$. These probabilities are assumed to be independent and identically distributed (i.i.d.) across players and across periods. (The probability of inertia in propensity adjustment need not be independent of the probability of being inertial regarding aspirations. We require only that each of of the four combined events—(adjust, adjust), (adjust, inertia), (inertia, adjust), (inertia, inertia)—occur with a probability greater than zero.)

Inertia and any one of a variety of perturbations allow us to show that ABARs are ergodic: they converge to a unique limiting distribution. The assumptions about perturbations are relatively innocuous. They may simply involve the possibility of small mistakes in each player's action choices or the exclusion of pure strategies.

Minor shocks to each agent's payoffs or state values (i.e., her aspiration level or action propensities) also yield the same conclusion. In the models presented in subsequent chapters, we generally assume perturbed payoffs.

Theorem 2.3. *An aspiration-based adaptive process is ergodic if it has inertia and any one of the following conditions hold:*

(i) Action trembles*: with a positive probability (which is i.i.d. across periods and independent across players), player i, instead of doing what he intended to do, "experiments" by randomly playing some action given by a totally mixed vector of probabilities over feasible actions. Further, in the stage game there is an outcome in which nobody gets their minimal payoff.*

(ii) Extreme propensities excluded*: neither 0 nor 1 is a feasible propensity value for any action for any player. Further, in the stage game there is an outcome in which nobody gets their minimal payoff.*

(iii) Stochastic payoffs*: every vector of actions produces a (nondegenerate) distribution of payoffs for every agent, where each distribution is finitely valued. Payoffs are i.i.d. across periods and independently distributed across players.*

(iv) State trembles*: with positive probability (i.i.d. over periods and independently across players) i's state can randomly tremble to any neighboring aspiration value and vector of propensities.*

Note that the conclusion of theorem 2.3 refers to a *distribution*. These types of models rarely yield point predictions. Instead, their typical prediction is that of a nondegenerate distribution of action propensities and associated payoffs.

Empirically oriented readers might be disinterested in results that hold at the limit. The cry goes up, "Dynamics! Dynamics! We want dynamics!"; i.e., only predictions that hold in real time matter empirically. We will examine dynamics whenever possible. But for several reasons limiting results have more empirical content than some empiricists realize.

First, there are trade-offs between different kinds of approximations. True, some models may make dynamic predictions, but as the literature on path dependence often reveals, many of these are not very sharp. Alternatively, a model may make a sharp prediction about what will happen in the limit. When we use the latter to analyze a real system the degree of approximation is about how close the system is to its probabilistic equilibrium. Using the former yields approximations; the predictions are fuzzy. There is a trade-off here; neither approach dominates the other.[23]

Second, some stochastic processes converge to their limits surprisingly quickly.[24] Furthermore, because the speed of convergence in ergodic finite Markov chains with stationary transition probabilities is geometric (because of matrix multiplication of probabilities), the further a system is from its steady-state distribution the stronger the tendency to move toward that limit.[25] Thus, approximating a system by its asymptotic properties is more likely to produce small errors than big ones, as the latter disappear relatively quickly.

Of course, whenever we can figure out dynamics well enough to make predictions, we will do so. Such results are also valuable.

2.2.7 Dynamics and Computational Models

Studying dynamics produces another kind of trade-off: computational modeling is often required. If one desires predictions that are both quantitative and analytically derived, one must often settle for predictions that hold in the limit. Fortunately, our discipline is less prejudiced toward computational models than it once was. Papers describing such models are now being published in the discipline's top journals in several subfields.

We have no religious fervor about computation: it is a tool—a useful one, especially for studying the dynamics of adaptive systems. In exploring the models in this book we usually proceeded sequentially: first we tried to get closed-form solutions; if we made little progress, then we eventually turned to computational modeling. We have no algorithm for calculating how long one should try analytical methods. Presently it is a matter of professional judgment: try until one either succeeds or the team reaches a consensus that analytical methods are not promising for the problem at hand. No impossibility

---

[23] As we'll see in the chapter on turnout, our model makes sharp quantitative predictions about turnout in the limit. It also makes dynamic predictions, but these are only qualitative, not quantitative. In one sense the quantitative equilibrium predictions have more empirical content, but to use them we must cross our fingers and hope that a given real system is close to its stochastic limit.

[24] For example, consider a two-state Markov chain, with states L and R, where the probability of leaving either state is 0.2. Suppose the process starts in state L for sure. The initial probability vector of (1,0) is far from the limiting distribution of (0.5, 0.5), yet by the end of period 4 the probability that the system is in state R is already 0.4304.

[25] For example, in the chain described in the preceding footnote, where the initial probability of being in state R is zero, the probabilities of being in that state in periods 1, 2, and 3 are 0.2, 0.32, and 0.384, respectively. The strongest kick toward stochastic equilibrium occurs initially, when the process is farthest from its limit. (Calculating these probabilities by hand will give readers a feel for why this is so.)

proofs are involved. Moreover, we would be delighted (though naturally a bit chagrined) if a colleague devised a closed-form solution for a problem that we treated numerically.

Our method might irritate two groups of scholars: those who argue that one should never compute and those who argue that one always should. We think the burden of proof should be on those who advocate these extremes. Regarding the never-compute position, we ask why one shouldn't compute after a long, unfruitful attempt with analytical methods? Is giving up better than computing? To our computation-only colleagues, we point out that the two methods can complement each other. Computational models can help us examine theories that we cannot (yet) solve in closed form; simple analytical models can help us understand what is going on in complex simulations. (We will exploit this complementarity extensively in chapter 4.)

2.3 The Evidential Status of Aspiration-based Adaptation

Any introduction to an unconventional family of theories should provide some empirical reasons for taking the set seriously. ABARs are somewhat unconventional in political science, but unevenly so. Theories based on these rules have two distinct though related elements. The first is aspirations; the second is adaptive change of action propensities in the light of aspiration-coded feedback. There is no doubt that human beings adjust their behavior in response to feedback. Indeed, this pattern—called the Law of Effect (Thorndike 1898) in psychology—is probably common to almost all animals, ranging from a fully rational Bayesian optimally solving a problem in statistical decision theory to bacteria responding to a food source. What is unconventional about ABARs—in particular, what differentiates them from from rational choice theories—is the notion of aspirations. Hence, we restrict our very brief tour of the literature to evidence relevant to aspirations and their properties.

Because aspirations and their levels are mentalistic concepts, they're not directly observable. Thus, we must rely on indirect evidence. Fortunately, there is quite a lot of that. But first, we mention a point on how to think about the evidence.

All the relevant data on aspirations that we know of involve tests of joint hypotheses. For example, psychological evidence that laboratory subjects often adapt via aspiration-based reinforcement learning probes the joint hypotheses that people have aspiration levels and that their subsequent propensity adjustments satisfy the axioms of reinforcement learning. (This is the most pointed evidence regarding ABARs.) Evidence that preference reversals can occur pertains to several joint hypotheses of Prospect Theory, including the premise that people compare alternatives to a reference point. (As noted in chapter 1, we regard the terms "reference point" and "aspiration level" as synonyms.) Data about the longitudinal stability of average national subjective well-being (Diener and Suh 1999) are relevant to the joint hypotheses that people's satisfaction is based on a comparison between how they're doing and their aspiration levels and that these aspirations adjust to changes in a person's income, with a relatively short lag. Hence, one cannot refer to an overview article entitled simply "Evidence Regarding the Existence of Aspirations." No such paper exists.

With this in mind, we turn briefly to the evidence, which can be divided into behavioral and hedonic.

2.3.1 Behavior: Learning in Repeat Play

There is much evidence that humans and other animals often behave consistently with the predictions of reinforcement learning (Bush and Mosteller 1955) and in particular with Thorndike's Law of Effect (1898), which is essentially our positive and negative feedback axioms, (A2.1) and (A2.2). It turns out that this is indirect evidence for aspiration-based behavior; as Hilgard and Bower stated in their well-known text on learning theory, experimental results on the effects of changing incentives "can be interpreted in terms of Helson's concept of adaptation level" (1966, p. 486), i.e., via aspiration levels.

This interpretation, however, is based on studies that used a rather weak research design in which predictions of a learning model were compared only to data. Tighter, more falsifiable studies have pitted reinforcement learning predictions against rational choice hypotheses, notably to test probability matching. (Probability matching is the hypothesis that in two-armed bandit problems with complementary reward probabilities—Left pays off with probability p and Right with probability $1 - p$, where $p > \frac{1}{2}$—the long-run choice probabilities will be p and $1 - p$, respectively.) The evidence is not easily summarized; even overviews reach different conclusions (e.g., Bower 1994; Vulcan 2000). In general, neither probability matching nor expected utility maximization is unequivocally supported. As the former implies, subjects do not settle down on the optimal action, and in many experiments they appear to asymptote on choice frequencies close to p (Bower 1994, p. 295). But sometimes they wind up choosing the better arm considerably more frequently than p (Vulcan 2000, p. 111), which is more consistent with expected utility theory.[26]

2.3.2 Behavior: Choice in Static Contexts

Perhaps the most dramatic confirmation of aspiration-based behavior is that of preference reversals: the reversal of a decision between options based on whether the choice problem is framed as involving a possible loss or as a possible gain.[27] This was quite dramatic because several researchers working on this problem were rather keen on finding disconfirming evidence. But the phenomenon just wouldn't go away (Hausman 1992).

These experiments provide evidence about the reality of aspirations via the confirmation of the joint hypotheses that people are comparing alternatives to reference points and that their reference points are influenced by the experiments' framing of the options.[28] As Kahneman and Tversky made clear in their pioneering paper (1979), a reference point is an internal standard of evaluation which (in the context of Prospect Theory) codes outcomes as gains or losses. The hypothesis that people use such a standard in many choice problems is arguably the theory's core premise. Regarding the theory's conceptual apparatus, it is clearly central: several other axioms, such as different attitudes toward risk for gains versus losses, wouldn't be meaningful claims without it. (Identifying a payoff as a gain requires a threshold, i.e., a reference point.) What is compared to what is fundamental in any coherent theory of choice,

---

[26] Unsurprisingly, subjects do better when they are given appropriate training (Shanks, Tunney, and McCarthy 2002) or better feedback (Friedman and Massaro 1998) and those with higher cognitive ability are more likely to behave optimally (West and Stanovich 2003). These effects are to be expected on the basis of Simon's scissors: when, e.g., subjects are appropriately trained, the gap between cognitive constraints and problem difficulty is eased, so performance improves.

[27] Preference reversals are predicted by Prospect Theory (Kahneman and Tversky 1979). As we've noted, this theory's fundamental postulate is that decision makers compare options to a reference point (a.k.a. aspiration level): those that will give payoffs above this point are coded as gains; those below, as losses. A second key assumption is that people are risk-averse regarding gains, and risk seeking regarding losses. These two assumptions together imply that if an experimenter can manipulate subjects' reference points, then he can change their choices, i.e., reverse their preferences. (The term "preference reversal" is slightly misleading. In experiments subjects are randomly assigned to one or the other framing of the choice problem; no single person actually reversed his or her decision.)

[28] The relevance of these experiments to the point at hand also depends on the validity of our claim that reference points and aspiration levels are merely different labels for the same idea.

and Prospect Theory takes a clear position on this: alternatives are compared to an internal standard, not just to each other.

Hence, we believe that many empirical studies of Prospect Theory [those about loss aversion and risk-seeking (avoiding) behavior for losses (gains)] test joint hypotheses including one on aspirations. The evidential status of Prospect Theory, like that of reinforcement theories, is thus relevant here.[29]

2.3.3 Hedonics

The study of happiness has been dormant for a long time. Recently, however, psychologists and economists have revived it (e.g., Kahneman, Diener, and Schwartz 1999; Easterlin 2001; Layard 2006). Two empirical patterns are especially relevant here. First, although sudden changes in life situation—winning the lottery, becoming a paraplegic—affect people's happiness, over time people adjust to many of these changes.[30] Especially money: for example, over a period in which average per-capita income in Japan rose fivefold, average subjective well-being responses to surveys barely changed at all.[31] This tendency seems so widespread that it has earned a name: the hedonic treadmill. Evidently aspirations for income are endogenous and obey adjustment rules covered by our axiom (A2.4).[32]

The second empirical pattern is that we compare our life situations to those of other people: a reference group effect (Merton and Rossi 1950). Suppose, for example, that we compare our income not only to our past income but also to how other people in our community or

[29] There is another side of Prospect Theory that is irrelevant for our present concerns: the axioms about subjective probability estimates. These and the premise about reference points are logically independent of each other. For a demonstration that a coherent Prospect Theory model can be constructed on the basis of the latter alone, see Munro and Sugden (2003).

[30] Not all: the loss of a job, for example, is hard to adjust to (Lucas et al. 2004).

[31] Are verbal responses about these subjective matters informative? Scholars working in the new hedonic psychology have addressed this important question. A variety of probes, including triangulation (e.g., peers tend to agree with a subject's self-assessment), strongly suggest that the responses are indeed meaningful (Layard 2006).

[32] For evidence that the counterintuitive hedonic treadmill is not the whole story for income, see Deaton (2008) and Stevenson and Wolfers (2008). Deaton reports that data support the conventional hypotheses (those which assume that improved material conditions directly impact happiness without the mediation of aspirations) that people in rich countries are on average happier than those in poor countries, and he infers that "the very strong international relationship between per capita GDP and life satisfaction suggests that on average people have a good idea of how income, or the lack of it, affects their lives" (p. 69).

society are doing—as, say, represented by average per capita income. This simple model of aspiration formation predicts that the rich will tend to be happier than the poor, as is the case (Easterlin 2001).

By itself this prediction is hardly surprising. (Moreover, classical utility theory generates the same implication.) It is the combination of this cross-sectional prediction and the above longitudinal one that is intriguing. To explain both types of changes in a single model with endogenous aspirations requires, we believe, both reference group effects and agents responding to changes in their own payoffs over time (Bendor, Diermeier, and Ting 2007).

Finally, it is worth noting that the binary evaluation of good versus bad appears to be a human universal (Brown 1991). When the underlying payoff variable has many values (e.g., money), this is consistent with the hypothesis that the people in question have an aspiration level that partitions the set of payoffs into two subsets: one good, the other bad. The ubiquity of binary coding suggests neurophysiological foundations; there is evidence for this (Hajcak et al. 2006).

All in all, there is considerable evidence that people have aspirations for important variables such as income, that these aspirations are a function both of our own experience and of the circumstances of relevant others, and that aspirations serve a number of important functions in our mental lives (subjective well-being) and in our choice behavior.

2.3.4 Complex Choice Processes

We do not, however, see aspiration-driven behavior everywhere. As we have noted several times, we believe that people normally optimize when choice situations are sufficiently simple. Thus, in such contexts they compare alternatives to each other, as classical decision theory requires. Furthermore, we suspect that in some settings (e.g., voting; see our discussion in chapter 5) decision makers make *both* kinds of comparisons: they compare options to each other and also to an aspiration level.[33] Hence, it is relevant to inquire whether our results are robust to this possibility: do they continue to hold when choice processes are complex, i.e., when they involve both types of comparisons?

We believe that our results are, in general, robust in this respect. But because this is a rather large topic, here we will restrict ourselves

[33] For example, there are reasons to believe that voters evaluate candidates both retrospectively and prospectively, which implies that they use both kinds of comparisons. We will discuss this further in chapter 5.

to reanalyzing just one finding. We will demonstrate that this chapter's first result, proposition 2.1, continues to hold if decision makers compare alternatives to each other as well as to their aspiration levels. Doing this rigorously requires that we stipulate how the dual comparison works. We do this now.

We represent the complex process via a weighted average equation. The weight, λ, is in $(0, 1)$, and $q_t(\alpha)$ denotes the probability that the agent selects action α in t based on both retrospection and prospection, while $p_t(\alpha)$ continues to denote the retrospectively based propensity. The function $\mathbf{I}(\alpha)$, which represents the prospective component, takes on a value of 1 if $\alpha = \alpha^*$, and 0 otherwise. It thus reflects the tendency of the agent to compare options prospectively against each other (and to get that evaluation right). Then we have the following.

(A2.5) For all t, $q_t(\alpha) = \lambda p_t(\alpha) + (1 - \lambda)\mathbf{I}(\alpha)$.

The following result uses this assumption to show that proposition 2.1 is not knife-edge: it continues to hold if a person compares alternatives to each other as well as to an aspiration level.

Proposition 2.3. *Suppose $n = 1$. The agent's probability of using action α in t is defined by (A2.5) with $0 < \lambda < 1$; the propensity component is a finite, stationary, and aperiodic Markovian ABAR. If payoffs are stochastic and there is a uniquely optimal action, then the agent plays suboptimal actions infinitely often with probability* 1.

More generally, we believe that the patterns produced by complex processes are qualitatively similar to those generated by pure aspiration-based adaptation.

CHAPTER THREE

Party Competition

THIS CHAPTER PRESENTS a behavioral model of elections based on satisficing (Simon 1955) coupled to the Schattschneider-Schumpeter-Downs macrohypothesis that in vigorous democracies major parties are structured to win elections. We model political parties as adaptive organizations that compete in a sequence of elections. Our central premises about decision making closely follow Simon's analysis: *winners satisfice* (the winning party in period t keeps its platform in $t + 1$), while *losers search.* Simon's general notion of an agent's aspiration level is thus represented here by the domain-specific hypothesis that winning an election is satisfying, while losing is not.

As noted in chapter 1, it is sometimes argued that although amateurs (voters) satisfice, professionals (politicians) optimize. However, we believe that this aphorism seriously underestimates the difficulty of optimizing in many electoral contexts. One feature that makes such problems hard is that politicians usually are uncertain about voter preferences. To be sure, parties conduct numerous polls; yet uncertainty often persists throughout campaigns and sometimes even *after* an election has been decided. (For example, the fierce debates among Democrats over John Kerry's loss in the 2004 presidential election indicate that even the past can be cloudy.) Many Downsian models simply ignore this uncertainty. Others incorporate it via a standard game-theoretic formulation, i.e., as a game of incomplete information, with each party's uncertainty depicted by subjective priors over the distribution of voter preferences. This approach's logic requires the parties to think about their uncertainties precisely and consistently, i.e., they have common knowledge about their respective prior distributions. This presumes a cognitive capacity for dealing with complexity and a level of coordination of their information bases that strikes even pure game theorists (Kreps 1990; Rubinstein 1998) as unrealistic. Hence, we present a behavioral alternative.

To lay bare the logic of satisficing and search in two-party competition, we present a stripped-down model. It assumes, as do most models of repeated elections, that voters' preferences stay put. Empirically, of course, these preferences do change over time, but posing the problem this way allows us to focus our analytical attention on how parties adapt and adjust their policies as they try to win office. Understanding how policies evolve given fixed voter preferences is a necessary first step for understanding their evolution in more dynamic settings.

The rest of the chapter is organized as follows. Section 3.1 reviews relevant literature. Section 3.2 presents the model and several implications.[1] Proposition 3.2 shows that if winners satisfice, then experimentation by losers is *necessary* for a well-defined type of electoral "progress." Proposition 3.3 demonstrates that if experimentation has certain weak properties, then it and satisficing by winners are *sufficient* to ensure that the sequence of winning policies converges to the policy space's top cycle set with probability 1.[2] Hence, if there is a majority-rule winner, then ultimately the incumbent party will espouse it. However, propositions 3.4 and 3.5 show, given weak assumptions about the out-party's search, that when a median voter exists, both parties do *not* stabilize at her bliss point. Thus, in contrast to both the Hotelling-Downs rational choice theory and Kollman, Miller, and Page's adaptive model (1992), full convergence is not predicted.

Section 3.3 investigates alternative specifications of the challenger's search behavior by endowing him with different degrees of sophistication and certain kinds of knowledge about the political terrain, following Kramer (1977), Miller (1980), Ferejohn, Fiorina, and Packel (1980) and Ferejohn, McKelvey, and Packel (1984). Section 3.4 analyzes whether our results are sensitive to changes in key assumptions. We present a computational model that provides results for ill-structured electoral environments: a multidimensional policy space where the Plott (1967) conditions do not hold (i.e., when there is no generalized median voter). Computational results show that in the long run winning policies are centrally located, and their dispersion is strongly correlated with the size of the uncovered set.[3]

---

[1] Proofs of these implications and other results of this chapter appear in Bendor, Mookherjee, and Ray (2006).

[2] The concept of a top cycle set is defined precisely in footnote 7. For now it suffices to know that it is a generalization of the idea of a majority-rule winner, usable when there is no median voter.

[3] The uncovered set is defined as follows (Miller 1980). Policy x covers y if (1) it is majority-preferred to y, and (2) all policies that are majority-preferred to x are likewise preferred to y. If there is no x that satisfies criteria (1) and (2), then we say that y is *uncovered*; all such policies form the uncovered set.

3.1 Related Work

Kollman, Miller, and Page (1992, 1998; henceforward KMP) pioneered work on adaptive parties. In their simulation model, winners satisfice; challengers generate platforms via adaptive search algorithms, and office-oriented ones then select the vote-maximizing platform. KMP showed that the distribution of winning platforms in a two-dimensional policy space tends to be centrally located. When the simulation is rerun in a unidimensional setting (the papers don't present results on this case), office-oriented parties converge to the median voter's ideal point (Page, personal communication, 1999).[4] Hence, *this* adaptive model yields the same long-run prediction as Hotelling-Downs.

Unfortunately, for several reasons KMP's impact on the field has been less than their papers deserved. First, in one sense KMP were too ambitious: they analyzed multidimensional policy spaces without examining the unidimensional setting. Second, in another respect, however, KMP were not ambitious enough: their papers settled for simulation results rather than analytical ones. This took their work out of the Downsian mainstream, which emphasizes mathematical models and analytical results. The combination of unorthodox substantive premises and an unfamiliar method of analysis may have limited its impact.

Third, there are many plausible ways to model bounded rationality. Hence, to get robust results we should posit *general properties of adaptation* (e.g., successful actions are more likely than unsuccessful ones to be repeated) rather than specific functional forms. Simulation is ill-suited to the general approach: a computer must be told exactly what kind of search rule to use. Sensitivity testing (which KMP did) can alleviate but not eliminate this problem. Indeed, because there are many types of bounded rationality, an efficient form of sensitivity testing is to establish results analytically.

This chapter complements KMP by using a different research strategy. First, we establish results that hold for the canonical Downsian setting: a unidimensional policy space and single-peaked preferences. Only then do we move to the less well-understood multidimensional environment. Second, we push analytical results as far as we can, turning to simulation only when necessary. Third, in the interest of generality and robustness, we specify a few general properties of adaptation rather than relying on detailed heuristics. These features

[4] If the set of platforms is finite, then one can prove that two of KMP's search rules yield convergence to the median voter with probability 1.

are interdependent—for modeling general properties of adaptation math is better than simulation—so they form a coherent approach with its own distinctive set of trade-offs.

3.1.1 Unorthodox Downsian Work

Although KMP were probably the first to make limited rationality *central* to models of party competition, they were not the first to incorporate aspects of bounded rationality in such models. Kramer (1977) and the matched pair of Ferejohn, Fiorina, and Packel (1980) and Ferejohn, McKelvey, and Packel (1984) (henceforth FFMP) were mostly Downsian in nature. They focused (Kramer 1977, pp. 311–315; Ferejohn, Fiorina, and Packel 1980, pp. 140–141; Ferejohn, McKelvey, and Packel 1984, pp. 45–46) on the so-called chaos problem, which arises out of the internal logic of the Downsian project (Ferejohn 1995). None of these papers made rationality a central concern. But in several ways they were unorthodox members of the program, and some of these respects involved nonoptimizing behavior.[5] Because these papers provide some interesting contrasts to the present work, we take a brief look at their features now.

First, all involve *status quo-based processes*: in Kramer's electoral model, today's winner keeps the same platform tomorrow; in FFMP's committee model, today's winning alternative is tomorrow's status quo. Though the authors do not give a cognitive interpretation for this,[6] we think there is a natural one: winners don't fix what is not broken. However, this satisficing interpretation of status quo-based processes is ours, not theirs. Indeed, this assumption fits awkwardly with the Downsian perspective.

Second, agents are myopic. FFMP make this explicit (Ferejohn, Fiorina, and Packel 1980, p. 144), but it also squares with Kramer's model in two ways: (a) That the winner keeps yesterday's platform is clearly myopic. (b) Kramer also assumes that the out-party selects a platform that maximizes vote share against the status quo policy. This is an example of what is now called myopic best response: an alternative is chosen today without regard for the long run.

Third, nonequilibrium (i.e., non-Nash) solution concepts are used. This, we believe, follows naturally from the agents' myopic qualities.

---

[5] We think that a behavioral program could embrace Kramer (1977) and FFMP as pioneering papers. For how a new program appropriates theories once part of an earlier one, see Laudan (1977, pp. 93–95).

[6] Kramer is especially terse about this assumption, saying only that "in each period one of the parties is elected, enacts the policy it advocated, and in the next election must defend this same policy" (p. 317).

Because we will compare our results with Kramer's and FFMP's in section 3.3, we defer a description of their findings until then.

3.2 The Model and Its Implications

We study a standard electoral game: a contest between two candidates or parties. A few modifications have been introduced to enhance analytical tractability. There is a finite set of citizens, $N = \{1, \ldots, n\}$, with n odd, and a finite set of policies or platforms, $X = \{x_1, \ldots, x_m\}$, with $m > 1$. (X may be huge, but finiteness is analytically useful for several results.) Each citizen has a strict preference ordering over policies. If the candidates adopt the same policy, then voters break their indifference by independently tossing nondegenerate coins. A voter's coin need not be fair; it might, e.g., be biased toward the incumbent. Voters may have different probabilities of voting for the incumbent or for either party. For simplicity we assume that all these random procedures are Markovian and stationary: they are independent of the electoral history prior to t and of t itself.

Since n is odd, the majority preference relation is also strict: for any two policies, x and x', either a majority of citizens strictly prefer x to x' (written $x \succ x'$) or they strictly prefer x' to x. Further, since the above assumption of indifference breaking means that individual voters always reach a decision, elections are conclusive even when the candidates adopt the same policy. (In these convergent outcomes, vote shares are random variables.)

We do not require spatial policies or preferences, but we can recover spatial settings (of different dimensionalities) when doing so is desirable. The following description of the majority preference relations induced by the above assumptions enables us to make this translation to a spatial framework. We partition the policy set into k disjoint subsets, $\{L_1, \ldots, L_k\}$, where $1 \leqslant k \leqslant m$, by iteratively applying the idea of the top cycle set.[7] Let L_1 be X's top cycle set. (As is known, L_1 cannot be empty.) Consider the reduced set, X/L_1. If this too is nonempty (it may not be), let L_2 denote the top cycle of X/L_1. Proceed in this way until all $x \in X$ are assigned to an L. This procedure must terminate since X is finite.

We call these subsets of X levels to suggest a mental picture: one can see the electoral environment as a series of levels or plateaus

[7] The top cycle set can be defined constructively. In our setting, a policy is in the top cycle set if and only if it is reachable from every other policy by a chain of strict majority preference.

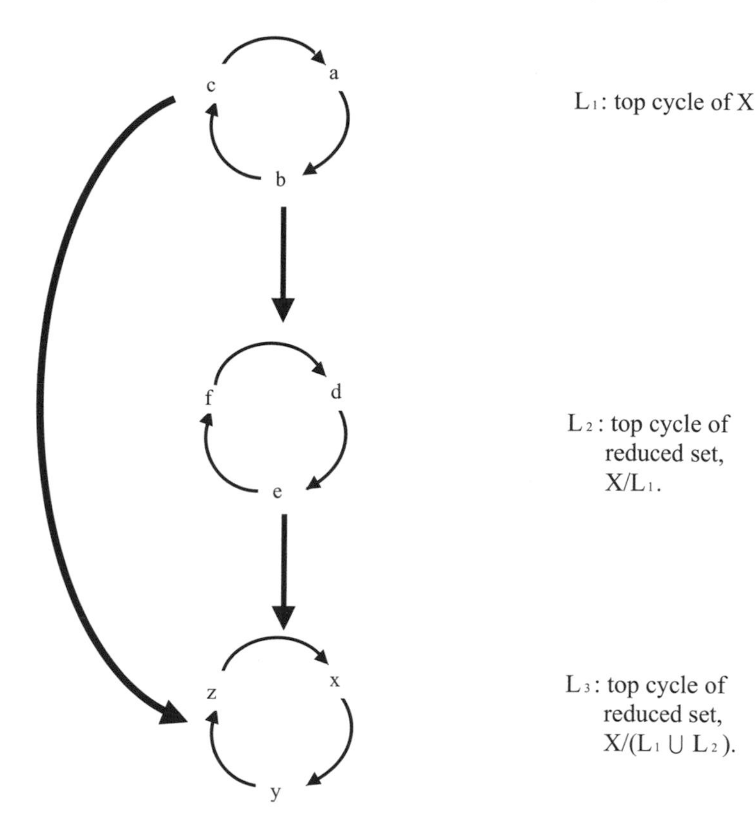

Figure 3.1. Three-level policy set.

(if $k > 1$). Each plateau electorally dominates those below it: each policy at a given level is majority-preferred to *all* policies at lower levels.[8] Further, every policy at a level *covers* (Miller 1980) all policies at lower elevations.[9] Within a level, however, no policy beats all others, nor does any policy lose to all others at its level. Thus, in nonsingleton levels, every two policies are joined by a majority-rule cycle. Hence, adaptive parties may get "hung up" on the cycles that pervade nonsingleton levels. Figure 3.1 gives an example of a policy set with three levels; each level has a cycle.

[8] This follows from two facts. First, no policy outside the top cycle set can beat anything in it (Austen-Smith and Banks 1999, p. 169.) Second, our assumptions rule out ties, so any platform in the top cycle must beat anything outside it.

[9] This implies that X's uncovered set is a subset of L_1, the uncovered set of X/L_1 is a subset of L_2, and so forth. But some policies in a given L_r may cover other policies in L_r (Bendor, Mookherjee, and Ray 2006).

Partitioning the policy set into levels is useful: it allows us to analyze concisely how the parties hill-climb—or plateau-climb—in the electoral landscape.

The partitioning also allows us to describe different majority preference relations. For example, let us use it to examine the classic spatial context: citizens with single-peaked preferences defined over a unidimensional policy space. For simplicity, assume that preferences are symmetric (e.g., quadratic utility). Symmetric preferences, plus our assumption that each voter's preference ordering is strict, together imply that the m policies are strictly ordered in Euclidean distance from the median voter's ideal point. Because the median voter is decisive here, the majority preference relation is identical to her preference ordering: the policy closest to her ideal point is the *Condorcet winner* (i.e., is majority-preferred to all other policies), the next closest policy loses to the Condorcet winner but beats everything else, and so on. Hence, in this classic setting the L-sets have a very simple structure. First, each L contains exactly one policy. Second, the policy in L_1 is the Condorcet winner, L_2's policy is the median voter's second most preferred option, and so on all the way down to L_m, whose policy is the farthest from the median ideal point. Thus, here the L's form a staircase, one policy per step, that leads up to the Condorcet winner.

The picture is naturally more complicated in most multidimensional policy spaces since these generically lack a generalized median. In such contexts the L's often are not singletons. Figure 3.2 depicts a two-dimensional space with three voters (again with symmetric, single-peaked preferences for simplicity) and six policies. The relatively centrist platforms, x_1, x_2, and x_3, form a cycle; each of them beats all of the more distant policies, x_4, x_5, and x_6, which also form a cycle. Hence, L_1 is composed of the more centrist policies, and L_2, the less centrist ones.

Consistent with idealizations that are standard in models of electoral competition, we assume universal turnout and sincere, error-free voting.[10] In short, it is assumed that if $x \succ y$, then x will defeat y in an election.

There is an indefinitely long sequence of elections, $1, 2, \ldots$, with one election per period. (At the start an incumbent party and its platform are randomly picked.) In every election the candidates simultaneously announce platforms; then citizens vote. The party that gets more votes wins the election and is the incumbent at the start of the next period.

---

[10] Proposition 6 of Bendor, Mookherjee, and Ray (2006) shows that our results are robust regarding these idealizations.

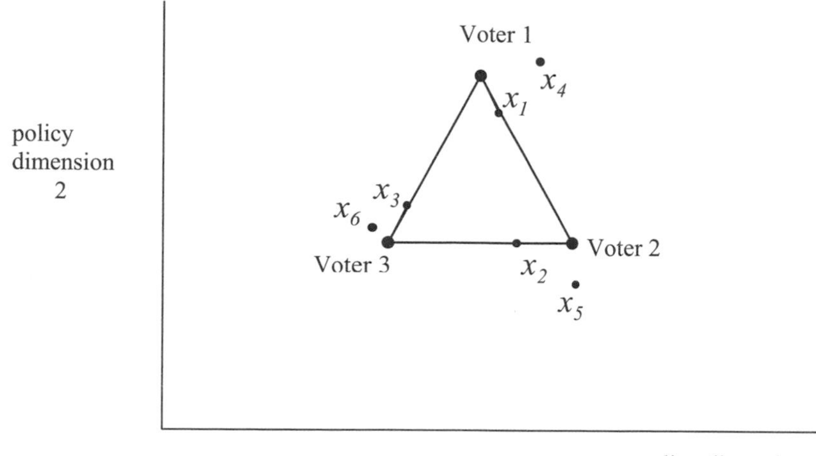

Figure 3.2. Levels in two dimensions.

The state variables of the associated stochastic process are the platforms of the incumbent, I_t, and the challenger, C_t. Thus, I_t is the policy that won the election in $t - 1$. We focus on how I_t—what Kramer (1977) called the *trajectory of winning policies*—evolves. (Because of I_t's importance we sometimes abuse terminology and refer to it as if it were *the* state variable.)

3.2.1 The Parties' Adaptive Behavior

The heart of the model is how the candidates respond to winning and losing. As already noted, we assume that winners satisfice (Simon 1955).

(A3.1) The winner of the election in t stands for reelection in $t + 1$ by keeping the platform that won him office in t.

In effect, the candidates have an implicit aspiration level in between the payoffs of winning and losing. Hence, winning is satisfying, and incumbents don't fix what is not broken.[11] [Apart from proposition 3.5, we do not explicitly model aspirations or their dynamics in this chapter. See Bendor, Mookherjee, and Ray (2001) for an overview of such models.] Similarly, losing is dissatisfying,

[11] Proposition 5.1 shows that under weak assumptions about aspiration adaptation, the candidates' aspirations will eventually move into the (l, w) interval and stay there (where l is the payoff for losing, and w the payoff for winning). So winning will be satisfying, but losing will not be.

and we follow Simon (1955) and Cyert and March (1963) in positing that dissatisfaction triggers search. Hence, our challengers (sometimes) search: in at least some elections they try policies that differ from their losing ones from the previous election.[12]

Before examining how challengers search, we report an important implication of satisficing which will help us understand which assumptions drive which conclusions. Proposition 3.1 refers to a stochastic process produced by the behavior of incumbents and challengers in the electoral environment of our k levels and (A3.1). So far, only part of this process has been defined: incumbents' (deterministic) behavior.[13] Randomness arises from the challenger's search, as we will see shortly.

Proposition 3.1. *Suppose (A3.1) holds. If I_t is in L_r, then thereafter it must be at that level or higher.*

Thus, assuming that incumbents satisfice ensures that electoral outcomes never slip downhill to lower plateaus.[14] The government's policy must either stay where it is or climb higher. The proof is simple. Suppose $I_t \in L_r$. The challenger either proposes a policy from a lower level or not. If it is lower, then the construction of the level sets plus sincere and flawless voting imply that the challenger must lose. Because winners satisfice, $I_{t+1} = I_t \in L_r$. If he proposes $x \in L_r$, then no matter who wins, $I_{t+1} \in L_r$. Finally, if the challenger proposes a higher platform, then he wins and satisficing by winners implies $I_{t+1} \in L_q$, where $q < r$. Induction does the rest.

Proposition 3.1 presumes nothing about the challenger. The result follows from the combination of the static electoral stage described by the k-levels and satisficing by winners. Recall, however, that we also assume error-free voting. Thus, the parties generate options that the voters test [per Simon's (1964) adaptive "generate-and-test" process], *and the test phase is flawless.* Error-free tests plus satisficing imply that the process cannot slip downhill.

So, half of the adaptive picture—how incumbents behave—acts as a *brake* on the process. The other half, how challengers search, supplies uphill momentum.

A key aspect of search is discovering new alternatives, as defined below.

[12] This is such a weak premise that we rarely label it a formal assumption. (We use it explicitly only in proposition 3.4.) If it didn't hold, then both parties would always keep the platforms they championed in period 1. This is neither realistic nor interesting.

[13] Proposition 3.1 can therefore analyze specific *sample paths.* It is not confined to probability distributions over a population of sample paths.

[14] Proposition 3.1 has bite only when there are multiple policy levels ($k > 1$).

Definition 3.1. A party *experiments* in period t if it selects a platform that it has never used before t. It *innovates* in t if it espouses a platform that neither party has ever used.

Because incumbents satisfice, they don't experiment. Only challengers can generate novel policies. The importance of this responsibility is underscored by the next result, which shows that experimentation's strong form—innovation—is *necessary* for upward progress, i.e., for the trajectory of winning policies to move uphill.[15]

Proposition 3.2. *Suppose (A3.1) holds. For all periods t and t', where $t < t'$, if I_t is in L_r and no challenger in $[t, \ldots, t']$ innovates, then with probability* 1 *$I_{t'}$ is also in L_r.*

The proof is simple. By proposition 3.1, winning policies never slip downhill. Thus, if $I_t \in L_r$, all prior winning platforms (hence losing ones as well) have come from level r or lower. Therefore, if no challenger innovates in $[t, \ldots, t']$, then all of them must have chosen platforms from level r or lower. But if so and no innovation occurs in $[t, \ldots, t']$, then the set of available policies in that era is in $(L_r \cup \cdots \cup L_k)$. So, $I_{t+1} \in (L_r \cup \cdots \cup L_k)$, whence by induction all winning policies in $[t, \ldots, t']$ must also be in $(L_r \cup \cdots \cup L_k)$. Hence, innovation is necessary for progress.[16]

The electoral dynamic need not grind to a halt if no one innovates: an incumbent can be beaten even if his opponent does not experiment, much less innovate. For example, suppose $L_r = \{x, y, z\}$ and $x \succ y \succ z \succ x$. Then the status quo policy can change endlessly without experimentation, as the parties follow the cycle. But this behavior cannot kick the trajectory of winning policies up to a higher plateau.

When does experimentation *suffice* for upward progress? Consider this condition.

(A3.2) There is an $\theta > 0$ such that for every history and in every election in which the challenger hasn't already tried everything, the probability he or she experiments is at least θ.

---

[15] As noted earlier, it is trivially true that search by challengers is necessary for upward progress. Proposition 3.2 is stronger: search *that yields systemic novelty* is required for progress. (By searching its memory for policies that have worked in the past but which it hasn't tried recently, a party could search without experimenting. And it could experiment without innovating.)

[16] Neither proposition 3.1 nor proposition 3.2 requires that the set of policies be finite.

The challenger has good reason to try something other than his last platform: it lost in the last election, and the incumbent has stayed put. Further, experimentation is reasonable because *everything* that the challenger has tried is electorally flawed.

Remark 3.1. If (A3.1) holds, then every platform that the out-party of $t > 1$ has used before t has lost at least once.

The proof is by contradiction. If Remark 3.1 did not hold, then the challenger in t must have, in some period $t^{\dagger} < t$, espoused a policy, x, that never lost. But satisficing implies that that party would have continued to uphold x in $(t^{\dagger} + 1, \ldots, t - 1)$, triumphing in all those elections. But then in t that party would be the incumbent, not the challenger.[17]

If we consider platforms that have lost in the past to be electorally damaged goods, then we see why (A3.2) would hold. Further, (A3.2) is a weak assumption about challengers: it says nothing specific about what they know or how sophisticated they are. A challenger might, e.g., know the entire policy set, have beliefs about voters' preferences about platforms, and sophisticatedly update those beliefs. Or she might grope about blindly. (A3.2) is only a summary statement about the effects of the out-party's knowledge and strategic sophistication: it always has some chance of experimenting (when that is possible). Moreover, (A3.2) does not presume any specific stochastic model or even any familiar class of stochastic models. In particular, (A3.2) is not Markovian: what happens today could depend on events in the distant past.[18]

Although (A3.2) is a weak assumption about experimentation, it and satisficing by incumbents ensure that the trajectory of winning policies converges to X's top cycle. Satisficing by incumbents and experimentation by challengers work well together: the former prevents the process from slipping downhill, and the latter provides upward momentum.

Proposition 3.3. *If (A3.1) and (A3.2) hold, then the trajectory of winning policies converges to and is absorbed by* L_1 *with probability* 1.

---

[17] Note that remark 3.1 does not depend on the voters' behavior. It is produced by the satisficing of incumbents.

[18] For example, the chance of experimenting could rise the more often the out-party loses, as, e.g., desperation to reclaim the White House sets in. And the magnitude of the increases could depend on *when* the losses occurred: e.g., the more recent the losses, the more the challenger wants to experiment. Because the party's memory is not itself a state variable in our model, this is not Markovian.

The proof relies on the fact that any level below L_1 is *transitory*: if I_t ever goes to such a level, (A3.2) ensures that eventually it must leave there and, by proposition 3.1, never return. Since all lower levels are transitory, long-run convergence to the top level is guaranteed. And proposition 3.1 implies that L_1 is absorbing: once a trajectory of winning policies reaches the top, it stays there.

Proposition 3.3 implies that if L_1 is a singleton, then the trajectory of winning policies converges to that unique platform. (The challenger may keep moving around; more on this shortly.) Thus, when a Condorcet winner exists, *the government's policy must converge to it.*[19]

Convergence to the top cycle can be established without presuming that the electoral dynamic belongs to a special class of stochastic processes. In particular, the process could have multiple limiting distributions.[20] (For an example, see Bendor, Mookherjee, and Ray 2006.) However, although convergence to a unique long-run distribution is not necessary for trajectories of winning policies to be absorbed into L_1, this property is sufficient for this convergence: as we show elsewhere (Bendor, Mookherjee, and Ray 2006), assuming that the process converges to a unique probabilistic equilibrium substitutes for positing that the challenger experiments.

It is important to note that the convergence of the I_t's into L_1 is not equivalent (even when L_1 is a singleton) to the famous Hotelling-Downs prediction that the parties adopt identical policies. In view of the facts—candidates in two-party systems rarely champion identical platforms (Levitt 1996; Ansolabehere, Snyder, and Stewart 2001)—that proposition 3.3 does not imply the median voter result is good for the model's empirical standing.

However, though this result does not imply complete convergence, it does not preclude it either. Proposition 3.3 is silent on the matter because it uses (A3.2), which does not say what challengers do once they can no longer experiment because they've tried all feasible platforms. This is unlikely if X is large, but it is not ruled out. To tie up

[19] Determining the speed of convergence requires search assumptions that are stronger than (A3.2). We explore this issue in the next section. For now, note that even an unsophisticated search can push winning platforms uphill rapidly. For example, if the challenger searches blindly, then the chance of moving up in one period equals the fraction of policies that are in plateaus above the incumbent's. Thus, if I_t is at a low level, then the probability of hill climbing in one election is substantial.

[20] In one important respect we needn't worry about the number of limiting distributions. By proposition 3.3, the electoral dynamic goes into L_1 for sure. So no matter where in L_1 it winds up, eventually the government's policy must be electorally undominated, beating all policies in lower levels.

this loose end, consider the following weak formalization of Simon-Cyert-March's idea that dissatisfaction triggers search. (In addition to formalizing Simon et al.'s general notion, (A3.3) also incorporates the innocuous domain-specific premise that losing an election is dissatisfying.)

(A3.3) There is a $\theta > 0$ such that for every history, the challenger in $t+1$ adopts a platform that differs from the one it lost with in t with a probability of at least θ.

This weak specification of problem-driven search ensures that the electoral process will not settle down into a Tweedledum-Tweedledee pattern. Note that (A3.3) is sufficiently weak—e.g., it is not Markovian—so that the next result cannot pin down the properties of the process's limiting distribution(s). But it can say what the process will *not* do.

Proposition 3.4. *If (A3.3) holds, then no state in which the parties adopt identical platforms is absorbing, nor is any set of such states.*

Proposition 3.4 implies that if the process converges to a unique limiting distribution, then that distribution must put positive weight on states in which the parties adopt different platforms. Further, if it has multiple stationary distributions, then all of them must put weight on circumstances in which the parties offer distinct policies. That parties don't converge to the same position emerges naturally from two weak behavioral premises: (1) losing can be dissatisfying and (2) dissatisfaction triggers search.[21]

3.2.2 How Robust Is Divergence?

Proposition 3.4 presumes that candidates are purely office-oriented. But many scholars have argued that they probably also care about policy (e.g., Wittman 1983; Calvert 1985) and, since passing legislation is easier with a big mandate, vote share as well (Milyo 2001). Is the divergence result robust with respect to assumptions about candidate motivation? We address this question now.

Let $\pi_i(w, v, x)$ denote candidate i's utility when she wins and obtains v votes, where x is the winning platform. Similarly, $\pi_i(l, v, x)$ is her utility or payoff when she loses. We then represent the standard assumptions about candidates' payoffs as follows. First, politicians prefer winning to losing: $\pi_i(w, v, x) > \pi_i(l, v, x)$ for any given $v \in [0, 1]$ and $x \in X$. Second, they prefer more votes to less, ceteris paribus: $\pi_i(w, v, x) > \pi_i(w, v', x) \Leftrightarrow v > v'$, and similarly for

[21] The finiteness of X plays no essential role in proposition 3.4.

$\pi_i(l, \cdot, \cdot)$. Third, they prefer policies closer to their bliss points, all else equal: $\pi_i(w, v, x) > \pi_i(w, v, x') \Leftrightarrow d(x, x_i) < d(x', x_i)$, and similarly for $\pi_i(l, \cdot, \cdot)$, where $d(x, x_i)$ is the distance between policy x and i's bliss point x_i.

Given multiple goals, one cannot assume that winning is always satisfying or that losing is dissatisfying. (For example, a winner with high aspirations who espoused a platform far from his ideal point may find the victory bitter.) Hence, we must make aspirations explicit, which entails replacing (A3.1) and (A3.3) by their more fundamental counterparts (A3.1′) and (A3.3′), below. These more basic assumptions are defined by a comparison of utility to aspirations, instead of (A3.1)'s and (A3.3)'s dependence on specific events (i.e., on winning and losing). (A3.1′) is thus a more general definition of satisficing, and (A3.3′) is a more general definition of search. In both, $a_{i,t}$ denotes candidate i's aspiration level at date t, and $\pi_{i,t}$, his utility.

(A3.1′) Satisficing: If $\pi_{i,t} \geqslant a_{i,t}$, then in $t+1$ candidate i espouses the same platform she used in t.

(A3.3′) Search: There is an $\theta_i > 0$ such that for all t and every history leading up to t, if $\pi_{i,t} < a_{i,t}$, then in $t+1$ candidate i espouses a platform that differs from her platform in t with a probability of at least θ_i.

Since aspirations are now explicit we must stipulate how they are formed.

(A3.4) There is an $\epsilon \in (0, 1)$ such that i's aspiration level adjusts by a rule that satisfies the following conditions for all t and all histories leading up to t:

(i) If $\pi_{i,t} > a_{i,t}$, then $a_{i,t} + \epsilon(\pi_{i,t} - a_{i,t}) \leqslant a_{i,t+1} < \pi_{i,t}$.

(ii) If $\pi_{i,t} = a_{i,t}$, then $a_{i,t+1} = a_{i,t}$.

(iii) If $\pi_{i,t} < a_{i,t}$, then $\pi_{i,t} < a_{i,t+1} \leqslant a_{i,t} - \epsilon(a_{i,t} - \pi_{i,t})$.

(A3.4) is quite general: it specifies only the direction of aspiration adjustment and some weak restrictions on speed—in particular, adjustment cannot become arbitrarily sluggish. We then obtain the following result, which shows that proposition 3.4's divergence conclusion is robust with respect to assumptions about candidates' goals.

Proposition 3.5 presumes that candidates have "qualitatively similar" motives, which means that they pursue the same goals: e.g., either both care about how many votes they get or neither does. Their preference intensities, however, may differ sharply. (Indeed, their utilities may be described by different functional forms.)

Proposition 3.5. *Suppose (A3.1′), (A3.3′), and (A3.4) hold. Candidates' motives are qualitatively similar. Then convergent outcomes are absorbing if and only if candidates care only about policy and not at all about winning or vote share.*

To see why the result holds, let us suppose that candidates care only about policy. Now consider a state in which both parties espouse the median voter's ideal point and have aspirations less than or equal to the party-specific payoff generated by that policy. Because candidates care only about policy, which side wins doesn't affect their payoffs; all that matters is that whoever wins will implement that platform, i.e., the median voter's bliss point. Because the corresponding payoffs are at least as big as the corresponding aspirations of the candidates, by (A3.1′) both parties will retain their platforms in the next period, and so on. Hence, this configuration is stable.

On the other hand, suppose that in addition to policy the candidates care about winning. Then both espousing the median ideal point cannot be stable because losing the election must sometimes be disappointing.[22] A similar argument holds if they care about vote share.[23] Hence, caring only about policy is necessary for stability.

Proposition 3.5 implies that if candidates care about all three goals (winning, votes, and policy), then the classical median voter outcome is unstable. Further, it is stable only if politicians put *zero* weight on winning—a knife-edged possibility that seems far-fetched.

This result may appear vulnerable to the following criticism: the parties might eventually become sophisticated enough to interpret a close loss (after, e.g., they've adopted similar or identical platforms) as resulting from chance factors that have nothing to do with their chosen policy. They may therefore infer that their platform choice was a good one. Thus, because the loser's policy is not really broken, the party doesn't see the need to fix it, whence convergence may be an absorbing outcome. However, this argument is

[22] This holds because aspirations and payoffs are stochastic—with identical platforms, which party wins is random—and aspirations are endogenous. The explanation for this part of the argument is somewhat involved, but to put it briefly, one side (say D) cannot always be content with a payoff produced by losing because sometimes D wins. This boosts its aspiration level, thus making a subsequent loss dissatisfying.

[23] If the parties have adopted the same platform, then votes are randomly cast, whence the argument of the previous footnote holds.

not compelling. When parties pick the same platform, voters will be indifferent between them, and the election outcome will be determined by stochastic factors such as arbitrary indifference-breaking rules, random voter turnout, or noisy vote counts. These will produce randomness in observed vote shares: the loser will end up with a vote share of less than half. Even a sophisticated party will find it hard to disentangle the impact of these stochastic variables from a genuine failure of its platform to appeal to a majority of voters. Because the temptation to second-guess its electoral strategy might be overpowering, the losing party is likely to engage in continued policy experimentation to improve its perceived chances of success in the next election.

At a more abstract level our behavioral model does not assume that agents know the game form, let alone that it is common knowledge. Parties may experience a disappointing loss, but that does not mean that they know precisely what would have worked instead.

Note that the KMP model and ours yield conflicting predictions when a median voter exists. Because the KMP challenger is trying (albeit myopically) to maximize his vote share, in the standard Downsian environment both parties end up espousing the median voter's bliss point, and so eventually take up identical platforms. Once that happens, the loser—however determined (hanging chads? the Supreme Court?)—will never move. In our model losing must eventually be dissatisfying even if the loser maximized his vote share; hence, the Tweedledum-Tweedledee pattern is unstable.

Thus, behavioral theories exhibit a pattern similar to that of rational choice theories. Some models predict convergence (Hotelling-Downs in the rational choice tradition; KMP in the behavioral framework); others predict separation (Calvert-Wittman for rational parties; our model for adaptive ones). Note, however, that the rationales for party separation are quite different. In the Calvert-Wittman model, policy-motivated parties (plus uncertainty) prevent convergence. In ours, all parties are office-motivated, but the dynamics of aspiration-based adjustments produces policy separation. Which model should be preferred is an empirical question. If Stokes' summary (1999) of the empirical literature—the two main parties rarely adopt the same platform—is accurate, then preference should be given to those theories in *both* programs (e.g., Wittman- or Calvert-type models in the rational choice program and the present aspiration-based theory in the bounded rationality framework) that make the more accurate prediction of nonconvergence.

3.3 Informed and/or Sophisticated Challengers

One can extend this model by making the challenger more informed and/or more sophisticated, hence sharpening his search for winning platforms. Regarding information, the extreme case would be to assume that the challenger knows the majority preference relation for each pair of platforms. Then, given varying degrees of strategic sophistication, the challenger might choose platforms that vote-maximize against the incumbent (Kramer 1977) or those that are in X's uncovered set (Miller 1980). Or one might posit an intermediate degree of information (e.g., the challenger has some chance of knowing what vote-maximizes against the status quo) and combine that with a degree of sophistication. Obviously, many extensions are possible. We can examine only a few prominent ones. Some are taken directly from the literature; others involve modifications. (The last case involves learning based on the feedback assumptions of chapter 1.)

3.3.1 Kramer's (1977) Model

Recall that incumbents in Kramer's model retain the platform that won them office, while challengers choose policies that vote-maximize against the status quo. His main result, theorem 1, says that the trajectory of winning platforms converges to the minmax set.[24] It need not stay there, but "Theorem 1 does ensure that a trajectory which jumps outside must immediately return toward the minmax set ..." (1977, p. 324). In contrast, our propositions 3.1 and 3.3 state that the trajectory is absorbed into the top cycle.

His model and ours yield different implications partly because they make different assumptions about what challengers know and/or can implement. Our challenger knows what he has tried in the past and has some chance of experimenting; Kramer's knows what vote-maximizes against the incumbent's policy. One might object to the latter because it gives challengers an unrealistic amount of information: to know *exactly* what policy vote-maximizes against the status quo is asking a lot of any decision maker or advisor. And presuming that the out-party is so well-organized, so immune to internal squabbles, that it can always *choose* a vote-maximizing option can also be

[24] A policy, x, is in the minmax set if the following properties hold. Consider the strongest alternative to x, i.e., the one that would garner the maximum number of votes, $M(x)$. The minmax set is composed of those policies which have the minimum $M(x)$. As Kramer notes, this generalizes the concept of a Condorcet winner; further, the minmax set always exists.

questioned. What, then, happens if challengers try to vote-maximize but occasionally "tremble" and mistakenly pick a platform that is not vote-maximizing? (For simplicity we make the standard assumption that following a tremble the challenger plays a fixed and totally mixed strategy: anything in X can be picked with positive probability.) The following result, which follows from proposition 3.3, gives the answer.

Remark 3.2. Suppose (A3.1) holds. With probability $1 - \eta$ the challenger selects a platform that vote-maximizes against the incumbent's policy; with probability $\eta > 0$ he trembles and plays a strategy that is totally mixed over X. Then the trajectory of winning policies converges to and is absorbed by L_1 with probability 1.

Hence, if the challenger can err in his effort to vote-maximize against the incumbent, then we recover the conclusion of proposition 3.3 even if the chance of error is arbitrarily small. Thus, though the challenger is trying to vote-maximize against the incumbent and usually does so, the process is led toward the top cycle, *not* to the minmax set (unless the two coincide). Why?

The reason is that the challenger's errors are filtered by the electorate, making the trajectory of winning policies drift toward higher plateaus in the short run and toward the top cycle in the long run. Proposition 3.1 tells us that given this electoral filtering, no mistake by the out-party can shove the dynamic down to lower levels. Further, since any kind of mistake is possible, the challenger has *some* chance of stumbling onto policies on higher levels. The voters approve of such mistakes, thus pushing the trajectory uphill—whether or not the minmax set and the top cycle coincide.[25]

Thus, regardless of the challenger's intentions, the electoral environment ensures that the dynamic is driven by winning per se rather than by the magnitude of victory. Consistent with Satz and Ferejohn's argument that "[when] we are ... interested in explaining ... the general regularities that govern the behavior of all agents ... it is not the agents' psychologies that primarily explain their behavior, but the environmental constraints they face" (1994, p. 74), the selection environment trumps the agent's intentions.

[25] This victory of the top cycle is hollow, strictly speaking, when it is the entire policy space. But proposition 6 of Bendor, Mookherjee, and Ray (2006) shows that if the top cycle is "almost" a strict subset of X, i.e., if the profile of voters' ideal points almost satisfies the Plott conditions, then I_t will spend most of its time in a strict subset of the policy space. (See subsection 3.4 for a detailed discussion of this robustness issue.) Because this subset of X and the minmax set can be disjoint (for an example see Bendor, Mookherjee, and Ray 2006), the thrust of remark 3.2 can hold even when the top cycle is everything.

This trumping holds quite generally; the Kramerian challenger's specific objective—to maximize votes against the status quo—was inessential in remark 3.2. As long as the challenger has some chance of trembling and playing a strategy that is totally mixed over X, the conclusions of remark 3.2 hold, *regardless* of the challenger's objectives. Thus, the parties could have different goals. For example, when the Democrats challenge, they could vote-maximize against the incumbent, but when the Republicans are the out-party, they select a policy that maximizes some ideological criterion (as in, e.g., Chappell and Keech 1986, p. 884). Or both parties could pursue a mix of office seeking and ideology, as in Wittman- or Calvert-type models. In the long run these goals do not matter. One could even allow for parties that suffer from Arrovian problems and so lack coherent preferences. All that counts is that the pattern of error gives the electoral mill enough grist to work on.[26] So long as this condition is met, the challenger could be as sophisticated and informed as one likes, with any kind of preferences; the end result is the same.

3.3.2 Miller et al. and the Uncovered Set

Miller (1980, p. 93) and others (McKelvey 1986; Cox 1987b; Epstein 1998) have argued that if x covers y, then x electorally dominates y. As Cox (1987b, p. 420) put it,

> If one accepts the extremely mild assumption that candidates will not adopt a spatial strategy y if there is another available strategy x which is at least as good as y against any strategy the opponent might take and is better against some of the opponent's possible strategies, then one can conclude that candidates will confine themselves to strategies in the uncovered set.

If we are to use the uncovered set as a solution concept, we must assume that challengers are both well-informed and relatively sophisticated. But expecting candidates to *invariably* pick policies in the uncovered set may be unrealistic.[27] Yet even a bit of information can help the challenger search, as the next result shows.

Remark 3.3. If (A3.1) is satisfied and for every history the challenger alights on X's uncovered set with positive probability, then the following hold.

---

[26] Thus, one can regard this as an evolutionary theory: blind variation is produced by error; selection is the electoral environment. We thank John Padgett for this interpretation.

[27] If they did, then the process would jump to L_1 in one period since X's uncovered set is a subset of L_1.

(i) I_t is in L_1 with positive probability for all $t > 1$.

(ii) If $\Pr(I_t \in L_1)$ is less than 1, then $\Pr(I_1 \in L_1) < \cdots < \Pr(I_t \in L_1)$.

(iii) $I_t \to L_1$ with probability 1 as $t \to \infty$.

Thus, even fragmentary information about the uncovered set's location and even crude understanding about the strategic value of uncovered policies can have substantial impacts in both the short run (parts (i) and (ii)) and in the long (part (iii)).

Now consider a less demanding possibility: the challenger might not know all of the uncovered set but may know policies that cover what he must try to beat today—the incumbent's platform. (This presumes that *some* alternative covers I_t. If not, then I_t is in X's uncovered set and so is already in L_1.)

First we establish the importance of the challenger finding something that covers the incumbent's platform. It is necessary: electoral hill climbing cannot occur without it.

Remark 3.4. Suppose (A3.1) holds. Consider any $r = 1, \ldots, k$. If I_t is in L_r and the probability that C_t covers I_t is zero, then I_{t+1} must also be in L_r.

The logic is straightforward. Any policy at higher levels, say any $x \in L_1 \cup \cdots \cup L_r$, covers any policy at lower ones, i.e., any $y \in L_{r+1} \cup \cdots \cup L_k$. Hence, if $I_t \in L_r$ and today's challenger has no chance of finding a platform that covers the incumbent's, then he has no chance of finding anything in $L_1 \cup \cdots \cup L_{r-1}$ since anything there would in fact cover I_t. Hence hill climbing cannot occur. Since proposition 3.1 ensures that the process cannot slip downhill, it must stay at the same plateau.

Now consider elections in which the challenger does have some chance of finding platforms that cover the incumbent's. The following assumption formalizes this idea.

(A3.5) For every history and in any election in which I_t is covered by some $x \in X$, with positive probability the challenger finds an option that covers the status quo.

(A3.5) neither implies nor is implied by (A3.2), which stipulates the possibility of experimentation.[28] But as the next result shows, their long-run effect is the same.

[28] (A3.2) does not imply (A3.5) because the challenger might experiment, but his set of possible new policies may not include anything that covers the status quo. For an example that shows why (A3.5) does not imply (A3.2), see Bendor, Mookherjee, and Ray (2006).

Remark 3.5. If (A3.1) and (A3.5) hold, then the trajectory of winning policies converges to and is absorbed by L_1 with probability 1.

Although the challenger is sophisticated enough to have a chance of finding a platform that covers the incumbent's, the process is *not* guaranteed to be absorbed into X's uncovered set (unless that set and L_1 coincide), though it will visit that set infinitely often. The reason: L_1 may have policies that are not in the uncovered set, and because any two policies in the same level are connected by a cycle, the trajectory of winning policies can leave the uncovered set.

3.3.3 FFMP (1980, 1984)

FFMP assume that new platforms come from a uniform distribution over the status quo's win set. (Policy x's win set is defined as the set of policies that are majority-preferred to x.) This is an intermediate degree of information and sophistication: less demanding than assuming that new options must cover the status quo but more demanding than assuming experimentation. However, FFMP posited a *uniform* distribution for computational reasons: they (1984) calculated bounds on the limiting distribution of winning platforms. This is unnecessary for qualitative results, and we shall disregard it. For our purposes the key part of FFMP's premise is that the challenger's search puts positive probability on anything that beats the incumbent's platform. As usual in this chapter, this assumption need not be forced into a Markovian mold.

(A3.6) Following every history, the challenger's search has a positive probability of finding any option that beats the status quo.

Because the set of policies that beat any x must include some in L_1, (A3.6) implies stochastic hill climbing in the short run and convergence to L_1 in the long run, just as remark 3.3 did.

Remark 3.6. If (A3.1) and (A3.6) are satisfied, then the following hold.

(i) I_t is in L_1 with positive probability for all $t > 1$.

(ii) If $\Pr(I_t \in L_1)$ is less than 1, then $\Pr(I_1 \in L_1) < \cdots < \Pr(I_t \in L_1)$.

(iii) $I_t \to L_1$ with probability 1 as $t \to \infty$.

Thus if challengers are as informed and sophisticated as FFMP posit, then long-term convergence to the top level is ensured, as is short-term progress.

3.3.4 Challengers Who Learn and Remember

Finally, we examine the possibility that challengers remember which platforms have done well in the past and which have done poorly (where doing well means winning, and poorly, losing) and adapt their propensities accordingly, per the basic feedback axioms of chapter 2.[29] Thus, the challengers need not be highly informed—for example, they may not know anything about the uncovered set—but they *are* adaptive: they learn what works and what doesn't.

Remark 3.7. Suppose (A3.1) holds. Parties have exogenously fixed aspirations in (l, w). With probability $1 - \eta$ the challenger selects a platform based on a propensity vector that changes in accord with assumptions (A2.1) and (A2.2); with probability $\eta > 0$ he tries a policy that has never lost him an election. (If no such policy exists, then his selection is based completely on his propensity vector.) Then the trajectory of winning policies converges to and is absorbed by L_1 with probability 1.

The proof is simple. By remark 3.1, we know that every policy that the challenger has tried prior to t has lost at least once. Hence, trying a policy that has never lost is equivalent to experimenting, in the sense of definition 3.1. Hence (A3.2) holds, which together with satisficing by incumbents yields the conclusion of proposition 3.3.

We know from remark 3.2 that the η-possibility of experimentation by challengers suffices, together with satisficing by incumbents, to drive the trajectory of winning platforms into level 1. Hence, one might wonder whether it is this assumption that does all the work in remark 3.7; perhaps learning by challengers is superfluous. In one sense that must be so, in light of remark 3.1. But we suspect that computational modeling would show that learning via ABARs can quicken the convergence to L_1.

In general, this section's findings show that endowing the challenger with more information and/or more strategic sophistication has a quantitative effect—convergence to L_1 is sped up—but does not affect the model's qualitative conclusions.

---

[29] As in the rest of this chapter, we assume here that winners satisfice. However, in this subsection we want to represent the possibility that challengers do not forget about the past performance of platforms that they have tried; yet, if satisficing were represented by propensity adjustment, it would entail setting the propensities for all other policies to zero, thus wiping out the memory of past victories and losses. Hence, although we assume that winners satisfice behaviorally—they keep the platform in $t + 1$ that won them office in t—we also posit that they continue to update a propensity vector in accord with chapter 2's feedback axioms. These axioms allow for gradual adjustment of propensities and therefore memory retention.

3.4 Robustness Issues

The price for analytical results is stylized assumptions. This means reshaping vague but plausible ideas (e.g., incumbents are often content with the platforms that won them office) into crisper but less plausible ones (incumbents *always* satisfice). To be sure, to theorize one must simplify: as Jonathan Swift observed long ago, the most realistic model of a phenomenon is the phenomenon itself. But it would be troubling if our results turned out to be knife-edge findings—if changing a premise a little altered the conclusions a lot.

Several features of our model might cause concern in this regard. As noted, assuming that incumbents invariably keep winning platforms exaggerates the plausible scenario it is meant to capture. Similarly, that x is majority-preferred to y may not *guarantee* that x will beat y: variations in, e.g., turnout or voters' errors, may change the outcome.

A more subtle concern, conceptually more serious than the above simplifications, is that our model seems to predict little in ill-structured environments where the Plott conditions fail. In such situations the top cycle may be the entire policy space. (It is well known that a multidimensional spatial voting setting is especially vulnerable to this problem.) But then proposition 3.3 is toothless, and our model apparently loses all predictive power.

Yet, as Ferejohn, Fiorina, and Packel (1980) and Ferejohn, McKelvey, and Packel (1984) argued, all is not lost. Although no policy is perfectly stable when the Plott conditions fail, some are probably more stable than others. To investigate this idea we resort to a computational model, which we now briefly describe.[30] (For links to a detailed description of the computer program, which is independent of the computational model in chapters 4, 6, and 7, see http://press.princeton.edu/titles/9352.html.) Because the simulation is a special case of our mathematical model—the policy space is finite, (A3.1) and (A3.2) hold, etc.—we focus on its distinctive properties: policies are set in a two-dimensional space, and voters have quadratic loss functions.[31]

[30] See Bendor, Mookherjee, and Ray (2006, pp. 189–191) for an analytical result that shows that the model is robust against small changes in key assumptions. Via a computational model we can examine the effects of big changes: e.g., when the voters' preference profile is far from having a generalized median.

[31] The following ensures that citizens have strict preference orderings over policies, as the analytical model requires: if policies x and y are equidistant from voter i's ideal point, then they are randomly and independently given different valence (nonspatial) values.

To ensure that the simulation results are easily interpretable, we make the search Markovian. Hence, the probability distribution of (I_{t+1}, C_{t+1}) depends only on the parties' current platforms and the transition rules created by the incumbent's satisficing and the challenger's search. We stipulate time-homogeneous search rules, so the (I_t, C_t) process is stationary. Hence, we can invoke powerful theorems for finite-state stationary Markov chains (e.g., Kemeny and Snell 1960) which tell us when such processes are ergodic (converge to unique limiting distributions). All of our computational results arise from ergodic processes. Thus, for any fixed set of parameter values, we will be scrutinizing the invariant distribution of the winning platforms. (More precisely, the output—for every fixed set of parameter values, 1,000 sample paths run for 1,000 periods—will closely approximate the corresponding invariant distribution.)

3.4.1 Results

We examine two types of results: (1) how different preference profiles affect the limiting distribution of winning platforms, and (2) how different search rules affect this distribution.

(1) The Effect of Preference Profiles. To measure a profile's symmetry, we use a standard metric: the size of the uncovered set. (At one extreme, if the uncovered set is a singleton, then a generalized median exists; at the other, it is the entire policy space. So the measure ranges from $1/m$ to 1.) The challenger's search rule is represented by a probability distribution over the policy space; here the distribution is single-peaked (a truncated normal). Thus, in t the challenger is more likely to choose a platform close to the one he espoused in $t-1$ than something far away.

The size of the uncovered set and the distribution of winning platforms are strongly related (figure 3.3). This reflects how the strength of centripetal forces varies across electoral environments. When the uncovered set is small, these centripetal forces are strong, so in the limiting distribution winning platforms are centrally located; when this set is big, the centripetal forces are weak, so winning platforms are scattered throughout the policy space.

This pattern complements an analytical result of Bendor, Mookherjee, and Ray (2006, pp. 189–191) which shows that the process is well-behaved for small perturbations to voter profiles. The computational results of figure 3.3 suggest that the process is well-behaved *globally*: the dispersion of winning platforms increases steadily as the uncovered set expands. But the electoral environment can mold the invariant distribution of winning platforms only if the out-party's

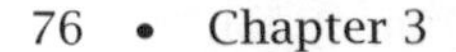

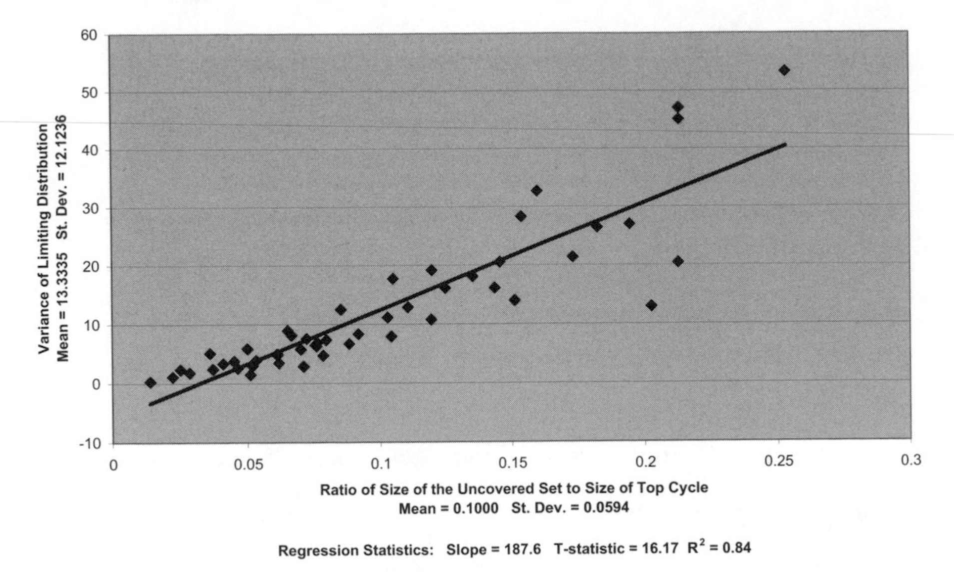

Figure 3.3. Winning platforms and the uncovered set.

search yields enough variety for the voters' selective forces to work on. So we now turn to the effect of different search rules.

(2) The Effect of Different Search Rules. The output in the first part of table 3.1 is based on naïve behavior by challengers: they search blindly, putting a probability of $1/m$ on every platform. Yet the size of the uncovered set and the long-run dispersion of winning platforms remain highly correlated: the main pattern—centrist platforms tend to win when the uncovered set is small—continues to hold. Hence, this pattern does not require search to be prospectively attuned to winning. Instead, what suffices is that challengers generate enough grist (variety) for the electorate's mill.

Table 3.1's second part shows that the relation between the uncovered set's size and the dispersion of winning platforms is reduced if the out-party's search is keyed to its policy preferences. This makes sense: that type of search creates a centrifugal force—the challenger being tugged back toward his ideal policy—that is independent of the size of the uncovered set.

Yet, although the pattern is weakened, it is still present, even in this extreme case when the challenging party is completely dominated by ideologues. (We have also studied searches that are a mix of the above pure types: the search centers on a policy that is a weighted average of the party's ideal point and its last platform. Results (unreported here) show that the system's long-run

TABLE 3.1
Relationship between size of uncovered set and dispersion of winning platforms.

Search rule	Mean uncovered set ratio	Mean variance of winning policies	β	R^2
Blind (uniform)	0.10 (0.063)	18.37 (18.58)	265.82 (14.92)	0.82
Ideological	0.09 (0.06)	10.51 (10.50)	98.25 (4.25)	0.27

Note: Standard deviations and absolute values of t-statistics are shown in parentheses.

tendencies are intermediate between those of the two pure search rules whose outcomes are reported in table 3.1.) Even ideological parties cannot completely ignore the strong electoral forces that exist when the uncovered set is small.

3.4.2 The Shaping Power of the Electoral Environment: Analytics Once More

Our computational results support the claim that the system is well-behaved even when the voters' preference profile is far from having a generalized median. But computational models must use specific assumptions—here, a two-dimensional policy space, quadratic utility, and a small electorate—so we now supplement these findings with an analytical one.

Since we computed when we couldn't derive general results analytically, we must simplify our analytical model *some*how. But this should be consistent with our substantive objective: to examine the electoral environment's centripetal forces. Therefore we should not constrain voters' preferences. Instead, we make our mathematical model tractable by simplifying the challenger's search: we assume that it is blind—uniform over X. This not only helps to ensure tractability; it is also substantively useful: since challengers search blindly, they cannot provide any directional tendencies to trajectories of winning platforms. Instead, such tendencies must be due to the selective forces inherent in the electorate (and on satisficing by incumbents).

Our last result shows that even if the top cycle is the entire policy space and nothing is assumed about the Plott conditions, the electoral environment can still impart some stochastic order to outcomes.

Proposition 3.6. *Assume (A3.1) and blind search. If $L_1 = X$ and x covers y, then the limiting probability that x is the incumbent's platform exceeds y's limiting probability.*

Thus, if the electoral environment has long strings of covering relations (e.g., x covers y, which covers z, which ...), then the limiting probabilities of winning policies will be structured by monotonicity (e.g., x is more likely than y, which is more likely than z, which ...).[32] Proposition 3.6 also implies that if a platform's long-run probability of being the government's policy is maximal, then *it must be in the uncovered set.* These properties provide a behavioral foundation for the claims of Miller et al. that if x covers y, then x electorally dominates y.

3.5 Conclusions

Our results emphasize how powerfully certain electoral landscapes shape the behavior of two competing, boundedly rational candidates. In highly structured electoral environments—those with many levels—electoral competition constrains the process greatly, even if challengers are ignorant and unsophisticated. Thus, our analysis is consistent with work in economics on zero-intelligence agents (e.g., Gode and Sunder 1993), which analyzes how much of market performance is due to the market environment rather than the intelligence of agents. Gode and Sunder concluded, "Adam Smith's invisible hand may be more powerful than some may have thought: when embodied in market mechanisms such as a double auction, it may generate aggregate rationality not only from individual rationality but also from individual irrationality" (p. 136). When the median voter exists, his or her hand is similarly powerful in guiding the trajectory of winning platforms.[33]

---

[32] Proposition 3.6 *cannot* be generalized by replacing "x covers y" with "x beats more policies than y does." Though the resulting conjecture—platforms that beat more rivals should eventually be more likely to be the government's policy—is intuitively plausible, it is not true in general. This is so even if one rules out spatially bizarre "preferred to" relations, e.g., x beats y even though the former loses to thousands of other platforms while the latter loses only to a handful.

[33] The parallel with models of zero-intelligence agents is incomplete: in a pure zero-intelligence model *both* candidates would choose platforms blindly, whereas our winners satisfice, which is fairly sensible behavior. We have not pursued that limiting case here. But even a cursory examination of the pure zero-intelligence model would reveal that the electoral environment strongly shapes the trajectory of winning policies.

We also investigated the effects of endowing challengers with more information and/or sophistication. The results show that their effect is quantitative, not qualitative: they tend to speed up hill climbing, making the trajectory of the winning platform converge faster to the top level.

A concern about this chapter's model is that slight perturbations of voters' preferences can create an ill-structured electoral environment and make many of our analytical results vacuous. But our computational results indicate that the process is well-behaved even when the preference profile is far from having a Condorcet winner.

We turn next to how voters choose, given the options made available to them by parties.

CHAPTER FOUR

Turnout

WE NOW TURN our approach to what is perhaps the most prominent anomaly for rational choice theory. As Fiorina (1990) famously suggested, the problem is both well known and straightforward: in large electorates, the chance that any single voter will be pivotal is very small. Consequently, the cost of voting will outweigh the expected gains from turning out and few citizens will vote.[1]

This prediction stands contrary to some of the most easily observed facts about elections. Since 1960, turnout in U.S. presidential elections has always exceeded 49 percent. Even turnout in midterm elections has always exceeded 36 percent during this period. It is furthermore well known that U.S. turnout rates typically trail those of most industrialized democracies. For example, since World War II, turnout in most U.K. general elections has exceeded 70 percent. Clearly, then, a prediction of low electoral participation is empirically problematic.

Strategic theories usually model turnout as a large team game (e.g., Palfrey and Rosenthal 1983). These typically posit two candidates and two types of citizens, where all members of each team have identical preferences. The preferences of each team are diametrically opposed. Each person can either vote for a candidate or stay home (shirk). Elections are decided by a simple plurality with a random tie-breaking rule. All members of the winning faction earn a positive payoff for winning (whether or not they voted); losers get nothing. Independent of the outcome, citizens bear an additive and private cost of voting. Because voting for the nonpreferred candidate is dominated for each voter, the relevant problem reduces to a participation game that simply involves the binary decision of whether to vote or stay home.

Strategic models of turnout typically do not predict that *no* voting will occur. If the cost of participating is not too high, then it will not be an equilibrium for everyone to stay home, for then a single voter could decide the election. Indeed, there are typically multiple equilibria with positive turnout. But the results of game-theoretic models of turnout have several highly unappealing features. First, no pure

[1] The classical version of the paradox of turnout was formulated as a decision-theoretic model by Downs (1957).

strategy equilibria exist, except in degenerate cases (e.g., if voting costs are zero or if the teams are exactly the same size). Second, the equilibria are asymmetric: some voters must play mixed strategies while others play pure ones. Finally, high turnout equilibria are not robust to the introduction of uncertainty over either preferences (Palfrey and Rosenthal 1985) and costs or the number of players (Myerson 1998). The robust equilibria have vanishing turnout.

The implication of vanishingly small turnout in team games follows by *jointly* assuming a certain behavioral model, such as expected utility maximization or Nash equilibrium, and making certain payoff assumptions as expressed by a normal form game: that voters care about outcomes and not, e.g., the act of voting per se, or that voting is costly. Thus, a solution to the anomaly must modify the behavioral model, the payoff assumptions, or both.

As Feddersen (2004) noted, the most prevalent response to this anomaly has been to modify the payoff assumptions. For example, citizens may have a sense of duty to vote that outweighs the cost of participation (Riker and Ordeshook 1968).[2] Empirically this may well be true, and we suspect that it does explain at least some turnout. But completely dispelling an anomaly in this manner raises obvious methodological concerns. To answer the question "Why do people vote?" simply by saying that people have a taste for it seems methodologically problematic.[3]

This chapter adopts a different approach. We leave the game structure, and hence payoffs, alone. As in the classical models, voting is costly and voters are motivated by outcomes. But instead of calculating expected utilities, our voters learn to vote or to stay home by a simple form of trial and error, as developed in chapter 2.[4] Their adaptation rules follow the axioms of ABARs generally and those of reinforcement learning (Bush and Mosteller 1955) more specifically. Actions that are successful today are more likely to be produced tomorrow; unsuccessful actions are less likely. This reinforcement learning is married to an aspiration level (Simon 1955), a threshold

---

[2] For a model where voters have altruistic preferences, see Feddersen and Sandroni (2006). Coate and Conlin (2004) develop a model of group rule-utilitarian voting. For models of group voting, see Morton (1991) and Herrera and Martinelli (2006). Schuessler (2000) has suggested models of "expressive voting." In a decision-theoretic formulation, Ferejohn and Fiorina (1974) assume that voters are regret minimizers.

[3] See, however, Feddersen and Sandroni (2006) for a model where the duty to vote is derived from more fundamental (here rule-utilitarian) principles.

[4] Kanazawa (1998) proposes an alternative stochastic learning model, along with an empirical test.

that partitions all possible payoffs into satisfactory and unsatisfactory ones, hence indicating which actions are coded as successes and which as failures. A voter's aspiration level itself adjusts to experience, reflecting prior payoffs.

The simulation results indicate that even if all the voters experience strictly positive costs of voting, turnout is substantial. Moreover, the model implies some of the main regularities from the empirical turnout literature, e.g., turnout is negatively correlated with participation costs and with differences in the relative sizes of factions. This is important because our approach not only proposes a solution to a hitherto unresolved puzzle but also preserves the insights of existing models.[5] We also derive a number of other implications, such as the duty to vote, that illustrate how ABARs generate collective behavior.

4.1 The Model

The model focuses on voters' turnout decisions under fixed candidate platforms. The electorate has n citizens and is divided into two factions: $n_D > 0$ "Democrats" and $n_R > 0$ "Republicans," with $n_D + n_R = n$. Voters are indexed by subscript i. Players interact at discrete time periods t according to the same one-shot game. In each period, each agent can choose either to vote or to shirk. Let $\alpha \in \{V, S\}$ denote the actions of voting and shirking, respectively.

Let $y \in \{w, l\}$ denote the outcomes of winning and losing, respectively. We use $\pi_{i,t}(\alpha, y)$ to denote agent i's realized payoffs at time t conditional on α and y. Where convenient, we also use $\pi_{i,t}$ to denote agent i's unconditional payoff at time t. In each period, $\pi_{i,t}(\alpha, y)$ is the sum of a deterministic and a random component. The random component is an independent and identically distributed shock, $\epsilon_{i,t}$, which is drawn from a uniform or normal distribution.

As is typical of turnout games, the deterministic component for each player depends on the action taken by the voter and on the outcome of the election (and hence on the actions taken all by players, i.e., the action profile). Whichever side turns out more voters wins the election. Ties are decided by a (not necessarily fair) coin toss. To make our model comparable with the other models throughout the book, the deterministic component can be described with a simple quadratic utility function in a spatial setting. Party platforms and

[5] Preference-based solutions frequently fail this second criterion. See, e.g., Palfrey and Rosenthal (1985) for a critique of regret minimization (Ferejohn and Fiorina 1974).

voter ideal points are located on a unidimensional space, with faction D voters located at -1 and faction R voters located at 1. Party platforms are characterized by the parameter $x \geqslant 0$, with the D-party located at $-x$ and the R-party located at x. Thus, x is a measure of how polarized parties are relative to the electorate.

If player i is part of the winning faction, then she or he earns a deterministic payoff regardless of whether she or he voted:

$$\overline{b} = -\frac{(x-1)^2}{2}.$$

Correspondingly, all members of the losing faction receive

$$\underline{b} = -\frac{(x+1)^2}{2}.$$

It will be convenient to adhere to the convention of letting $b = \overline{b} - \underline{b} = 2x$ denote the net benefit of winning.

Each player's deterministic cost of voting is c. Normally, it is assumed that $b > c > 0$, so that voting is undominated. Of course, the turnout paradox can be directly avoided by assuming that voters have a duty to vote or, equivalently, a "negative cost" of voting (Riker and Ordeshook 1968). This is equivalent to setting $c < 0$, which will be investigated as a special case below. Payoffs are additive in the benefits and costs. Thus, for the deterministic component, winning voters get $\overline{b} - c$; winning shirkers get $\overline{b}$. Losing voters get $\underline{b} - c$; losing shirkers get $\underline{b}$.

Note that the costs and benefits of voting are homogeneous within each faction. This allows us to keep the model comparable to earlier, game-theoretic analyses of turnout, such as the Palfrey and Rosenthal (1985) model.

The heart of the model is the learning behavior of each agent, where action propensities as well as aspiration levels respond to experience. In its most general form, this behavior follows the rules of ABARs laid out in chapter 2. However, to implement the model we must make several additional assumptions about the specific form of adaptation used by voters.

In every period t, every actor i has a propensity (probability) to vote, denoted $p_{i,t}(V) \in \{p^1, \ldots, p^l\}$, where $l > 1$ and each propensity value is between 0 and 1. That citizen's propensity to shirk is thus $p_{i,t}(S) = 1 - p_{i,t}(V)$. For convenience, we often abbreviate the vote propensity as $p_{i,t}$. These probabilities are independent across citizens. As with any ABAR, each citizen also has an aspiration level, denoted $a_{i,t}$. Note that we assume that all agents have the same set of possible propensity levels. Similarly, all agents have the same set of aspiration levels.[6] The sets of propensity and aspiration levels are fixed over time.

Depending on $p_{i,t}$, an action is realized for each i. This determines whether i's faction won or lost and whether i voted, which together establish the deterministic component of i's payoff. The randomly determined realized payoffs are then compared to aspiration levels, which may lead to the adjustment of turnout propensities or aspirations for the next period. Consistent with chapter 2, we also allow for the possibility that voters are sometimes inertial. Recall that with probability ε an agent does not adjust his turnout propensity in a current period. Similarly, with probability ε an agent does not adjust his aspiration level. These probabilities are mutually independent and identically distributed across both agents and periods. We call any agent who is noninertial for both turnout and aspirations *alert*.

For our specific ABAR we use the well-known Bush-Mosteller reinforcement rule, which is defined as follows. If an actor who takes action α and who is noninertial in a given period codes the outcome as successful (i.e., if $\pi_{i,t} \geqslant a_{i,t}$), then

$$p_{i,t+1}(\alpha) = p_{i,t}(\alpha) + \lambda(1 - p_{i,t}(\alpha)),$$

where $\lambda \in (0, 1]$ represents the speed of learning or adaptation, given a successful outcome. Similarly, if the outcome was coded as a failure, then

$$p_{i,t+1}(\alpha) = p_{i,t}(\alpha) - \lambda p_{i,t}(\alpha),$$

where $\lambda \in (0, 1]$. Finally, aspiration adjustment is implemented by stipulating that tomorrow's aspirations are a weighted average of today's aspiration level and today's payoff (Cyert and March 1963):

$$a_{i,t+1} = (1 - \nu)a_{i,t} + \nu\pi_{i,t},$$

where $\nu \in (0, 1)$.

Because we assume a finite state space—hence finitely many turnout propensity values and aspiration levels—these transition rules are approximate. The actual values of $p_{i,t}$ and $a_{i,t}$ are rounded for all i and t. Thus, this combination of adjustment rules is indeed a special case of an ABAR.

Our model is naturally formalized as a discrete-time, finite-state Markov process. In any period t, each agent i is characterized by vote propensity, $p_{i,t}$, and an aspiration level, $a_{i,t}$. Hence, a state in this process is described by n pairs of propensities and aspirations. Transitions between states are governed by a combination of the propensity and aspiration adjustment axioms and the payoff environment

---

[6] In the simulation program, finiteness follows from the program's internal representation of floating-point numbers.

of the turnout game. Because these transitions are stationary—they do not depend on the date—we have a stationary Markov process. Our goal is then to study the long-run behavior of this process.

As with most games of interest, it is difficult or impossible to derive quantitative properties of the limiting distribution analytically. We therefore use a computational simulation which enables us to examine the important quantitative features of the process's limiting distribution, such as the average level of turnout. It is important to note that because the computational model satisfies all of the premises of the general model defined in chapter 2, theorem 2.3 continues to hold: the simulation must converge to a unique limiting distribution. This result provides theoretical foundations for our simulations in two ways. First, because we know that the process will converge to the same limiting distribution from all starting states, our simulation results do not depend on the initial state (provided, of course, the program is run long enough). Second, an alternative interpretation of the limiting distribution is that it also gives the long-run mean fraction of time that the process occupies a given state. Therefore, by considering a single run (for each parameter configuration), we can capture the limiting behavior of our process as if it were run for many different initial states.

However, the simulation approach is limiting in two ways. First, all simulation results depend on the specific functional form given by the Bush-Mosteller model and the specific payoff distribution. Second, any conclusion drawn from a simulation holds, strictly speaking, only for the chosen parameter configuration. To address both problems we also derive a few analytical results that capture the general properties that drive the simulation runs and partially characterize turnout levels.

4.2 Main Results

4.2.1 Basic Simulation Results

Our simulation software allows us to test quickly a large number of parameter configurations of interest. However, the number of parameters is large, and for much of the subsequent discussion we will be interested in varying only one or two at a time. Thus, unless otherwise stated, our simulation runs use a set of parameter values described by table 4.1.

The first, and most fundamental, question is, do adaptively rational agents learn to vote in significant numbers? The answer is

TABLE 4.1
Default simulation parameters.

Number of simulations	1,000
Number of voters (n)	50,000
Factional split (n_D)	25,000
Party platform extremity (x)	1
Voting cost (c)	0.2
Shock distribution ($\epsilon_{i,t}$)	$\sim N(0, 0.1)$
Turnout propensity adjustment	Bush-Mosteller
Turnout adjustment (λ)	0.1
Initial turnout propensity distribution ($p_{i,1}$)	All 0.5
Aspiration adjustment and payoffs	Linear with stochastic quadratic payoffs
Aspiration adjustment (ν)	0.1
Initial aspiration distribution ($a_{i,1}$)	Center of payoff distribution

yes. In our first run the electorate has 50,000 voters evenly divided between two factions. Even with so many citizens, the average turnout over 1,000 simulations at $t = 300$ is 50 percent. Figure 4.1 shows that in this run, the distributions of voter propensities are more or less identical at periods 100, 200, and 300, and quite different from the initial distribution at period 1. This supports the notion that each simulation had settled into its limiting distribution by period 100.

To demonstrate that these turnout levels are robust, we can also start the simulation with turnout propensities that are far from the final steady state. Instead of using initial turnout propensities that are normally distributed around 50 percent, the following runs set initial turnout propensities to zero. The average turnout over time is plotted in figure 4.2, and the distributions of turnout propensities at periods 5, 15, and 100 is plotted in figure 4.3.

Here we see that participation is about 40 percent by period 20 and soon afterward stabilizes at 50 percent. Reassuringly, figure 4.3 shows that by the 100th period, the distribution of voting decisions is indistinguishable from those in figure 4.1. These results illustrate the content of theorem 2.3: the outcomes of this ergodic process are independent of the endogenous variables' starting values. Varying the values of exogenous variables can, of course, affect the speed at which participation breaks out. For example, raising the adjustment parameter λ would increase turnout in the early periods.

As a corollary, it is reasonable to expect that high levels of turnout will also moderate over time. In the following runs we start with

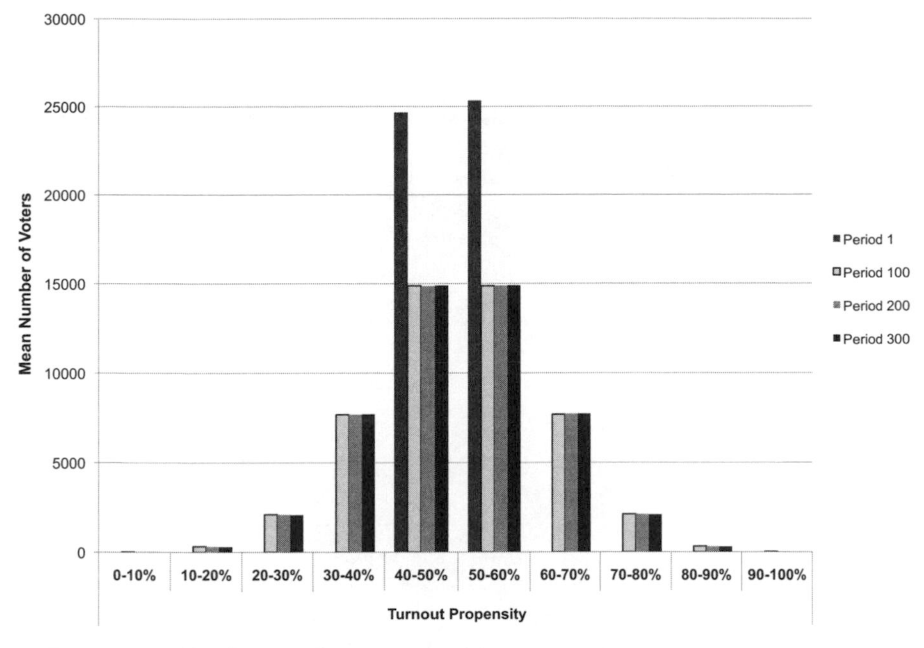

Figure 4.1. Distribution of vote propensities.

unrealistically high turnout propensities ($p_{i,1} = 0.9$) and aspirations ($a_{i,1} = 1$). This perhaps best describes a newly democratized country, where citizens have high expectations about the democratic process and are highly motivated to participate in the first elections.[7] Analogously to figures 4.2 and 4.3, figures 4.4 and 4.5 show that voting eventually converges to the now-familiar steady state.

What causes and sustains the breakout of participation? As this finding is central to most of the results in this chapter, it is worthwhile to try to understand it. Consider the dynamics of a single hypothetical simulation. Suppose that $n_D = n_R = 5{,}000$, $\overline{b} = 0$, $\underline{b} = -1$, $c = 0.2$, initial propensities are $p_{i,1} = 0.01$, initial aspirations are $a_{i,1} = -0.5$, and the payoff shock is distributed uniformly over $[-0.1, 0.1]$. Suppose Democrats win in period 1: 50 Democtrats vote and only 49 Republicans do so. The key question is, What happens to people's dispositions to vote after this election? Because everyone starts with intermediate aspirations, all the winning Democrats find

[7] This reflects the experience of newly democratized countries in eastern Europe. Dalton and Klingemann (2007, p. 15) write that "Election turnout was often fairly high in the immediate post-transition elections in eastern Europe, but has subsequently declined in most nations."

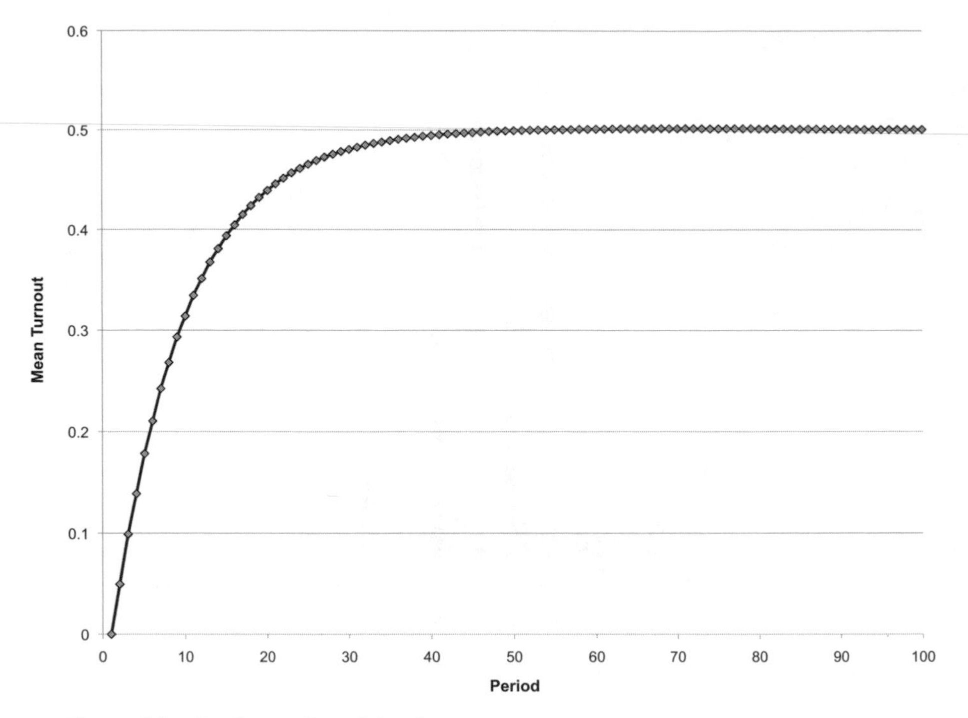

Figure 4.2. Breakout of participation.

winning and voting to be satisfactory. (Even with a bad random shock to payoffs, the worst payoff a winning voter can get is −0.3.) Hence, these 50 Democrats are mobilized: their vote propensities rise after the election. However, the slothful behavior of their comrades, who enjoyed a free-riding payoff of between −0.1 and 0.1, is also reinforced. So this is not the place to look for the explanation of a major breakout of participation. The key is the effect that the Democratic victory had on their *shirking opponents.* The best payoff that a shirking Republican could get in period 1 was −0.9 (i.e., −1 plus a maximally good shock). Because this is less than their initial aspiration level, *all shirking losers are dissatisfied with staying home.* Hence, in the next period all such Republicans—the overwhelming majority of their team (4,951)—will increase their probability of voting. We call this *loser-driven mobilization.*

The story is not over. In period 2 the Republicans, having been mobilized by their loss in the previous election, are likely to win. All Republicans who actually voted will have that behavior reinforced, but all their free-riding comrades will have that action supported as well. Thus, once again, focusing on the winners does not explain why

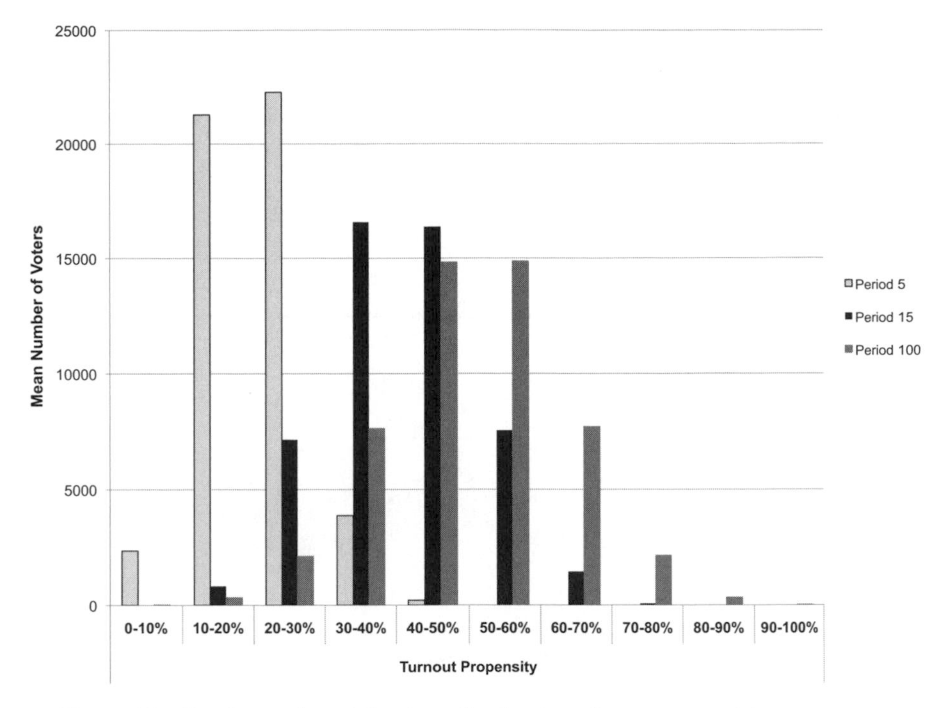

Figure 4.3. Breakout of participation, distribution of vote propensities.

many citizens eventually turn out. We must again look at the losers—in this period, the Democrats. In period 2 almost all Democrats stay home and get a payoff of −1 on average. With aspirations adjusting slowly, and hence still close to −0.5, these players will code payoffs that are about −1 as failures. So now the Democrats' shirking is inhibited. Hence, more of them turn out in period 3, and loser-driven mobilization continues. The mobilization of one side begets countermobilization, in pluralist fashion.[8]

Finally, we can understand why participation would break out even if all voters began with very low aspirations. In the worst case, all shirkers might be satisfied with staying home regardless of the election outcome. While one might think that this should stop loser-driven mobilization, happy slothfulness cannot endure because aspirations adjust to experience. Aspirations will rise even if one's side loses; they will rise even more if one's party wins the election. And once a citizen's aspiration equals −1, shirking and losing will

[8] When participation is costly, the Pareto-optimal symmetric outcome is for everyone to stay home. Thus, mobilization and countermobilization result in an escalating arms race of effort that is collectively inefficient.

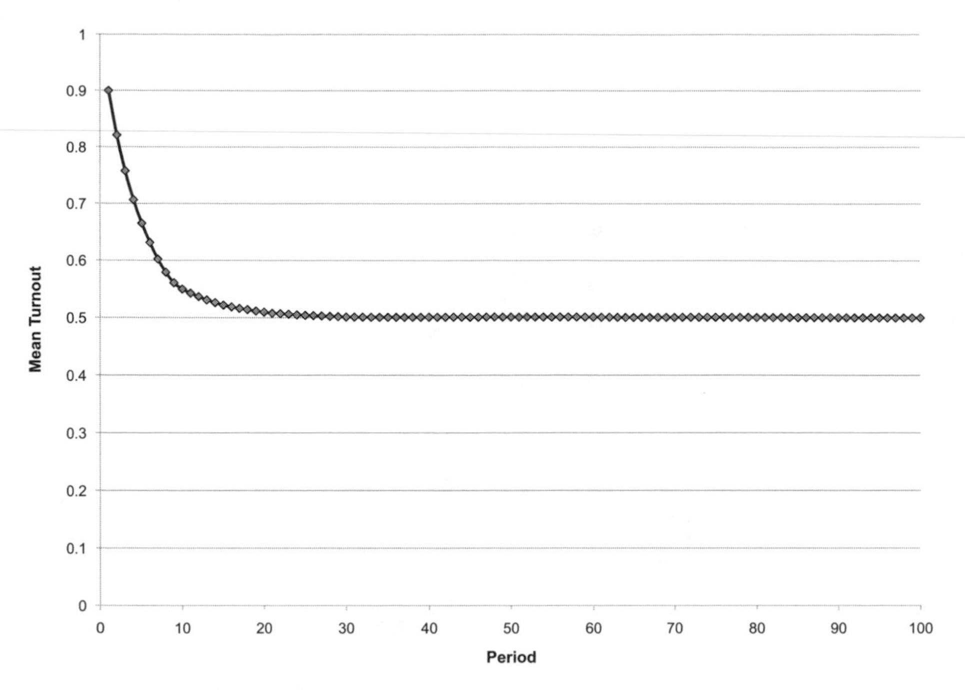

Figure 4.4. Collapse of participation.

be dissatisfying more than half the time. Thus, while shirking and winning continues to be fine, shirking and losing quickly becomes unsatisfactory. Once again, a process of loser-driven mobilization is triggered, as dissatisfied losing shirkers become more inclined to vote.

4.2.2 Explaining Participation: Analytical Results

The mobilization we observe occurs follows naturally from the model laid out in chapter 2. Indeed, we can illustrate why much of it does not depend on the specifics of the Bush-Mosteller mechanism used in the simulation but is instead driven by much more general properties of trial-and-error learning. The following two results do not analytically predict nonnegligible turnout, but they do develop some of the central intuitions for why it occurs.

Our first result establishes some conditions under which a majority of voters become more or less inclined to vote. It rests on three important observations about the distribution of action propensities in society. The first is a simple property about aspirations and electoral payoffs. Let $\pi_{V,w}^{\min}$ and $\pi_{S,l}^{\max}$ denote the minimal possible payoff from voting and winning and the maximal payoff obtained from

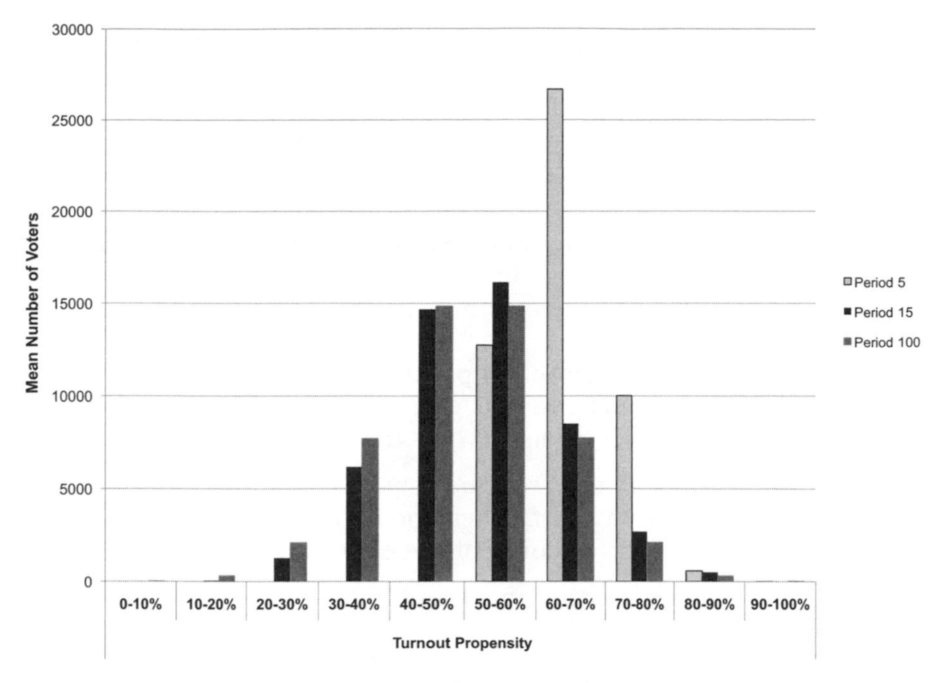

Figure 4.5. Collapse of participation: distribution of vote propensities.

shirking and losing, respectively. We also say that an actor is satisfied if the corresponding action is coded a success and dissatisfied if it is coded a failure.

Remark 4.1. If $a_{i,t} < \pi_{V,w}^{\min}$ for all people in the winning faction and $a_{i,t} > \pi_{S,l}^{\max}$ for all people in the losing faction, then all winners are satisfied by the outcome in t while all losers are dissatisfied.

This condition identifies situations in which everyone's satisfaction is determined exclusively by the collective outcome. Winners get payoffs of either $\pi_{i,t}(V, w)$ or $\pi_{i,t}(S, w)$ depending on whether they voted or stayed home. So if all winners have aspirations below $\pi_{V,w}^{\min}$, then they are all content with the outcome. Similarly, losers get payoffs of either $\pi_{i,t}(V, l)$ or $\pi_{i,t}(S, l)$, so if their aspirations exceed $\pi_{S,l}^{\max}$, then losing is unacceptable.

The second observation characterizes which citizens become more inclined to vote and which become less inclined. Given the conditions of remark 4.1, which citizens will increase their propensity to vote in period 2? To answer that question we need only the assumptions about ABARs, which are much more general than those of the Bush-Mosteller rule used in the simulation.

Remark 4.2. Suppose $a_{i,t} < \pi^{\min}_{V,w}$ for all people in the winning faction and $a_{i,t} > \pi^{\max}_{S,l}$ for all people in the losing faction. If adjustment is by any arbitrary mix of ABARs, then $p_{i,t+1}(V) > p_{i,t}(V)$ or $p_{i,t}(V) = p_{i,t+1}(V) = 1$ for all alert winning voters and all alert losing shirkers, and $p_{i,t+1}(V) < p_{i,t}(V)$ or $p_{i,t}(V) = p_{i,t+1}(V) = 0$ for the other alert citizens.

It is obvious that winning voters increase their propensity to participate: they voted and were pleased with the outcome. A bit less obviously, so will losing shirkers, as all losers were displeased with the outcome.

The third observation involves political demography: how many citizens are either winning voters or losing shirkers? We say a win is conclusive if the winner got more votes than the loser (no coin toss).

Remark 4.3. If a party wins conclusively and has at most one more member than the losing party, then the number of winning voters plus losing shirkers is a majority of the electorate.

To see why, suppose that the Republicans win. Hence we have more Republican (winning) voters than Democratic (losing) voters. But given that $n_R \leqslant n_D + 1$, there must be at least as many Democratic shirkers as Republican ones.

Combining these remarks yields a few simple conditions under which a majority of citizens will become mobilized (increase their propensity to vote). It is sufficient that aspirations are not too high for winners and not too low for losers, the winning faction is not too large, the election is conclusive, and vote propensities are not already maximized.[9] Importantly, voters become mobilized even if shirking by all citizens is a Nash equilibrium, which occurs if $c > b/2$. Note that these conditions restrict neither the size of the electorate nor how people adapt. The electorate may be very large, and citizens may use different ABARs that adapt at different speeds.

The notion of loser-driven mobilization that we discussed earlier falls naturally out of this analysis. For example, consider circumstances in which everyone is fully disposed to shirk at $t = 1$, as in figures 4.2 and 4.3. Because aspirations are endogenous, they typically increase rapidly into the intermediate region of $(\pi^{\max}_{S,l}, \pi^{\min}_{V,w})$. Once this happens, the run will satisfy all of the conditions for increased mobilization. Thus, after most elections (i.e., whenever elections are conclusive) at least half of the noninertial citizens will become more inclined to vote. However, because the speed of learning is relatively

[9] Note also that this is hardly the only set of conditions that yields increased vote propensities.

low ($\lambda = 0.1$), relatively few people actually turn out in period 2. Given that winning voters and losing shirkers are more than half the community, this implies that most of the newly mobilized are losing shirkers. Thus, in the beginning mobilization is loser-driven.

We know from the simulations reported thus far that mobilization does not continue indefinitely. It is therefore important to consider why turnout levels stabilize. One answer is suggested by remark 4.1, which provides the key intuition about how behavior is mediated by aspiration levels. The hypothesis of the remark is that winners' aspirations are low enough so that winning is gratifying even if one paid the costs of participating, and losers' aspirations are high enough so that losing is dissatisfying even if one avoided those costs.

If, contrary to remark 4.1, winning citizens had high aspirations and losers had low aspirations, then we can reverse the mobilization story: voters will demobilize. To see this, suppose that $p_{i,t}(V) > 0$ for each citizen i. If $a_{i,t} \in (\pi^{max}_{V,w}, \pi^{min}_{S,w})$ for winners and $a_{i,t} \in (\pi^{max}_{V,l}, \pi^{min}_{S,l})$ for losers, then after the election all shirkers will be content with their payoffs while all voters will be dissatisfied. All (noninertial) citizens therefore become less inclined to vote.[10] As with the mobilization story, demobilization requires only very weak assumptions about the nature of trial-and-error learning: only the qualitative properties of ABARs were assumed. Thus, citizens may differ substantially in how they learn.

Obviously, given that demobilization is universal, the electorate's expected average propensity to vote falls (or, because of inertia, remains unchanged). Clearly, a situation in which all alert players are becoming more likely to stay home is unstable. Hence, this one-sided domination cannot be a long-run probabilistic equilibrium. Over time, members of the dominating faction will learn to free-ride on their comrades' efforts. This will make the race competitive again.

Since the assumptions about aspirations in the demobilization story are so extreme, it is worth asking how they may come about. The proximate cause is that recently one faction has been winning by wide margins. Winning produces payoffs of either $\pi_{i,t}(V, w)$ or $\pi_{i,t}(S, w)$, and thus a sufficiently long string of victories will drive the winners' aspirations above $\pi^{max}_{V,w}$. Meanwhile, the corresponding long run of defeats will send the losers' aspirations below $\pi^{min}_{S,l}$. Such runs may occur because one faction is much larger than the other. (As we will see in section 4.3, changing the relative sizes of the factions in the simulation does affect turnout as this reasoning indicates.) But

[10] If $(\pi^{max}_{V,w}, \pi^{min}_{S,w})$ and $(\pi^{max}_{V,l}, \pi^{min}_{S,l})$ are empty, then the conclusion holds vacuously.

even with evenly sized factions, a string of victories may occur by chance.

The mobilization and demobilization stories are different from a demographic or head-counting sense. In the latter, the electorate's average propensity to vote falls. But in the former, the fact that more citizens will increase their propensity to participate than will decrease that tendency does not necessarily imply that the electorate's average propensity to turn out rises. To flesh out this point, consider the following numerical example. Suppose that a citizen starts with a vote propensity of 0.01 and an aspiration of -0.2. She votes, and her faction wins the election. Since this result is satisfactory, her propensity to vote rises. If her speed of adjustment is $\lambda = 0.1$, then her vote propensity becomes $0.01 + 0.1(0.99) = 0.109$. Now consider another citizen from the same faction who shirked in the election. Since she is also satisfied with the outcome, her propensity to vote falls or, equivalently, her propensity to shirk rises. Since she started with a shirk propensity of 0.99, this probability increases to just $0.99 + 0.1(0.01) = 0.991$. Thus, although the propensities of the two voters move in opposite directions, the quantitative rise in the first citizen's voting propensity (0.099) swamps the rise in the second citizen's shirking propensity (0.001). Beginning from a low proclivity allows a citizen to adjust upward considerably, while beginning from a high propensity does not. Indeed, in this example the districtwide average vote propensity would rise if more than 1 percent of the district became more mobilized.

Since typical elections are likely to result in both mobilization and demobilization, we are interested in saying more about general movements in the average participation propensity in the electorate. It is clear from the preceding example that this requires some consideration of not only how many people adjust in each direction but the extent of their adjustment as well. For example, the symmetric Bush-Mosteller rule suggests that very high propensities for any action tend to be self-limiting, as satisfied people cannot increase those inclinations by much.

We can use definition 2.2 to make a general statement about how citizens using ABARs might produce high levels of mobilization. The result, proved in Bendor, Diermeier, and Ting (2003a), depends on weak monotonicity, symmetry, and action invariance. It can be easily verified that the Bush-Mosteller rule satisfies all three.[11] (The distinctive feature of the Bush-Mosteller rule is linearity: i.e., adjustment

[11] Note that symmetry fails if the speed of propensity adjustment is different for successes than for failures.

magnitudes are linear in the status quo propensity.) With these properties, our main analytical result shows that the breakout of participation illustrated in figures 4.2 and 4.3 holds for a rather large class of adaptive rules under a broad range of parameter values. In particular, this generalization of the Bush-Mosteller rule shows that linearity plays no essential role in the outcome of the preceding example. Part (b) parallels part (a) by reversing some of its key assumptions and invoking action invariance.

The proposition, proved in Bendor, Diermeier, and Ting (2003a), uses the following notation: $\overline{p}_t$ denotes the districtwide average propensity to vote at period t, and $E[\overline{p}_t]$ denotes its expected value prior to period t.

Proposition 4.1. *Suppose that all voters adapt by the same weakly monotonic and symmetric ABAR.*

(a) *If*

(i) $a_{i,t} < \pi_{V,w}^{\min}$ *for all people in the winning faction and* $a_{i,t} > \pi_{S,l}^{\max}$ *for all people in the losing faction,*

(ii) *the election is conclusive and the winning faction is not larger than the losing faction by more than one voter, and*

(iii) $p_{i,t}(V) \leqslant \frac{1}{2}$ *for all* i*,*

then $E[\overline{p}_{t+1}] > \overline{p}_t$.[12]

(b) *If*

(i) *the ABAR is action-invariant,*

(ii) *winners with* $a_{i,t} \in (\pi_{V,w}^{\max}, \pi_{S,w}^{\min})$ *and losers with* $a_{i,t} \in (\pi_{V,l}^{\max}, \pi_{S,l}^{\min})$ *are a majority, and*

(iii) $p_{i,t}(V) \geqslant \frac{1}{2}$ *for all* i*,*

then $E[\overline{p}_{t+1}] < \overline{p}_t$.

The two parts of proposition 4.1 give us a clear understanding of the dynamics of turnout in the simulation, given (for example) a start of nearly complete apathy. Initially, demographic mobilization and the ceiling effect—per-capita amounts of propensity change—reinforce each other: most citizens increase their propensity to vote, and because they began with little inclination to participate, increasers have more adjustment room than decreasers. Eventually,

[12] We have extended proposition 4.1(a) (Bendor, Diermeier, and Ting 2001) to cover asymmetric rules, which respond more to negative than to positive feedback. For evidence of this "negativity bias," see Baumeister et al. (2001).

however, mobilization is self-limiting because one or both of the underlying factors reverse themselves. First, once the community's average propensity to vote exceeds $\frac{1}{2}$, the ceiling effect favors shirking: there is now more room to decrease than to increase. Second, one side may run off a string of victories, which will send some of the winners' aspirations above $\pi_{V,w}^{\max}$ and some of the losers' aspirations below $\pi_{S,l}^{\min}$. If this happens to enough people, the demography of mobilization will turn around: now a majority of people will become less inclined to vote, and turnout will start to fall.[13]

These analytical results strongly suggest that the results in figures 4.2 and 4.3 do not depend on the details of the simulation program. Rather, they are the consequence of a few simple mechanisms that are instantiated by the parametric setting of this run. In this sense the analytical results also serve as a sweeping sensitivity test for that run and reduce the need for laboriously investigating a large number of other parametric configurations.

4.3 Variations in Participation

Our main result thus far is the emergence of substantial turnout in large electorates. While this may address the anomalous prediction of negligible turnout generated by many rational choice models, such models are successful in explaining *variation* in turnout (Hansen, Palfrey, and Rosenthal 1987; Shachar and Nalebuff 1999). Thus, we need to consider whether the adaptive model can do as well as its rational choice counterparts at comparative statics predictions.[14]

[13] Proposition 4.1(a) gives only a partial explanation of the outbreak of participation because it requires all voters to have a propensity of at most $\frac{1}{2}$. Of course, the result describes a sufficient condition for increasing average propensity to participate, not a necessary one. So it does not rule out the fact that mobilization continues in that run even after some $p_{i,t}(V)$'s exceed $\frac{1}{2}$. Likewise, part (b) of the result does not rule out decreases in average vote propensities when some propensities fall below $\frac{1}{2}$.

[14] One type of variation that we do not consider here is that of voter-specific participation patterns over time. Fowler (2006) adapts our basic model to address the possibility of habitual voting, whereby citizens either usually vote or usually abstain. In his model, citizens adjust voting propensities by equal increments (e.g., increases and decreases in voting propensities in each period are fixed at 0.01). This prevents the large downward (respectively, upward) adjustments for citizens with high (respectively, low) voting propensities implied by the Bush-Mosteller adjustment rule. The modified functional form also sits within the family of ABARs and like many other ABARs does not change the qualitative results reported here. We conjecture that habitual voting would be even better characterized by a logistic adjustment function, whereby propensity adjustments are small for extreme propensity values and large for moderate ones.

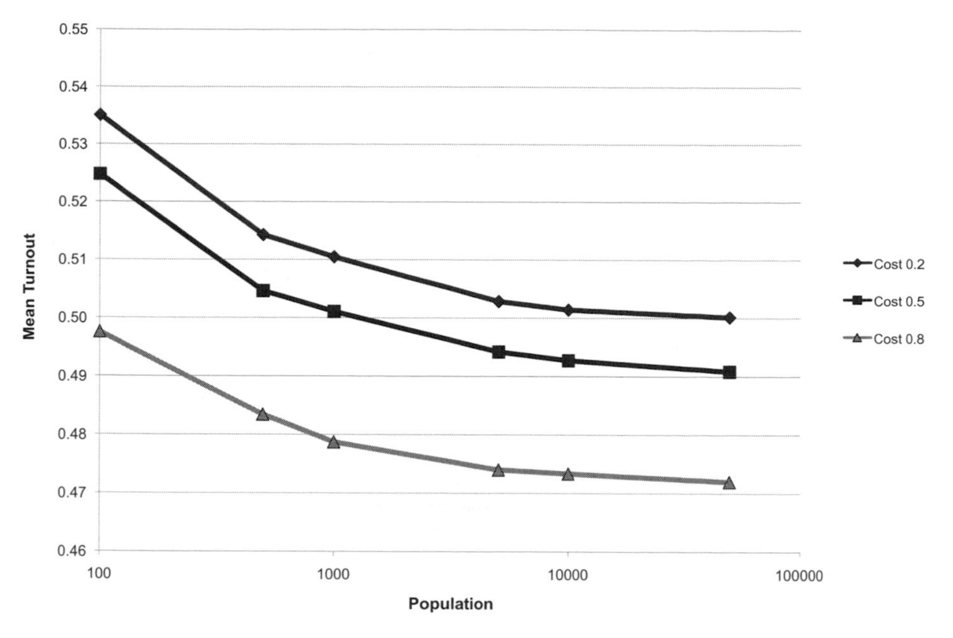

Figure 4.6. Turnout by population and cost.

A comparative statics analysis examines how changes in the model's exogenous parameters (e.g., cost of participation) affect its endogenous variables (e.g., participation levels). In a probabilistic framework, this requires that we study how the properties of the (unique) limiting distribution (e.g., *expected* turnout) change as an exogenous parameter varies.

4.3.1 Voting Cost and Population Size

The literature on turnout provides intuitive comparative statics with respect to voting cost and population size. A well-known empirical regularity is that higher costs are correlated with lower turnout. Additionally, turnout should decrease as the population increases in size. In game-theoretic models of turnout, participation quickly approaches zero as the population size increases. Figure 4.1 implies that this is not the case in our model (fortunately, given turnout data in large electorates). Nevertheless, participation should be affected to some degree by n.

Figure 4.6 illustrates these comparative statics by graphing the average period 300 turnout over 1,000 simulations across three different values of c (0.2, 0.5, and 0.8), and six values of n (50, 100, 500, 1,000, 5,000, 10,000, 50,000).

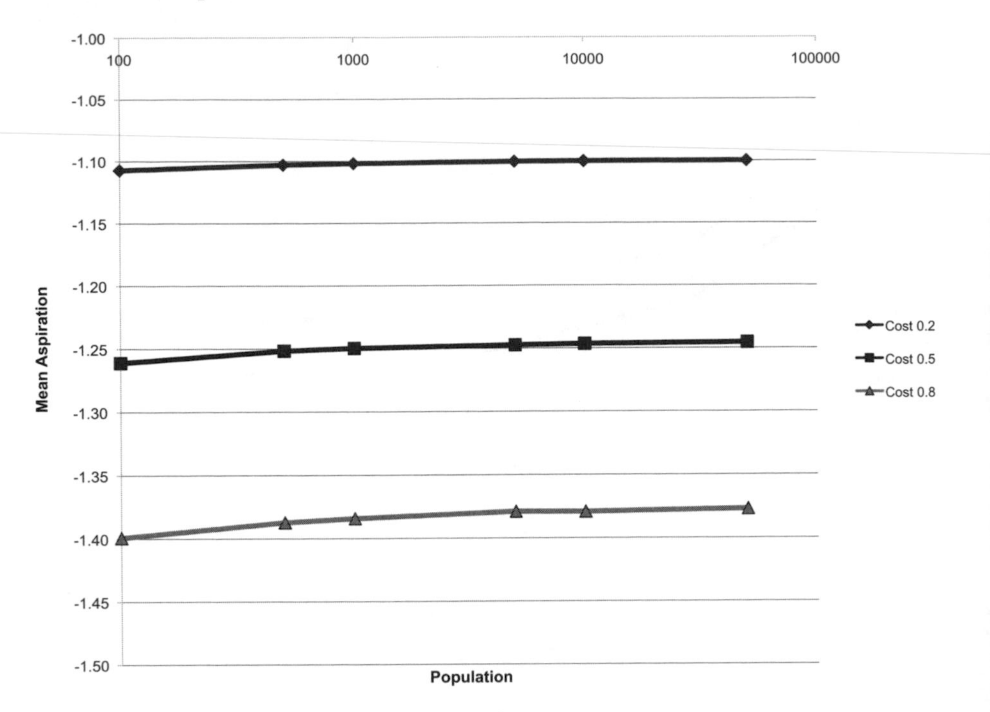

Figure 4.7. Aspirations by population and cost.

Our results are consistent with both relationships. Higher costs of voting do depress participation in elections. Observe, however, that even a substantial change in cost leads to only a moderate decrease in turnout. This perhaps surprising finding is an instance of a more general phenomenon in models of aspiration-based learning: the effects of changing payoffs on behavior are muted by aspirational mechanisms (March 1994). This holds because aspirations adjust to experience—here, payoffs. Hence an increase in the cost of voting is partly absorbed by lower aspirations in the steady state. Figure 4.7 illustrates this by graphing the average aspirations of voters across the runs done in figure 4.6.

Next, consistent with the data of Hansen, Palfrey, and Rosenthal (1987), our computational model predicts that turnout decreases in n. Notice that the decline in turnout is nonlinear, dropping relatively quickly for n below 100. Turnout is significantly higher in small, committee-sized forums than in large legislative districts. The principal intuition behind this result is that pivot probabilities still matter (albeit experientially rather than prospectively): when n is small, each agent's likelihood of swinging the election is nontrivial. Thus, given realistic aspirations, voting is more likely to satisfice in an election with low n. Note finally that figure 4.7 suggests that aspirations are increasing in n. This follows from the lower turnout rates for high populations. Since both parties win with equal probability, average payoffs and hence aspirations are higher when citizens vote less often.

4.3.2 Faction Size

There are two good reasons for examining the effects of varying faction sizes. First, we are of course interested in knowing what happens in common cases where uneven factions compete electorally. Second, the astute reader may have noticed that when faction sizes are exactly equal, there exists a pure strategy Nash equilibrium in which everyone votes. Hence in this very specific context both game-theoretic models and our adaptive one predict high turnout. Thus, it is worth seeing whether our model continues to generate high turnout when factions are of different sizes. In this context, game-theoretic models predict low turnout (e.g., Palfrey and Rosenthal 1985; Myerson 1998). They also predict that turnout in both factions will decline in the asymmetry in faction sizes, and that turnout will be higher in the smaller faction. These predictions have been tested successfully with field data (Shachar and Nalebuff 1999) and in experiments (Levine and Palfrey 2007).

Figure 4.8 plots turnout levels and victory proportions for the larger faction (D) as a function of the size of the larger faction. Note first that when the larger faction has only 50.1 percent (25,050 of 50,000) of the voters, the turnout results are almost indistinguishable from those of the initial simulations in figure 4.1. Turnout approaches 50 percent, but the advantaged side wins about two-thirds of the contests. As one faction becomes substantially larger than the other, turnout in the steady state drops in both factions. Additionally, the smaller faction turns out at a somewhat higher rate. Finally, the decline in turnout correlates neatly with an increase in the proportion of victories for the advantaged faction. Beyond a 55–45 split, faction sizes do not matter: turnout is fairly constant, and the larger faction wins every election. This happens because the lopsided races cause voters' aspirations to reflect these certain election outcomes. Their turnout adjustments then depend only on their payoff shocks and voting choices. Since these adjustments affect voters of both factions identically, both sides turn out in equal proportions.

The lower level of overall turnout can be explained through the polarization of aspirations. Winning most of the contests drives

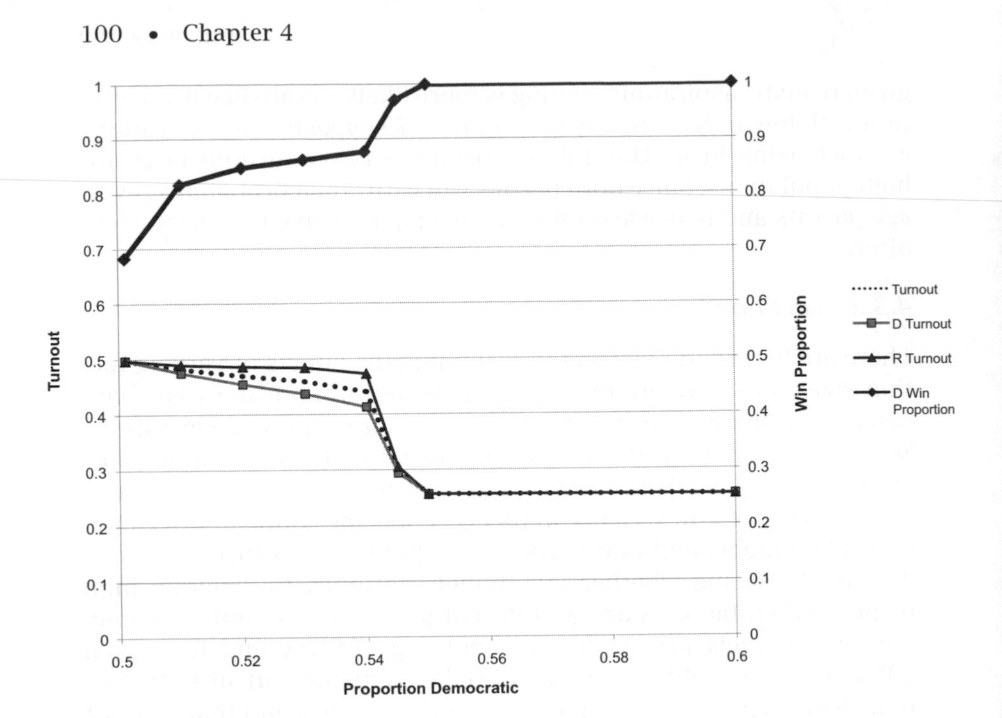

Figure 4.8. Turnout and win proportions with uneven factions.

the majority's aspirations up and the minority's aspirations down. The movement of aspirations out of the intermediate range of $(\pi_{S,l}^{\max}, \pi_{V,w}^{\min})$ results in demobilization, as we explained in the previous section. A string of victories makes the majority complacent: their aspirations become so high that only the highest payoff, winning and shirking, satisfices for many of them. (This holds probabilistically because payoffs are stochastic.) Voting is therefore inhibited, regardless of the electoral outcome, and the majority faction's average vote propensity falls. Meanwhile, the series of losses have reduced the minority's aspirations so much that for many of them losing and shirking has become acceptable. Shirking is then reinforced regardless of the electoral outcome, reducing the smaller faction's average vote propensity. As figure 4.8 illustrates, the drop in overall turnout is not drastic for moderately asymmetric factions, as shirking is frequently inhibited in the smaller faction and occasional victories do occur. The higher rate of inhibition of shirking in the smaller faction is in part responsible for its higher turnout.

The contrast between this result and the comparative statics on voting costs illustrates the highly nonlinear nature of aspiration-based learning. Aspirations partially absorb changes in voting costs and result in "small," if intuitive, differences in voting behavior. On the other hand, aspirations amplify the effect of changes in faction size and yield qualitatively "large" differences in participation.

Interestingly, before aspirations fall out of the intermediate zone in these simulations, participation rates actually remain high.[15] This happens because intermediate aspirations imply that winning is satisfactory and losing is unsatisfactory. Members of the majority faction are then in what learning theorists call a *benign* environment: no matter what the action, it is likely to be reinforced. Thus, prior dispositions toward both voting and shirking are strengthened. By contrast, members of the minority faction are in what learning theorists call a *malign environment*: no matter the action, the feedback is likely to be negative. Defeat will probably induce shirking for a citizen who is inclined to vote, and mobilization for a citizen who is inclined to shirk. Consequently, initially apathetic and initially mobilized tendencies are both dampened. But for both factions, participation does not systematically degrade—as long as aspirations remain intermediate.

4.3.3 Ideology

While platforms in this chapter are fixed, we can still examine the effects of exogenous changes in platform positions. One conjecture is that reductions in b, the difference in the policy benefits of electing the preferred candidate, decrease turnout. Given realistic aspirations, lower values of b will increase the likelihood of negative reinforcement of participating after voting and winning, or positive reinforcement of staying home after shirking and losing. Figure 4.9 plots the effect of ideological extremism (as summarized by the absolute value of the party platform positions, x) on turnout.

Note that at $x = 0$, both platforms are identical. This removes any policy motivation for voting. As a result, we would expect turnout to be low since in the absence of a payoff shock shirking would dominate voting. In fact, turnout drops to about 25 percent. As we saw in figure 4.8, given the parametric assumptions of our simulation this is approximately the level of turnout that can be sustained when voting almost certainly yields a lower payoff than not voting. Beyond $x = 0.5$, turnout increases only very slightly. For these values of x, it is very unlikely that voters will receive the "wrong" feedback from

[15] We show elsewhere (Bendor, Diermeier, and Ting 2003a) that this pattern holds more generally for action-invariant Bush-Mosteller adjustments. In particular, we show that if aspirations remain intermediate, one-sided electoral competition does not systematically degrade participation propensities. Under the conditions, if $p_{i,t} \leqslant \frac{1}{2}$, then $E[p_{i,t+1}] > p_{i,t}$, and if $p_{i,t} > \frac{1}{2}$ and the probability that i is pivotal in t is sufficiently low, then $E[p_{i,t+1}] < p_{i,t}$.

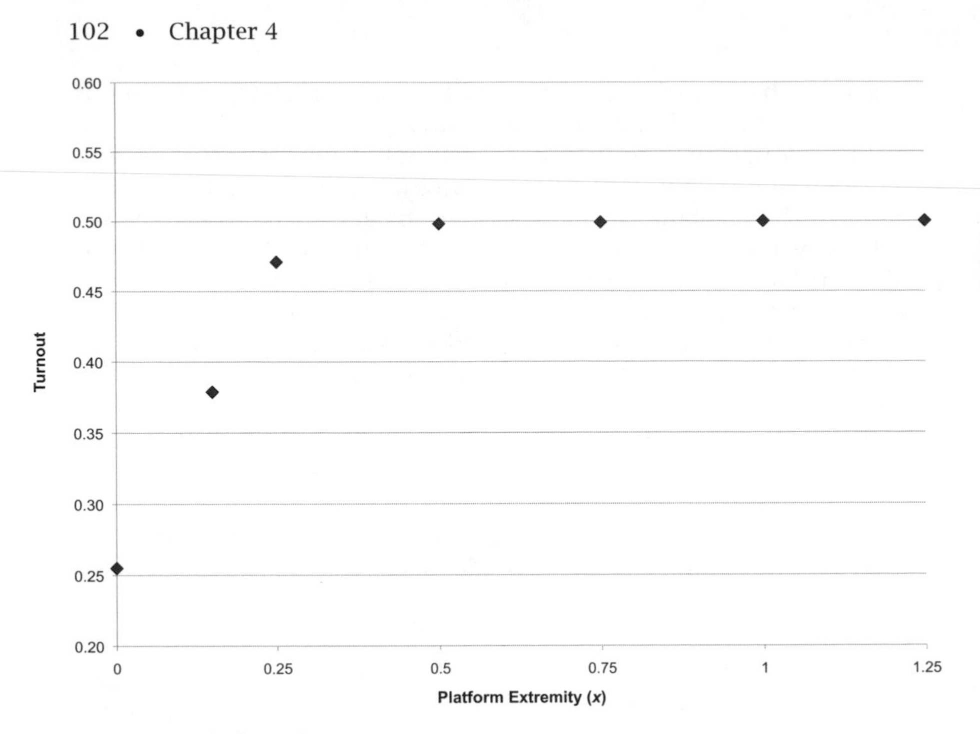

Figure 4.9. Ideological extremity.

an election outcome, and hence these games are structurally more or less identical.

The runs in figure 4.9 are based on the cost of voting being 0.2. Hence, they presume that there is no benefit to voting when the platforms are identical, but there is a nonnegligible cost to doing so. What happens if this cost is also close to zero? Our next result, proposition 4.2, shows analytically that turnout is substantial under Downsian convergence, provided that the costs of voting are sufficiently small. Further, this holds in arbitrarily large electorates. This result also provides a quantitative, analytically based estimate of average turnout under the above parametric conditions. As this result is new, we provide a formal proof in appendix A.

As usual, obtaining analytical results requires making some simplifying assumptions. The main simplification, compared to this chapter's computational model, is that here we assume aspirations are exogenous. (They may, however, vary across citizens.) It is important to note that exogenously fixing aspirations does not bias the result toward any particular outcome. As we will see in a moment, ergodicity continues to hold: there is a unique limiting distribution over turnout propensities for any vector of aspirations. Moreover, for a wide variety of payoff distributions—those in which the payoff shock has unbounded support—the aspiration levels' values have little effect on the expected level of turnout in the limit, provided that the costs of voting are sufficiently low.

Further, in many respects the assumptions of proposition 4.2 are more general than those of the computational model. First, the electorate may be of any size. Second, we are not restricted to quadratic loss functions regarding the deterministic component of payoffs. All that is required is that $b_i = 0$ for all i when the parties adopt the same platform. Indeed, voters can have different utility functions. Third, the policy space can be multidimensional. Fourth, a wide class of payoff shocks is allowed; we are not restricted to the uniform. Fifth, the result holds for a large class of ABARs. Unlike the computational model, which presumes Bush-Mosteller adaptation, the next result requires only quite general properties used by most of the models in this book: Markovian ABARs with stationary transition probabilities that are magnitude-insensitive. Thus, proposition 4.2 provides a sensitivity test in several ways. In particular, it shows that in stable two-party systems where the costs of participating are positive but small, on average about half the electorate should participate under a wide range of assumptions.

Proposition 4.2. *Suppose $b = 0$. Citizens adjust actions via an arbitrary set of stationary Markovian ABARs that are magnitude-insensitive. Aspirations are exogenously fixed; they may differ across citizens. For all i, ϵ_i has a continuous density with finite mean and variance. If $\Pr(a_i > \epsilon_i) > 0$ for all i, then in the limit average turnout is approximately one-half of the electorate for c close to zero.*

The intuition underlying this result is given in figure 4.10, which shows the payoff distributions for voting and shirking when $b = 0$, the costs of voting are small but positive, and the payoff shock is normally distributed.[16] When c is small, the probability of being dissatisfied by staying home is nearly equal to that produced by voting, for any fixed aspiration level—low, intermediate, or high. The ABARs studied in this book are continuous processes: small parametric differences produce small changes in the state variables. In particular, small differences in the probability of negative feedback (dissatisfaction) have small effects on the propensity to vote. This is especially

[16] Note that if the shock is normally distributed—indeed, if it has any unbounded density—then the critical property of $\Pr(a_i > \epsilon_i) > 0$ holds for every exogenously fixed aspiration level.

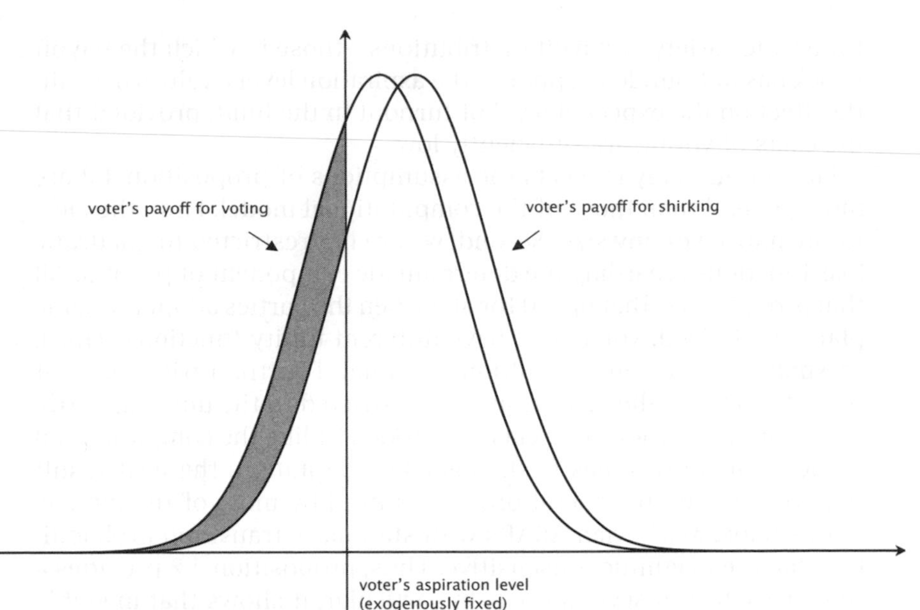

Figure 4.10. Payoff distributions for voting and shirking, $b = 0$. The shaded area represents the differences in the probability of being dissatisfied with voting versus the probability of being dissatisfied with staying home. The area falls continuously to zero as $c \downarrow 0$.

easy to see for the simplest ABAR: satisficing. If citizens use this rule and who wins the election does not affect payoffs ($b = 0$), the relevant stochastic process reduces to a set of two-state Markov chains, where the states are "vote" and "shirk" and each voter's process can be examined in isolation (again, because $b = 0$). A typical voter then switches from voting to shirking if she is dissatisfied with participating and is alert, and does the opposite if staying home is dissatisfying and she is alert. Intuitively, we have a dynamic equilibrium (hence, the limiting probabilities of voting and shirking) when the process is just as likely to change from state A to state B as it is to go in the opposite direction. Thus, small differences in the probability of dissatisfaction in each state must have small effects on the limiting probabilities.

4.3.4 The Duty to Vote

One response to the turnout anomaly was to change the payoff assumptions. The most influential of these attempts was Riker and Ordeshook's famous "D"-term, intended to capture a "duty to vote." Formally, assuming a large enough D-term is equivalent to

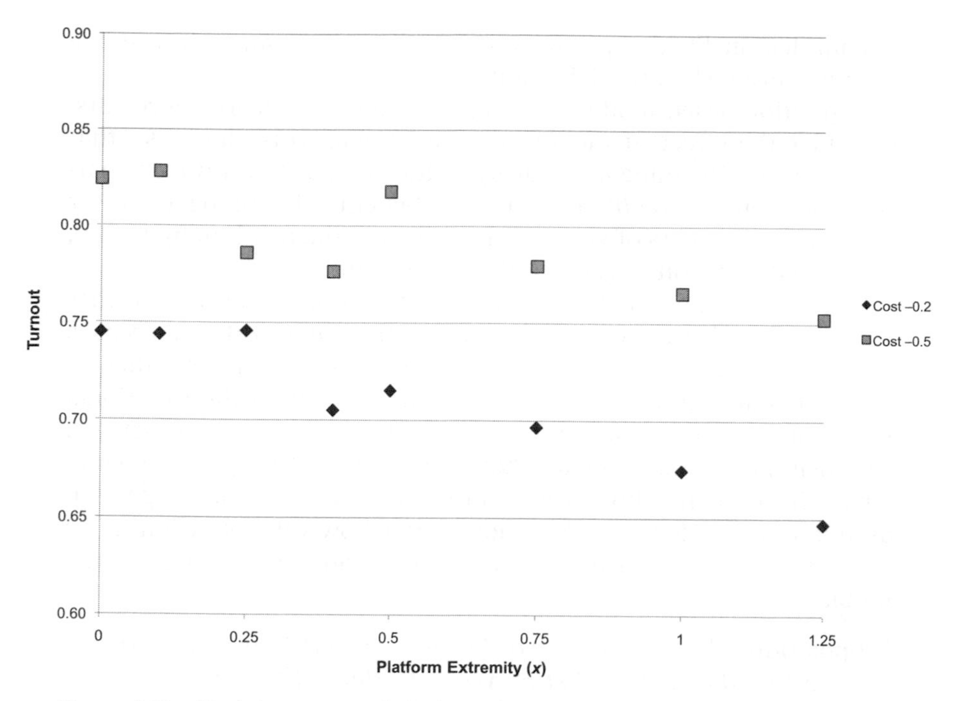

Figure 4.11. Negative costs and ideological extremity.

assuming negative costs of participation—whence participating is a strictly dominant strategy. Rational choice theory predicts that people would then always vote, but what happens in our model is surprising. Consider figure 4.11, which plots the average turnout when voting costs are negative ($c = -0.2, -0.5$) and for different values of the party platform polarization parameter, x.

The figure reveals that turnout does increase with negative costs. Yet even when the cost is low (i.e., the duty to vote is high), it does not climb nearly as high as predicted by rational choice theory. That is, our aspiration-based model *does not necessarily select strictly dominant actions.*[17] This seems strange until we recall the mediating effects of aspirations. When costs are negative, aspirations end up much higher than they are when costs are positive. Hence losing and voting is still usually dissatisfying. Consequently, losing voters often

[17] This also holds in the case of the Prisoner's Dilemma. As Karandikar et al. (1998) have shown in the two-player case, the strictly dominated cooperative outcome will occur most of the time, provided aspiration updating is sufficiently slow and trembles are small.

become less inclined to participate, so full turnout cannot be a stable outcome even when participation costs are negative.[18]

Aspiration-based models can imply even more surprising results. Consider the effect of moving the party platforms closer, so that the benefits of winning are sharply reduced. Counterintuitively, participation tends to be *higher* when the benefits of winning are lower (given negative costs of voting). This reverses the result in figure 4.9, where platform convergence reduced turnout.

While these runs may seem pathological, they illustrate a rather general effect. The counterintuitive effect that mobilization increases when the value of winning falls to zero is not peculiar either to the particular parameter values in figure 4.11 or to the functional forms of the simulation model. The next result, proven in Bendor, Diermeier, and Ting (2003a), shows analytically that patterns similar to those of the above runs can be derived under more general assumptions.[19] Hence, it does not matter how valuable winning is; the pure intrinsic motivation of civic duty leads to greater expected mobilization.

Proposition 4.3. *Consider two districts, A and B, with* $c < 0$ *and* $\epsilon_{i,t} = 0$ *for all* i, t*, such that in A,* $b = 0$ *(thus* $\pi_S^{\max} = \pi_{S,w}^{\max} = \pi_{S,l}^{\max}$ *and* $\pi_V^{\min} = \pi_{V,w}^{\min} = \pi_{V,l}^{\min}$*), while in B,* $b > 0$*. Assume that* $p^1 < p_{i,t} < p^l$ *for all* i*. Then for any arbitrary collection of ABARs:*

(i) *If in district A* $a_{i,t} \in (\pi_S^{\max}, \pi_V^{\min})$*, then* $p_{i,t+1} > p_{i,t}$ *with probability* 1 *for all alert citizens in A.*

(ii) *If* $\pi_{S,w}^{\min} \geqslant \pi_{V,l}^{\min}$*, then the conclusion in (i) cannot hold for district B: for arbitrary faction sizes,* $p_{j,t+1} < p_{j,t}$ *with positive probability for any* j *in B.*

(iii) *If, in addition to the conditions in (i) and (ii), everyone in both districts uses the same symmetric and action-invariant Bush-Mosteller rule and* $\overline{p}_t^A \geqslant \overline{p}_t^B$*, then* $E[\overline{p}_{t+1}^A] > E[\overline{p}_{t+1}^B]$*, where* $\overline{p}_t^j$ *denotes the average period* t *vote propensity in district* j*.*

Proposition 4.3 implies that if initially the districts start out with the same average vote propensity, then after period 1 the expected

---

[18] Alternatively, reconsider exogenously fixed aspirations, as in the previous subsection. If the random shock is unbounded (e.g., it is normally distributed), then shirking can produce a dissatisfying payoff even when $b = 0$, and staying home first-order stochastically dominates voting, as in figure 4.10. And since shirking can always disappoint, eventually the agent will again try his hand at participating.

[19] For a more detailed analysis of the counterintuitive effects of aspiration-mediated change, see Bendor, Diermeier, and Ting (2003b).

vote propensity in district A, where $b = 0$, will exceed the expected propensity in B at every date. The result is driven precisely by the fact that people in district A are motivated *only* by their sense of civic duty. As they do not care about the collective outcome, they have only two expected payoffs: $\overline{b} - c > 0$ for voting and $\overline{b}$ for shirking. Because everyone's aspirations are realistic, in district A, they will tend to be in $(\overline{b}, \overline{b} - c)$. Hence, for people in this district participating is always gratifying, while shirking never is. Consequently, voting is always reinforced and shirking is always inhibited, regardless of the electoral outcome. Thus, in the case of degenerate payoff distributions, in district A everyone's propensity to turn out rises in every period until they reach 1, where they will stay. In contrast, in district B people care about winning. This implies that losing while voting can be disappointing. If this occurs—and such an outcome is always possible—then the losing voters will become less inclined to vote.[20]

Note that proposition 4.3 holds for an extreme comparison, between a district where winning is worthless and one where winning is worth more than the private satisfaction of doing one's civic duty. Yet, despite this, the district where winning is worthless has a higher expected turnout than the one where winning not only is worth something but also is the more important payoff.

4.4 Conclusions

As a further proving ground for a mathematical model of adaptively rational behavior, we have developed a basic model of electoral participation. Because important parts of the model—in particular, payoffs—are highly similar to well-known games of voter turnout, it provides a basis for comparing predictions against its rational choice counterparts.

We believe that the model performed quite well. Most importantly, it predicts substantial turnout in very large electorates and even when voting is costly for all citizens. Reinforcement learning, mediated by endogenous aspirations, seems to lead naturally to substantial turnout under a wide array of parametric configurations. Indeed, it has been hard to *suppress* participation in the computational model. Additionally, it is consistent with most of the empirical regularities that determine levels of turnout. Finally, it provides

[20] Our result is consistent with the intriguing finding by psychologists that adding extrinsic rewards can impair the performance of actions for which people are already intrinsically motivated. For a review see Deci, Koestner, and Ryan (1999).

new predictions, e.g., when voters feel a duty to vote or when their aspirations (in, for instance, new democracies) are unrealistic.

The following chapter considers a natural next step, which is to consider voters' choices among candidates. Following this, we will then be able to integrate campaign strategies with a full model of a mass electorate.

CHAPTER FIVE

Voter Choice

TWO OF THE MOST robust findings about American voters are that few of them have coherent, detailed ideologies and few know much about politics. Donald Kinder summarizes decades of survey research on ideology: "Precious few Americans make sophisticated use of political abstraction. Most are mystified by or at least indifferent to standard ideological concepts, and not many express consistently liberal, conservative, or centrist positions on government policy" (1998, p. 796). Regarding information he reports that "the depth of ignorance demonstrated by modern mass publics can be quite breathtaking" and "the number of Americans who garble the most elementary points is ... impressive" (p. 785). Luskin's summary is harsher: most voters "know jaw-droppingly little about politics" (2002, p. 282; see also Delli Carpini and Keeter 1996 and Converse 2000).

As is well known, these empirical regularities contrast sharply with premises about voters in standard spatial models. In most Downsian formulations, citizens are assumed to have well-worked-out ideologies in their heads—so, e.g., in unidimensional models a host of issue positions are reduced in a consistent way to preferences over a single left-to-right spectrum—and to know a lot about politics: e.g., they know where candidates stand in the commonly constructed (Stokes 1963) ideological space or at least have unbiased estimates of these positions.

This gap between what we know empirically and what we assume theoretically was recognized long ago by Stokes: "[Downs'] model includes some cognitive postulates that need to be drastically qualified in view of what is known about the parties and electorates of actual political systems" (1963, p. 369). And though the empirical critique *has* had some influence on theorizing—e.g., the work of Enelow and Hinich (1984) and Hinich and Munger (1994) clearly reflects concerns with standard spatial premises about voters—the debate has been hampered by the failure of the critics to create their own models of electoral competition.

However, nearly 40 years ago Key (1966) sketched out an alternative: a verbal theory of retrospective voting. Fiorina eloquently captured the heart of the idea.

> [C]itizens ... typically have one comparatively hard bit of data: they know what life has been like during the incumbent's administration. They need *not* know the precise economic or foreign policies of the incumbent administration in order to see or feel the *results* of those policies. And is it not reasonable to base voting decisions on results as well as on intentions [i.e., campaign promises]? In order to ascertain whether the incumbents have performed poorly or well, citizens need only calculate the changes in their own welfare. If jobs have been lost in a recession, something is wrong. If sons have died in foreign rice paddies, something is wrong. If polluters foul food, water or air, something is wrong. And to the extent that citizens vote on the basis of such judgments, elections do not signal the direction in which society should move so much as they convey an evaluation of where society has been.
>
> (Fiorina 1981, pp. 5–6; emphasis in the original)

Key's ideas are plausible, but they leave important gaps. In particular, how do voters evaluate governmental performance? How do they decide that an incumbent has "performed poorly or well"?

One way to make these notions more precise—a way that we think is close to the spirit of Key's argument—is to posit a concept central to this book: aspirations. In the context of voter choice, aspirations are internal evaluation thresholds which code an incumbent's performance as good or bad, satisfactory or unsatisfactory. Once an incumbent's performance has been assessed in this manner, the *direction* of the voter's stance toward the incumbent politician or party is determined: good performance is rewarded with increased support, and bad with less support. Notice that this evaluation need not be reasonable. It is perfectly consistent with our approach for voters to withdraw their support for politicians even though their discontent is based on events (e.g., shark attacks or droughts) that are clearly beyond the control of public officials. For evidence of these phenomena, see Achen and Bartels (2004).

This notion forms the basis for the behavioral model of voter choice we introduce in this chapter. However, to implement it in the context of voter choice we must deploy our theoretical framework in a slightly different way than we used it in chapters 3 and 4.[1] In both party competition and voter turnout, parties and voters respond to outcomes directly derived from their own actions. If a party's platform loses, it tries something else. If a voter's turning out increases her payoffs, she votes more often. While we could implement the

---

[1] The possibility of this variant was noted in chapter 2. As explained on pp. 25–26, the variant we use in this chapter is consistent with the underlying axioms of aspiration-based adaptation.

same rule here—if a voter's choice of candidate results in a better payoff from the eventual winner of the election, the voter takes that action more often—this would force the voter to ignore pertinent, readily available information: the party identity of the incumbent. Doing so could lead to odd chains of events. Suppose, for example, James votes for a Democrat, but the Republican wins, and once in power the Republican's policies consistently produce poor outcomes for James. Key's theory, and intuition, would predict that James would become still less likely to vote for a Republican, given the poor outcome he just received, but this is the opposite of what the rule of the previous two chapters would have him do. Since he voted for a Democrat, and that was the action that resulted in his subjectively bad outcome, he should decrease the probability that he will vote for a Democrat instead. In a model of a two-party system without abstention, that means he must *increase* his likelihood of voting for a *Republican* instead!

This chapter therefore presents a richer model which allows voters to use the identity of the incumbent's party in their decision making.[2] Section 5.1 presents this model, along with a few definitions necessary to structure later results. These results fall into two sets. The first set, presented in sections 5.2–5.4, predicts that voters will sort into parties and describes the polarization that arises from varying degrees of voter misperception. These are quite general, obtaining across a wide range of substantive settings, including limited-information environments and those in which voters vary substantially in terms of cognitive capabilities. Additionally, they hold for a large class of retrospective voting models, even when voters are partly prospective, as in Downs's model.

The second set of results returns to this book's core purpose and explores the difference between naïve and sophisticated retrospective voting (RV). Because the empirical literature indicates that the modal American voter is not very sophisticated, we focus most of our efforts on establishing properties of naïve RV. In the first of the sections devoted to this analysis (section 5.5), we examine

[2] Of course, some voters may not possess this knowledge, particularly in districts that do not list the present occupation of all candidates. However, such voters would not likely be able to adjust propensities in the manner of the previous chapters either. After all, to do so would require turning out to vote and remembering for whom you voted, and yet never discovering who won the election even while apportioning full credit or blame to the person for whom you previously voted. Such behavior would seem to stretch the "bounded" in bounded rationality a bit too far to talk meaningfully about learning over time.

whether unsophisticated voting can produce optimal electoral outcomes. Our modeling approach allows us to consider aggregate electoral outcomes in large populations of voters all responding independently to an incumbent, an advance over the common assumption of a single representative voter. Section 5.6 examines how institutional effects—direct versus representative democracy—can save naïve retrospective voters from themselves.

5.1 The Model

We consider two parties, Democrats (D) and Republicans (R), who contest a sequence of majority-rule elections in periods $0, 1, 2, 3, \ldots$. Voters may vote for party D's or party R's candidate in that election; they cannot abstain. In period t each voter has probability $p_{i,t}$ of voting for the candidate from party D in the election that begins period $t+1$. Since there are only two parties, the probability of voting for the candidate from party R is just $1 - p_{i,t}$. We call $p_{i,t}$ voter i's vote propensity.[3] An election begins each period; the winner of this election is the office holder throughout the period and is the incumbent in the following period's election. Each voter receives a payoff from the office holder during the period, arising from an unspecified combination of the office holder's effort and policies, as well as factors such as terrorist attacks, business cycles, or droughts that are not fully controlled by the office holder. We assume that these payoffs are in general stochastic. Payoffs may differ by voter and by party but not within each party: all office holders within a party are assumed to provide identical payoffs to a given voter. This simplification is made so that we can focus on party-oriented voting rather than on attachment to a specific candidate.

As in all flavors of retrospective voting, voters can respond either positively or negatively to the incumbent's performance, and it is this response that drives the model's dynamics. We make the model tractable by dichotomizing the incumbent's performance: each voter gets either a low (l) or a high (h) payoff from the incumbent.[4] As we

[3] Although the model permits a restriction of vote propensities to binary values of 0 and 1, it does not require this assumption. Thus, deterministic voting is a special case of this model.

[4] Although assuming binary payoffs does involve a loss of generality, it is worth noting that any set of preference orderings over a finite set of outcomes can be represented either by deterministic payoffs, one for each ordinal rank, or by only two payoffs, if the latter are stochastic. Since the probability of getting the higher payoff can vary continuously, we have as many degrees of freedom as needed.

will see shortly (proposition 5.1), this enables us to suppress aspirations, which makes the model much more tractable, while simultaneously retaining the spirit of aspiration-driven adaptation.[5] Because these two properties appear inconsistent, we must explain how we pull off this trick.

Recall from chapter 2 that given our basic axioms of aspiration-adjustment (A2.4), a person's aspiration level must eventually become realistic: in the limit, it must eventually move into the interval of feasible payoffs, $[\underline{\pi}, \overline{\pi}]$, and stay there. In the present context of binary payoffs, realistic aspirations seem to imply that eventually an agent would regard the low payoff as unsatisfactory—a property that turns out to be central to our modeling strategy of suppressing aspirations. However, propensity-adjustment axiom (A2.1) categorizes ties between payoffs and aspirations as positive outcomes. This implies that if aspirations converged exactly to the l payoff, then an agent would always be content no matter how poorly the incumbent performed. To prevent this unrealistic possibility, we tighten up the aspiration-adjustment assumptions by ruling out arbitrarily slow adaptation. As proposition 5.1 demonstrates, this ensures convergence to the *open* interval of (l, h), thus guaranteeing that the low payoff eventually becomes dissatisfying.

(A5.1) For each agent i, there is an $\epsilon_i \in (0, 1)$ such that i's aspiration level is updated via a rule that satisfies the following conditions:

1. If $\pi_{i,t} > a_{i,t}$, then $a_{i,t+1} \in [a_{i,t} + \epsilon_i(\pi_{i,t} - a_{i,t}), \pi_{i,t})$.
2. If $\pi_{i,t} = a_{i,t}$, then $a_{i,t+1} = a_{i,t}$.
3. If $\pi_{i,t} < a_{i,t}$, then $a_{i,t+1} \in (\pi_{i,t}, a_{i,t} - \epsilon_i(a_{i,t} - \pi_{i,t})]$.

Any aspirational dynamic governed by (A5.1) ensures that no matter what the agent initially aspired to, he or she will eventually come to regard the h payoff as a success and the l payoff as a failure.

The next result says this more precisely. It is proved in a more general form in appendix A. All proofs of subsequent results can also be found in appendix A unless otherwise noted.

Proposition 5.1. *Consider a decision-theoretic problem in which the payoffs are either l or h and every feasible action produces either payoff with positive and stationary probability. If aspirations adjust via (A5.1), then the following conclusions hold.*

[5] Explicitly representing endogenous aspirations has been a formidable problem in the formal modeling of adaptive behavior.

(i) *If* $a_{t'} \in (l, h)$*, then with probability* 1 $a_t \in (l, h)$ *for all* $t > t'$.

(ii) *Suppose aspirations start outside* (l, h)*: either* $a_0 \leqslant l$ *or* $a_0 \geqslant h$*. Then* a_t *moves monotonically toward* (l, h) *and is absorbed into* (l, h) *with probability* 1 *as* $t \to \infty$.

Under these assumptions, decision makers whose aspirations adjust in accord with (A5.1) will eventually become dissatisfied with l and so will become less inclined to use an action that just delivered that payoff, and they will become more disposed to an action which has just produced an h-payoff. Thus, proposition 5.1 provides an analytical warrant for suppressing aspirations from models with binary payoffs.[6]

For the present model, proposition 5.1 implies that if citizens adjust aspirations in ways consistent with (A5.1), then eventually they will come to regard h's as satisfying and l's as dissatisfying. So their propensity to vote for the incumbent will rise if they get a high payoff and will fall if they get a low one. Thus, we use reduced versions of chapter 2's basic ABAR axioms: here, action propensities adjust directly in response to payoffs without the mediation of aspirations. These reduced versions are stated precisely below. For convenience, we will call any rule that satisfies (A5.2) and (A5.3) a *propensity-adjustment rule*, or PAR.

(A5.2) Positive Feedback: If $\pi_{i,t} = h$ and the incumbent is D, then $p_{i,t} \geqslant p_{i,t-1}$, and this conclusion holds strictly if $p_{i,t-1} < 1$. If $\pi_{i,t} = h$ and the incumbent is R, then $p_{i,t} \leqslant p_{i,t-1}$, and this conclusion holds strictly if $p_{i,t-1} > 0$.

(A5.3) Negative Feedback: If $\pi_{i,t} = l$ and the incumbent is D, then $p_{i,t} \leqslant p_{i,t-1}$, and this conclusion holds strictly if $p_{i,t-1} > 0$. If $\pi_{i,t} = l$ and the incumbent is R, then $p_{i,t} \geqslant p_{i,t-1}$, and this conclusion holds strictly if $p_{i,t-1} < 1$.

Thus, binary payoffs and proposition 5.1 together enable us to have our analytical cake and eat it too: in these contexts it is reasonable to suppress aspirations from the model, yet it remains true that

[6] Of course, we must acknowledge that *something* is lost by assuming binary payoffs and suppressing aspirations. The former assumption is often not the most natural way to represent choice situations in which a great many payoffs are possible. The latter assumption makes it impossible for the present model to represent explicitly aspirational dynamics or their effects. Both of these issues are addressed in chapter 6.

vote propensities are modified as if aspirations guided propensity changes.[7]

Because payoffs are binary, the relations between parties and voters are represented by the probability that a particular party gives the high payoff to different citizens. Thus, we assume the following properties, described by the corresponding terms and notation:

(1) A voter i's *type* is described by two parameters, $h^D_{i,t}$ and $h^R_{i,t}$, where $h^D_{i,t}$ denotes the probability that voter i gets the h payoff from the D party in period t. The meaning of $h^R_{i,t}$ is analogous.[8] Though these two are sufficient to define voters' types, we will for clarity also use $l^D_{i,t} = 1 - h^D_{i,t}$ and $l^R_{i,t} = 1 - h^R_{i,t}$ to denote the probability of voter i's receiving a low payoff from D or R, respectively. Thus, voters with the same h-probabilities are the same type. (Abusing terminology somewhat, we will refer to voters of type i, type j, etc.) When these probabilities are assumed to be stationary over time, we write them as h^D_i, etc. When they are nonstationary, then the probabilities change by an exogenous process. For example, disasters such as hurricanes can lower the chance of a high payoff, as can partly exogenous processes such as business cycles or a 9-11 attack (Achen and Bartels 2004).[9]

(2) We say that a type i voter has *liberal interests* if $h^D_i > l^D_i$ and $h^R_i < l^R_i$; conservative interests are defined analogously.[10] We state the notion this way—voter i *has* certain kinds of interests—because we do not assume that a voter understands the underlying structure of his interests, as he would if he had a well-worked-out political ideology. When comparing voters, we say that the interests of a type i voter are *more liberal* than those of a type j if $h^D_i > h^D_j$ and $l^R_i > l^R_j$. The former concept

[7] Some readers may find it more natural to think of this chapter's model as having explicit aspirations; if so, then merely assume that $a_{i,t} \in (l, h)$ for all i, t. This is equivalent to the approach adopted here, i.e., suppressing aspirations and assuming that propensity adjustments depend solely on payoffs.

[8] Note that $h^D_{i,t}$ and $h^R_{i,t}$ need not sum to 1. A voter might, for example, be unlikely to get good payoffs from *either* party.

[9] One could think of the economic payoff that a Democratic incumbent gives a voter of type i as having a policy component plus an exogenous random shock. Both combine to make $h^D_{i,t}$ fluctuate over time. What the model requires is that either of the following hold: (1) the nonstationarity of $h^D_{i,t}$ is due to exogenous changes in the distribution of the random shock, or (2) there is some deterministic exogenous trend to $h^D_{\cdot,t}$ that affects all voters similarly.

[10] Near the end of the chapter we use a specific version of the model which presumes a one-dimensional policy space. There it is natural to presume, given that this is a party-oriented model, that D's policy is to the left of R's.

is stronger than the latter: if i's interests are liberal and j's are conservative, then i's interests are more liberal than j's; the converse does not hold because i's interests could be more liberal than j's yet be conservative nonetheless.

We complete the model specification by noting that we need more structure on the nature of adaptation than is given by axioms (A5.2) and (A5.3): many of this chapter's results are restricted to rules that are *order-preserving.* This property constrains the set of possible PARs in an intuitively appealing way: a rule is order-preserving if the same outcome applied to two different propensities preserves the ordering between the two.[11] For example, a voter who begins a period with a propensity of $\frac{1}{2}$ and subsequently gets a high payoff from a D must adjust her propensity to a value at least as high as she would have had she instead begun the period with a propensity less than $\frac{1}{2}$—lower propensities cannot leapfrog higher ones.

5.2 The Endogenous Emergence of Party Affiliation

In this section we show how party affiliation can emerge endogenously, even if voters lack political ideologies and only retrospectively evaluate governmental performance. The key to understanding this result is the difference between a *sample path* and a *distribution* over sample paths. Sample paths are somewhat unpredictable in our framework and in stochastic models generally. To see this, consider the following example. Suppose there are three voters in a district, each of whom is likely to be dissatisfied, as $h_k^D, h_k^R < \frac{1}{2}$ for each. Voters i_1 and i_2 have identical interests, and each is more likely to get a high payoff from a D than from an R. Voter j's interests are different: he is more likely to get a good payoff from an R than from a D. They all start off without party affiliations: $p_{i_1,0} = p_{i_2,0} = p_{j,0} = \frac{1}{2}$.[12] Because responses to incumbents are stochastically determined—a voter with a time-independent $h_k^D = 0.3$ has a 30 percent chance of having a good experience with a Democratic incumbent—a potential two-period voting history could unfold as follows. First a D wins by

[11] A bit more formally, recall from chapter 2 that $\delta_{i,t}^{+}(\alpha, p_{i,t}(\alpha))$ denotes the expected increment in propensity for a success and that $\delta_{i,t}^{-}(\alpha, p_{i,t}(\alpha))$ denotes the expected decrement for a failure. Then order preservation states that whenever propensity x is at least as big as propensity y, then $x + \delta_{i,t}^{+}(x) \geqslant y + \delta_{i,t}^{+}(y)$. The condition on failures is analogous.

[12] We assume throughout this chapter that each voter starts off with a unique probability of voting D. Allowing for nondegenerate probability distributions over different initial propensities of voting D would complicate matters unnecessarily.

chance, but only voter i_1 gets a good payoff from her. By the assumptions of positive and negative feedback, $p_{i_1,1}$ will then exceed $\frac{1}{2}$, while $p_{i_2,1}$ and $p_{j,1}$ will be less than $\frac{1}{2}$. Suppose this yields an improvement in R's chances that in turn results in an electoral victory for R in period 2. This time, both i_1 and i_2 get bad payoffs from the incumbent (R), but j's experience with R is good. Again by (A5.2) and (A5.3), the propensities of i_1 and i_2 to vote Democratic will rise while j's will fall.[13]

The values the propensities will have at the end of this exercise depend on the particular form of the PAR in use, but whatever the form, we now have a weak ordering over vote propensities: $p_{i_1,2} \geqslant p_{i_2,2} \geqslant p_{j,2}$. Further, $p_{i_1,2} > \frac{1}{2} > p_{j,2}$. A piece of this ordering matches conventional wisdom: given i_1's interests, she is more likely to get high payoffs from a D incumbent than is j, and indeed i_1 ends up leaning more toward D than j does. Other parts, however, clash with conventional wisdom. For one thing, i_1 has become affiliated with D, and j with R, even though no h in this example exceeds $\frac{1}{2}$. Individuals who usually get poor payoffs from both parties will still end up liking one of them, at least for a little while. For another, i_1 and i_2 have different vote propensities despite having identical interests. As Achen put it, here "[t]he voter's political history is the only causal variable" (1992, p. 198); citizens' current voting tendencies reflect their life experiences with the two parties, as Jackson (1975) and Achen (1992) have argued. Accordingly, we cannot in general discuss what happens to any specific voter, as this is partly based on chance. Instead we will speak of the relative probabilities that voters with different interests will travel on different sample paths defined by distributions over their vote propensities.

With this concept in hand, we are ready for our first major result.[14] Proposition 5.2 concerns the ex ante probability of voting for D: i.e.,

---

[13] This example describes one possible sample path. In general, when viewed from time $t-1$, $p_{i,t}$ is a random variable. As with any random variable, it has a probability distribution. Thus, agents have probability distributions over their propensities to vote D or R. This is analogous to chapter 4, where citizens have probability distributions over their propensities to turn out.

[14] To keep the analysis clean, we analyze voters who adapt by the same propensity adjustment rule. This allows us to attribute differences in retrospective voting tendencies to differences in interests, not in PARs, which is preferable given the greater empirical interest in the former. Of course, all else equal, variations in PARs also affect voting. For the three-voter example given in the text, if i_2 had reacted much more strongly than i_1 to negative outcomes, then i_2's propensity to vote D at the end of period 2 might have been greater than i_1's, despite having received fewer good outcomes from Democrats. The model as stated allows us to explore variations in PARs systematically as well, but this must wait for future work.

the unconditional probability that a particular citizen will vote D at date t, given only the parameters' values at t_0. (This is equivalent to the expected propensity of voting for a D at t, given the parameters' initial values.) We use $P_{i,t}$ to denote this unconditional probability. Here and in other results we refer simply to "the probability," without modifiers.

Proposition 5.2 (Bendor, Kumar, and Siegel 2010). *Suppose voters i and j are part of the same electorate and use the same order-preserving PAR. If their interests satisfy $h^D_{i,t} > h^D_{j,t}$ and $h^R_{i,t} < h^R_{j,t}$ and if $p_{i,0} \geqslant p_{j,0}$, then $P_{i,t} > P_{j,t}$ for all $t > 0$.*

Proposition 5.2 describes a probabilistic relation between interests and vote propensities. Though our simple three-person, two-period example indicated that individual voters may achieve nearly any voting pattern, regardless of interests, on average voters more likely to get satisfactory payoffs from Democrats and bad ones from Republicans will tend to vote for Democrats more often, as long as they accurately assess the quality of the outcome (we relax this later). The proposition focuses on pairs of voters, but applying it iteratively yields an expected, ex ante ranking of all voters. Polarization—here represented as differences in the likelihood of voting for each party—is a natural consequence of voters' sorting into the party more likely to give them satisfactory payoffs.

This sorting happens generally, for any size electorate and any composition of interests among the voters, and it holds regardless of the fine structure of adaptation. Highly sophisticated voters can coexist happily with quite naïve ones in the model. By the same token, proposition 5.2 implies that a rich informational environment is not necessary for voter sorting. Citizens don't need to be either well-informed or well-equipped to discern the quality of candidates or their policies; they sort appropriately (i.e., in accord with their interests) if they merely respond to subjective measures of their own welfare. Finally, because PARs can change over time, the result allows for empirically plausible age effects. For example, voters seem to adjust their vote propensities less as they get older (Jennings and Markus 1984), an effect which can be captured via a PAR that decreases the magnitude of $|p_{i,t+1} - p_{i,t}|$ as t increases.

Proposition 5.2 is limited in one important way, however: it is confined to voters in the same electorate. While these voters can respond differently to an incumbent, they still experience the same one. This is important. It allows us to speak in relative terms: if voter i is more likely than j to get good payoffs from D and bad ones from R, then i will ex ante be expected to vote more often for D. Yet this is not necessarily true across electorates. Consider, for example, an i and j who live in separate jurisdictions, so they respond to different incumbents in each period. Further assume that both i and j are likely to be ill-served by both parties: their h's are all less than $\frac{1}{2}$. If i lives in a heavily partisan electorate in which Democrats are always elected and j lives in an equally partisan one in which Republicans always win, then i will frequently be dissatisfied with D's performance and j with R's, leading j to have *higher* D-propensities than i, despite being more likely than i to get low payoffs from D.

Thus, more than one's own interests matter when comparing across electorates: the makeup of each electorate matters as well. Remark 5.1 identifies conditions for this ecological effect to affect propensity orderings. As in the previous paragraph, remark 5.1 posits two middle-of-the-road voters, i and j, who are likely to get unsatisfactory payoffs from both parties, either because the parties have been captured by activists who are ideologically extreme or because their governments don't know how to cater to the interests of those in the middle. Both i and j belong to electorates which provide them with what should be their optimal outcomes, i.e., the party more likely to make them happy always wins (perhaps because a majority in each electorate has the appropriate $h^{\bullet}_{k,t} = 1$).

Remark 5.1 (Bendor, Kumar, and Siegel 2010). Assume that voters i and j, in electorates A and B, respectively, use the same order-preserving and symmetric PAR. In electorate A Democrats always win; in electorate B Republicans always win. Voter i has $\frac{1}{2} > h^D_{i,t} > h^R_{i,t}$, and voter j has $\frac{1}{2} > h^R_{j,t} > h^D_{j,t}$. If $p_{i,0} = p_{j,0}$, then $P_{i,t} < P_{j,t}$ for all $t > 0$.

Dissatisfied middle-of-the-road types can thus end up voting "out of order." What about more extreme voters, i.e., those likely to get good payoffs from only one of the parties? Proposition 5.3 recovers the ordering of proposition 5.2 for all voters, both within and across electorates, assuming their interests are sufficiently extreme.

Proposition 5.3 (Bendor, Kumar, and Siegel 2010). *Suppose i has $h^D_{i,t} > \frac{1}{2} > h^R_{i,t}$ while j has $h^D_{j,t} < \frac{1}{2} < h^R_{j,t}$. If they use the same order-preserving and symmetric PAR and $p_{i,0} \geqslant \frac{1}{2} \geqslant p_{j,0}$, then $P_{i,t} > \frac{1}{2} > P_{j,t}$ for all $t > 0$.*

Like its single-electorate predecessor, proposition 5.3 has definite, testable implications at the individual level.[15] In addition to the effect of sorting by interests discussed previously, both propositions illustrate how conditional responses to exogenous shocks can translate into electoral outcomes. For example, the outbreak of war is likely to alter voters' h's, the probabilities that they will get satisfactory payoffs from the incumbent. If the direction or magnitude of these changes is correlated with voter interests before the war, so that, say, voters with low values of $h_{i,t}^{R}$ find these values decreased more than voters with high values of these parameters, then the above propositions suggest that the electorate's degree of polarization will change after the onset of war, with increasing changes the longer the war goes on. Greater spread of antiwar movements during wartime would be one consequence of this.

Proposition 5.3 also has implications at the aggregate level. One relates to the outcome of elections. Compare two districts, A and B, of equal size and composed of voters who satisfy the requirements of proposition 5.3. If there are more voters like i in A than in B and more like j in B than in A, then we have the intuitively sensible prediction that D is more likely to win in A than in B. This prediction holds regardless of the level of dispersion of interests among voters of each type; it also extends to districts of different sizes. A second relates to how the party affiliations of voters and electorates shift over time. Suppose that propensity adjustment slows down over time, as discussed above. Then, a model that also had overlapping generations of voters and correlated payoff shocks (per Roemer 2001, p. 51) would yield cohort effects: a generation of new and hence volatile voters affected by the same experience (e.g., the Great Depression) would tend to align with the party that most often produced satisfactory outcomes when these voters were young. This could lead to a shift in citizens' party identification if this early experience took them off the path induced by parental or peer socialization. As these voters aged, however, subsequent life experiences would have an ever-decreasing impact on their voting tendencies—their party identifications would harden over time. If the cohort were big enough, this could produce an electorate that consistently voted for one particular party. This state of affairs would continue until the appearance of a new, sufficiently large generation that, in response to a new common experience, could turn the tables on its elders and switch the electorate's voting behavior.

[15] Also like proposition 5.2, this result yields the conclusion that i's probability distribution over his propensity to vote Democratic first-order stochastically dominates j's, provided that the PAR is symmetric as well as order-preserving.

5.3 Misperceptions

Although the kind of retrospective voting studied in this chapter is cognitively simple, it depends on a vital input: a citizen's perception of her payoffs. And since payoffs in a model of voting depend on public policies and the evaluation of the latter is far from easy—policy evaluation is a speciality in its own right—a realistic theory must allow for the possibility that ordinary citizens may err in evaluating an incumbent's performance. (That means, in the context of this chapter's model, allowing for the possibility that a voter believes she got a high payoff when in fact she received a low one, or vice versa.)

Further, it is essential to know whether payoff misperceptions affect party-oriented voting. It is obvious that *systematic* errors could have such effects: e.g., if a left-leaning citizen always perceived his payoff as being low when the incumbent was Republican, no matter what the R's performance was, then he would vote for Democrats more often than he would absent this bias. The more interesting question is whether *un*biased misperceptions can affect party-oriented voting.

Our first result on misperceptions shows that the conclusions of propositions 5.2 and 5.3 are robust with respect to unbiased mistakes—fortunately, given that many voters are quite ignorant of governmental conduct. (Note that this and the other misperception results allow error rates to change over time: e.g., citizens might evaluate incumbents more accurately as they acquire more information about politics over time.)

Proposition 5.4 (Bendor, Kumar, and Siegel 2010). *Suppose the hypotheses of proposition 5.2 (or proposition 5.3) hold. Further, citizens misperceive their payoffs with probability $\psi_t \in (0, \frac{1}{2})$, which is independently and identically distributed across voters and independently over time and over the realized payoffs to the voters. Then the conclusion of proposition 5.2 (or of proposition 5.3) obtains.*

It is well-established that citizens vary greatly in their political sophistication (e.g., Delli Carpini and Keeter 1996; Kinder 1998; Luskin 2002). Hence we should expect them to make errors of misperception at different rates. The next result examines an interesting effect of this variation in sophistication.

Proposition 5.5 (Bendor, Kumar, and Siegel 2010). *Suppose there are two types of voter, where i has liberal interests and j has conservative interests. At date t, sophisticated i's have error probability $\psi^S_{i,t}$, while unsophisticated i's make mistakes with probability $\psi^U_{i,t}$,* *with $\psi^S_{i,t} < \psi^U_{i,t} < \frac{1}{2}$ for all t. Similarly, sophisticated j's err in t with probability $\psi^S_{j,t}$, and unsophisticated ones do so with probability $\psi^U_{j,t}$, with $\psi^S_{j,t} < \psi^U_{j,t} < \frac{1}{2}$ for all t. Otherwise the hypotheses of proposition 5.3 hold. Then, ex ante, a sophisticated i is more likely to vote for a D than is an unsophisticated i, who is more likely to vote for a D than an unsophisticated j, who in turn is more likely to vote for a D than a sophisticated j, for all $t \geqslant 1$.*

Thus, the more sophisticated voters—those who are better at evaluating governmental performance—polarize to a greater degree than less sophisticated ones, which is consistent with the picture of "Independents" drawn in *The American Voter* (Campbell et al. 1960, p. 143). Further, proposition 5.4 implies that voting tendencies converge as evaluation errors become more common.

The last result in this section examines the effect of biased errors on voting propensities. Proposition 5.6 relies on a notion of perceptions having a partisan bias: one's errors are skewed in favor of one of the parties and against the other one. This bias could arise from a top-down processing of information: e.g., someone who thinks, perhaps unconsciously, "if D is in power, then my payoff must be good; if R is in power, then my payoff must be bad." Bartels (2002) provides evidence that partisan-biased political perception has substantial effects, "perpetuating and reinforcing sharp differences in opinion between Democrats and Republicans" (p. 138).

Proposition 5.6 (Bendor, Kumar, and Siegel 2010). *Suppose the hypotheses of proposition 5.2 hold, except that i_1's misperceptions have a more partisan bias in favor of D than i_2's do. If they have the same underlying interests, then i_1's expected propensity of voting for D is greater than i_2's for all $t \geqslant 1$.*

5.4 Retrospection and Prospection Combined

Probably most voters use some combination of retrospection and prospection in order to make their decisions: they can evaluate the incumbent's performance *and* compare the candidates' platforms to each other (Fiorina 1981) or do one or the other in different races (Nadeau and Lewis-Beck 2001).[16] In this section we combine these

[16] Note that the mental operations in aspiration-based retrospective voting and in Downsian prospective voting are quite different. In the former voters compare realized payoffs to an internal standard of evaluation. In the latter they compare what they will get from one party versus another. As suggested in chapter 1 (footnote 20), one can build internally consistent models in which actors carry out both kinds of comparisons.

two elements in a straightforward extension of our basic model and then show that the conclusions of proposition 5.2 continue to hold in this more complex setting.

For the prospective component we use a standard spatial model in a one-dimensional policy space. Both the incumbent and the challenger espouse platforms. (We don't need to assume that platforms are fully binding on parties if they reach office. As many scholars have noted, this is one reason why voters might not put much weight on such promises. Further, platforms can vary with time, as long as this variation is exogenous to voters' propensities. Thus, we allow platforms to change as different factions or candidates take control of the party.) Voters observe these platforms and, when thinking prospectively, compare the parties' platforms to their ideal points. The retrospective component also has a spatial aspect, as spelled out by the following assumption.

(A5.4) $h^{x}_{i,t}$, the probability that a voter gets the h payoff with x, is strictly decreasing in $|z_i - x_t|$, where z_i is voter i's ideal point in policy space X (a compact and convex subset of $\mathbb{R}^n$) and x_t is the policy enacted by the incumbent in period t.

The two components are combined by the following weighted-average equation. The weight, λ, is in (0,1), and $q_{i,t}$ denotes the probability that i votes Democratic in t based on both retrospection and prospection, while $p_{i,t}$ continues to denote the retrospectively based propensity. The function $\mathbf{I}_i(D, R)$, which represents the prospective component, takes on a value of 1 or 0 if D or R's platform (D_t or R_t), respectively, is closer to i's ideal point and is $\frac{1}{2}$ if they are equally close.

(A5.5) For all i and all t, $q_{i,t} = \lambda p_{i,t} + (1 - \lambda)\mathbf{I}_i(D, R)$.

Observe that for simplicity and to satisfy an important ceteris paribus condition, the weight is constant across voters. An interesting question for future research is how the weight on platforms varies as a function of voter sophistication. [This matter is not obvious: e.g., Fiorina (1981) anticipated that more sophisticated citizens would vote less retrospectively but reported (p. 49) that this hypothesis wasn't supported by the evidence.]

Proposition 5.7 (Bendor, Kumar, and Siegel 2010). *Suppose both candidates announce platforms in unidimensional policy space with* $D_t \leqslant R_t$ *and the winner implements a policy such that* $x^D_t < z_{MV} < x^R_t$ *at every date* t*, where* MV *represents the median voter. If (A5.4) and the assumptions of proposition 5.2 hold, except that*

(A5.5) replaces pure retrospective voting, then the conclusion of proposition 5.2 still obtains.

This result presumes citizens who are more cognitively sophisticated than the most naïve retrospective voters. Whereas the latter may not have a spatial framework in their minds (much less embed parties' platforms and their own ideal points in a policy space), the former can carry out these mental operations. Further, citizens covered by proposition 5.7 can unify, albeit in a simple linear way, retrospective and prospective assessments.

But it turns out that these differences in sophistication do not alter the qualitative voting patterns generated by the crudest retrospection. On reflection this makes sense. Spatial models typically build in a direct connection between citizens' interests and party-oriented voting: voters are presumed to have a good understanding of their interests (in standard models one might say that their understanding is complete) and act accordingly. So the prospective component in the equation in (A5.5) is tugging citizen i in the right direction, toward the party that will better serve her interests.

Hence, although proposition 5.7 is a reassuring robustness result, which shows that our prior findings based on purely retrospective voting are not fragile, knife-edge results, and although it uses premises that are more plausible than those involving pure retrospection, one could argue that proposition 5.2 is more surprising: it shows how little is required of citizens in order for partisan voting to emerge endogenously.

5.5 Voter Sophistication and Electoral Outcomes

Thus far we have examined properties shared by a broad swath of retrospective rules. However, we believe that an important kind of theoretical competition will occur *within* the RV family. This requires understanding differences within this family. Given the literature's focus on the sophistication of voters, it is natural to focus on naïve versus sophisticated retrospective rules.

The class of naïve RV rules that we examine here includes satisficing, the Bush-Mosteller rule (perhaps the best-known example of reinforcement learning), and many others. The set is identified simply by adding stationarity to (A5.2) and (A5.3). Such rules adjust vote propensities in a way that is independent of time. In contrast, nonstationary rules keep track of time. Clearly, both types of rules belong to the RV family, but the latter attend to a variable that the former ignore and in that sense are more complex.

We show here that, except in rather special circumstances, stationary RV rules do not produce optimal electoral outcomes even over the course of many elections. To demonstrate how PARs representing such naïve RV rules fall short of optimality, we examine two simple but theoretically important cases. In the first case the electorate has just one voter; in the second, infinitely many. The first case is useful because in such electorates the voter is always pivotal; hence, we can study the suboptimality of PARs in splendid isolation, without the complexities arising from collective choice processes. The second case is useful because a Law of Large Numbers makes the aggregate outcome—which party wins the election—deterministic and thus easier to analyze. In both cases we investigate whether citizens eventually learn to do what is best for them, i.e., to vote consistently for the party that better serves their interests.

Remark 5.2. Suppose $n = 1$ and the voter uses a stationary PAR. If $\max\{h_t^D, h_t^R\} < 1$ for all t then the citizen never settles down on one party: both parties are elected infinitely often with probability 1.

The empirical content of remark 5.2 is simple: the voter will inevitably be dissatisfied with the incumbent at some point in her history, leading to a decrease in the propensity that she will vote for candidates from that incumbent's party in the future, resulting in a nonzero probability of kicking the incumbent's party out of office. Its consequences for social optimality are of more substantive interest, however. Assume that $h_t^D > h_t^R$ for all t (or vice versa), so one of the parties produces candidates more likely to make the voter happy, on average. Yet a voter using a stationary PAR will never settle on this optimal candidate.[17] Because optimal PARs are generally nonstationary and so more complex,[18] it is unlikely that many cognitively constrained voters ever achieve optimality in their voting.

Interestingly, however, partisan bias in perceiving payoffs improves matters for certain classes of voters. It does so for a simple

[17] This property should not be very surprising by now. At several points in this book we have seen that agents who adapt via stationary ABARs will use suboptimal actions infinitely often with probability 1. (Proposition 2.1 is a fairly general statement of this.) A simple example is that of a satisficing agent playing a two-armed bandit with normally distributed payoffs of equal variance. Suppose the payoff of L has mean zero and R's has mean 1. If the aspiration level is exogenously fixed, then R is optimal in a strong sense: it first-order stochastically dominates L. Nevertheless, it is easy to see that the agent will play the suboptimal arm infinitely often.

[18] That such rules do, in fact, exist can be rigorously established along the lines of Kiefer and Wolfowitz (1952).

reason: such a bias pushes certain voters in the direction they should go, given their interests. In particular, this type of misperception makes voters less likely to notice that incumbents of the optimal parties—those that would better serve their interests—perform poorly, whence these voters are less likely to impatiently reject such incumbents who happen to give them objectively low payoffs. The next result states the effect comparatively. To see the normative implication in a clear way, simply posit that the perceptions of citizen j are unbiased.

Remark 5.3 (Bendor, Kumar, and Siegel 2010). Suppose the assumptions of proposition 5.6 hold. Citizens i and j have identical interests and reside in the same electorate; given these interests, voting for D is their optimal choice. If voter i's partisan misperception bias in favor of D strictly exceeds j's, and $p_{i,0} \geqslant p_{j,0}$, then in all future periods i will be more likely than j to vote optimally.

Suppose that j's perceptions are unbiased. Then he sees part of the world correctly—indeed, j never errs when evaluating the current government's performance—but this makes him too inclined to turn against the imperfect yet optimal party. To paraphrase Voltaire, the perfect is the enemy of the best (Bendor and Kumar 2005). In contrast, i sees the world through rosy, D-partisan lenses, and this evaluation bias partly substitutes for the general piece of knowledge that D is the optimal party for this voter.

However, although fortuitously biased mistakes push a voter in the right direction, they are unlikely to produce optimal voting even in the long run. What about the effects of having many voters? Will an abundance of voters produce optimal collective judgment, as in Condorcet Jury Theorems?

Part (iii) of the next result is confined to PARs that have the property of *equal adjustment*. For any given propensity, a PAR in this class changes a given propensity by the same amount (up or down), though the amount of adjustment can differ for different propensities.[19]

Remark 5.4. Suppose there are infinitely many voters, all of the same type. All voters' PARs are stationary, symmetric, and order-preserving. The start is unbiased—$p_{i,0} = \frac{1}{2}$ for all i—and $h_t^D > h_t^R$ (analogous results hold for $h_t^R > h_t^D$).

(i) If $h_t^D > h_t^R > \frac{1}{2}$ for all t, then whichever party wins the first election is elected thereafter, with probability 1.

[19] Formally, equal adjustment implies $\delta_{i,t}^{+}(x) = \delta_{i,t}^{-}(x)$ for all propensities x.

(ii) If $h_t^D > \frac{1}{2} > h_t^R$ for all t, then two paths can occur: (1) the initial incumbent is D, who is elected thereafter, or (2) the initial incumbent is R, but R is defeated in the first election and never wins office again.

(iii) If $\frac{1}{2} > h_t^D > h_t^R$ for all t and the PAR additionally satisfies equal adjustment, then every incumbent eventually loses office, with probability 1.

As might be expected, the type of voter present in the population dictates the outcome of all elections. Further, because the population is infinite, the process locks onto its predestined outcome swiftly. What is less obvious is that there is only a narrow band over which a Jury Theorem–like result obtains.[20] If $h_t^D > h_t^R > \frac{1}{2}$, then a problem of excessive inertia can arise: the first party in office is "good enough" for all subsequent time. The flip side of (i)'s statement is (iii)'s: if $\frac{1}{2} > h_t^D > h_t^R$, then neither party's candidate is good enough, and the government cycles. Only when the electorate's interests line up just right—i.e., when $h_t^D > \frac{1}{2} > h_t^R$ (or $h_t^R > \frac{1}{2} > h_t^D$)—does the electorate settle on the socially optimal party quickly and stay there.

The limited ability of large populations to lead to social optima has normative consequences, particularly if we assume that voters are cognitively constrained. For example, assume that voters' $h_{i,t}$'s can vary with time but are formed by the relation of outcomes to endogenous aspirations, rather than via rational calculus. If a citizen's aspiration level is the unweighted average of her realized payoffs, then as time passes, no matter how good a party is for voters at first, eventually aspirations will approach average outcomes and $h_{i,t}$ for that party will approach $\frac{1}{2}$.[21] At this point, regardless of how bad a challenging party might have been for the voters in the past, they will quite likely toss the incumbent out and try the challenger again. Thus, we often end up in category (iii) of remark 5.4, effectively choosing between the lesser of two evils.

Overall, then, we see that Achen (1992) was right: important kinds of retrospective rules are suboptimal. Remark 5.2 shows that

[20] The results of remark 5.4 continue to hold under a complex choice process along the lines of (A5.5). Naturally, the introduction of a direct and flawless comparison of the parties will expand the parametric region in which the benign outcome (ii) occurs. Further, the higher the weight on the prospective component—$1 - \lambda$ in the equation in (A5.5)—the bigger this parametric region will be.

[21] Consider that "rapid economic growth in countries such as Japan and France has been accompanied by a virtually flat line for SWB [subjective well-being]" (Diener and Suh 1999, p. 441). This seems to reflect what psychologists now call the *hedonic treadmill*: by adjusting to experience, higher aspirations reduce some of the potential psychic benefits of greater wealth.

suboptimality persists even as time goes to infinity. Remark 5.4 shows that it can persist even as the number of voters goes to infinity. These theoretical results are important not because we observe time or populations increasing without limit; they matter because they demonstrate that retrospective voting can fall short of optimality for fundamental reasons.

5.6 Institutions and Unsophisticated Retrospective Voters

In some ways, however, remarks 5.2 and 5.4 are too pessimistic: they reflect how naïve retrospective voters can behave suboptimally, but they do not examine how the voters' agent—the incumbent—might improve matters. The next results show that representative democracy ameliorates problems caused by unsophisticated retrospective voting.

To see the value added by representation we first analyze how retrospective voting fares under direct democracy. Under the latter institution citizens vote directly on policies, as they do for state initiatives and referenda. We consider a single-issue area. An initial policy is randomly selected to be the status quo in t_0. Citizens respond to policies as discussed in the section covering prospection; in particular, (A5.4) determines their interests. [Per the objections of Stokes (1963), we do not assume that voters understand their actions in the framework of (A5.4). The assumption is merely our way of representing their underlying interests, as in Achen and Bartels (2002).] If the status quo policy wins majority approval in the current election, then it continues in force for another period. If the voters reject it, then a new policy becomes the status quo. (For what follows we do not need to specify how the new policy is selected.)

We say that a policy is *stable* if, once installed as the status quo, it wins approval from the electorate thereafter with probability 1. Hence a stable policy is an absorbing state in the corresponding stochastic process. Voters continue to vote retrospectively, based on what they observe (their realized payoffs), using PARs to update their propensities to vote for the status quo policy.

Remark 5.5 (Bendor, Kumar, and Siegel 2010). Suppose that (A5.4) holds. If the PAR is stationary, then policy x is stable only if it gives an h payoff to a majority of citizens with probability 1 for all $t \geqslant 1$.

Remark 5.5 immediately implies that if no policy can *guarantee* good outcomes to any citizen (which seems plausible!), then no policy is stable, given a stationary retrospective rule. This is true even if the electorate is completely homogeneous. Thus, Achen and Bartels (2004) are right to be concerned about what they call "blind" retrospective voting: in an imperfect world, where no policy elicits positive responses with certainty, even the best policy will eventually be discarded in a direct democracy.[22]

Now let us see how representative democracy fares.

Remark 5.6 (Bendor, Kumar, and Siegel 2010). If the hypotheses of remark 5.5 hold, then the following conclusions obtain.

(i) A fully informed incumbent who maximizes the probability of staying in office in the current election is stable only if there is a policy she can implement which generates high payoffs to a majority of citizens with certainty at every date.

(ii) If no such policy exists but the electorate is homogeneous, then no incumbent is stable but every incumbent implements the electorate's common ideal point.

Retrospective citizens who respond naïvely to stochastic outcomes still vent their frustrations in the voting booth, punishing incumbents for anything from wars to shark bites. Yet despite this type of behavior, office-oriented politicians can protect the voters *from themselves.* They do so not out of benevolence but because pleasing the voters is the best way to win reelection and so to enjoy the perks of office.[23]

---

[22] Again, analysis based on Jury theorems might lead one to think that this implication of remark 5.4 is still too pessimistic. In particular, perhaps it is quantitatively unimportant for large electorates: if there are a great many voters, then discarding an optimal policy might be an extremely unlikely event. This intuition is half right: under otherwise standard assumptions (independent errors and so forth), the chance that ABAR-driven voters will make this mistake under direct democracy gets arbitrarily small as the electorate increases without limit (Bendor, Kumar, and Siegel 2010). Even here, however, the bad news in remark 5.4 asserts itself: if the optimal policy in a spatial setting is stable, then so are infinitely many suboptimal ones. (This is essentially part (ii) of remark 5.4 with a continuum of alternatives.) ABAR-driven voters do not cope with the trade-off between type 1 and type 2 errors as well as utility-maximizing ones do.

[23] Part (ii) is stated in terms of a unique social optimum, but the result is not fragile. Suppose our normative theory requires that socially optimal policies be Pareto-efficient. Given this, one can show that if the electorate is nearly homogeneous, then a myopically support-maximizing politician will implement a policy that is close to a socially optimal policy, if such policies exist. (If they don't exist, then the matter is moot: no intelligible claims about the suboptimality of democracy can be made.)

5.7 Conclusions

We have seen that a large class of retrospective rules—including some that are quite naïve—produce important patterns of voting behavior, in particular endogenous polarization (proposition 5.2). Thus Key was right: citizens don't need ideologies. They can get by, in an important practical sense, with retrospective voting.

There are, however, significant and empirically testable differences within the large family of retrospective rules studied here. For example, some PARs (e.g., bang-bang satisficing) can produce highly volatile voting behavior, especially if both parties usually produce poor payoffs which are accurately perceived by voters. In contrast, other adaptive rules or retrospective evaluations can generate habitual behavior: e.g., chronic partisan bias in perceptions can produce significant habituation via a tendency to overestimate the performance of one party. Alternatively, habituation could arise from the use of a particular PAR. Consider, for example, a logistic adjustment rule in which propensities trace out the logistic function $1/(1 + e^{\beta x})$ by adding (subtracting) constant increments to x given positive (negative) feedback. Here, a few increases (decreases) in propensity rapidly carry a voter to the flat part of the logistic function, which changes slowly with additional feedback. Thus, a voter using such a PAR would change her propensity only a little once habituated as a Democrat or a Republican, even after several outcomes that would otherwise tend to push her away from her chosen party. And whether people develop habitual party affiliations can be tested by longitudinal individual-level data.

Another discriminating property, though one that probably interests theorists more than empiricists, concerns the optimality of retrospective voting. Many backward-oriented rules—stationary ones—do not guarantee optimal voting even in the ultralong run. But even these are sensible heuristics: they produce behavior that is directionally consistent with voters' interests and are well-adapted to the informational and cognitive constraints shouldered by most citizens.

Of course, retrospective voting requires an input: a voter's evaluation of how the incumbent performed. It is known that citizens' knowledge of governmental performance varies enormously. This difference in the inputs to retrospective rules has significant effects: proposition 5.5 showed that more knowledgeable citizens are more polarized. As more than a few scholars have suggested, many centrist voters, instead of being exemplars of classical democratic theory (well-informed citizens who use their knowledge to render considered judgments), know less than their more polarized peers.

We have focused on the behavior of voters and have mostly assumed exogenously fixed parties. This is a common modeling assumption (e.g., Palfrey and Rosenthal 1985; Achen 1992; Bendor, Diermeier, and Ting 2003a) but its justification is tractability, not verisimilitude. In related work (Bendor, Kumar, and Siegel 2007) we close the loop by considering how rational parties would behave, given retrospective voters. The next chapter takes a different tack, combining the models of chapters 3–5 into an integrated behavioral model of two-party elections.

CHAPTER SIX

An Integrated Model of Two-Party Elections

EACH OF THE LAST three chapters has presented a model of some aspect of the electoral process. In each case—party competition, voter turnout, and voter choice—we held all other electoral factors constant in order to focus tightly on the aspect of interest. Although this measured approach allowed for clean analyses, the price was rather high: each model froze some important features of elections that vary in the real world. In the turnout model in chapter 4, for example, citizens never change party identification; they can choose to stay home, but they cannot vote for the opposition. Conversely, in chapter 5's model, voters could change parties, but they could not choose to drop out of electoral politics altogether.

These focused models were useful stepping stones, but it is time to combine them into a coherent whole. In this chapter we let all three components of chapters 3–5 vary simultaneously: citizens choose whether to participate or to stay home; those who turn out decide which side to support; parties compete by offering alternative platforms to the electorate.[1] Hence, we can address questions about relations among these endogenous variables. For example, one might wonder whether chapter 4's robust patterns of participation were artifacts of rigidly (and unrealistically) fixed parties. Would the adaptive search of parties for better platforms impair turnout? In particular, would citizens stay home in greater numbers if the parties learned to adopt similar platforms? Or consider voter choice. In chapter 5 we considered vote choice in the context of static parties and full turnout, not in the messier reality where parties search for better platforms and voters may stay home. How often do adaptively retrospective citizens vote accurately—in accord with their interests—when parties can change their platforms substantially? Conversely, would searching for new policies still help challengers discover popular platforms when voters are not error-free Downsian automata?

[1] In this sense this chapter is closely related to Ledyard's (1984) seminal game-theoretic model of two-party competition with turnout. While the model has been well known for its stark conclusion (in the equilibrium both parties locate at the median and nobody votes), the model's perhaps more important insight was a discussion of the normative properties of two-candidate elections: the adopted electoral platform maximized the sum of voters' utility functions.

Further, this chapter's model also allows for greater heterogeneity within each coalition. The turnout model, for example, kept matters simple by assuming that everyone in the same faction got the same payoff if their candidate won. Here citizens on the same side can get different payoffs. Hence, the model can analyze the effects of voter heterogeneity. For example, suppose citizens have different ideal points over a unidimensional policy space. Who will turn out more often: moderates or people on the wings?

Clearly, integrating the focused models of party competition, turnout, and voter choice opens up a wealth of questions—more than we can address in depth here. It also presents problems. Each of the behavioral models in the previous three chapters generated complex dynamics; hence, our ability to derive analytical results was limited. Combining all three produces a model that is much more complex: its parameter space is far too large to explore completely, and its interactions too complex to allow deductive analysis. Accordingly, we neither rigorously derive results nor search the parameter space comprehensively. Instead, we focus on a series of empirically interesting questions that the model can address and vary only those parameters necessary to illustrate the behavior in question. This does reduce generality somewhat. Fortunately, this cost is mitigated by our earlier analytical results. Further, the integrated computational model lets us explore a far wider set of electoral behaviors than is permitted by extant models, a benefit that we think outweighs the disadvantages of these complex simulations.

Moreover, thanks to the work of the previous chapters, this complexity can be penetrated: now that we understand the internal workings of the three simpler models, we can productively study their interactions and the ensuing outcomes. To do this, however, we must create a computational model that instantiates the models of chapters 3–5. We describe such a model below in sufficient detail so that a reader with some training in programming can reproduce it. For complex models such as ours, replicating results is particularly important, and so this chapter's computational model is available as a companion to our book. Two programs are provided. One has a graphical user interface that uses RePAST 3[2]; this program works well as an exploratory tool. All figures in this chapter relating to electoral *dynamics* were obtained via this program. A second, which has no graphics, is useful for batch runs. All figures relevant to the system's *mean* behavior were obtained via this program. Both programs

[2] See http://repast.sourceforge.net/repast_3/index.html for more information.

are available on the book's website (see http://press.princeton.edu/titles/9352.html for links to this site). Accompanying technical documents there and in appendix B fully describe their operation. We encourage readers to use these models as they go. In particular, exploring the graphical version can enhance and deepen insights described here. As an added bonus, the program contains settings we do not explore in this book; we hope these will suggest further research to other scholars.

6.1 Full Computational Model for Two Parties

The core of any election model is the interplay between voters and politicians. The rules mediating these interactions were all specified in earlier chapters; here we merely describe how they operate in the computational model. We begin with voters. As described in chapters 4 and 5, adaptive voters are defined by their probabilities of turning out and of voting for a particular party, along with their aspiration levels and their payoff functions. We keep all four elements here, with a few minor changes. In chapter 5 we suppressed aspirations in order to derive some analytical results; here aspirations are explicitly represented and are endogenous. In chapter 4 all voters of a particular faction had identical payoff distributions; here voters have heterogeneous preferences.

All aspects that define voters (turnout propensity, vote propensity, aspirations, and payoffs) must be specified precisely by the computational model; a simulation cannot use general functional forms. As a rule, we aim for the most general formulation that is feasible, providing multiple options in some cases. This drives up the number of parameters as noted above but also allows for more wide-ranging theoretical exploration.

Payoffs and aspirations are tightly linked in the model. Payoffs have three components. The first is a loss term that grows more negative the more the incumbent's actions in office diverge from a citizen's bliss point. We offer two options for this term: quadratic (the default) and piecewise-linear. As described in chapter 5, the voter need not know or understand her ideal policies to be able to react to the policies enacted by the incumbent. The second is a fixed cost (c) of voting. As discussed in chapter 4, this typically represents the effort and opportunity cost involved in all aspects of voting, but a duty to vote can also be represented, i.e., by $c < 0$. The third and final component is a random variable (ϵ_i) that represents random outcome shocks beyond the control of any incumbent. The model allows these to be normally or uniformly distributed. Shocks are assumed to be uncorrelated across voters. Put together, the payoff to voter i, under the default quadratic loss, is

$$-\tfrac{1}{2}(x_t - z_i)^2 - \mathbf{1}_i c + \epsilon_i,$$

where x_t is the policy adopted by the winning candidate, z_i is i's bliss point, and $\mathbf{1}_i$ is one if i voted and zero otherwise.[3]

Aspirations for each voter are initially set by default to equal the expected payoff she would receive were she to turn out half of the time and split her votes equally between the parties.[4] Aspirations adjust as in chapter 4: a linear combination of previous aspirations and present payoffs, so that

$$a_{i,t+1} = (1 - \nu)a_{i,t} + \nu\pi_{i,t}.$$

As always, when a citizen's payoffs exceed aspirations, the outcome is deemed a *success* and propensities to try the associated actions (e.g., turn out and vote Democratic) are increased; when payoffs fall short of aspirations, the outcome is called a *failure* and the relevant propensities decrease. If payoffs equal aspirations, no adjustment takes place. As in the previous chapters, we use inertia to ensure ergodicity.[5] Initial vote and turnout propensities are tunable parameters in the model. Though we often default to setting each action—vote or do not vote; vote for one party or vote for the other—as equally likely to avoid biasing the initial dynamics, several other options are available in the program; we will describe those explored here as they are introduced.

Action propensities could adjust in many different ways that would be consistent with the basic axioms of adaptation laid out in previous chapters. For consistency, here we use the Bush-Mosteller rule from chapter 4. Under this rule the new propensity is a linear combination of the old propensity and either one (if a success) or zero (if a failure):

$$p_{i,t+1} = (1 - \lambda)p_{i,t} + \lambda\mathbf{1}_{\pi_{i,t} \geqslant a_{i,t}}.$$

For purposes of comparison the model can turn off propensity adjustment, using instead several different benchmarks. For turnout

---

[3] The names of the parameters in the executable program differ from those listed here, primarily so as to be readable without reference to this book.

[4] The executable program has options for different distributions of initial aspirations, so as to examine independently their effect on dynamics. (Because the process is ergodic, differences in initial aspirations vanish in the long run.)

[5] We use one parameter in the model, ε, to regulate inertia in all model adjustments. Inertial behavior is checked independently at each opportunity to adjust. The default value of ε is 0.01.

we turn off propensity adjustment and fix participation at 100 percent for an entire run. When this is done, citizens are like those in chapter 5: they always turn out; what they adjust is the propensity to vote D or R. For vote choice there are two diametrically opposed benchmarks. One is perfect Downsian behavior: as in chapter 3, a Downsian citizen always votes for the party whose position is closer to her own bliss point, regardless of past events. At the other extreme, citizens vote randomly: they toss fair coins. These benchmarks are included to enhance our understanding of the model and how results are generated. By freezing behavior for one component—forcing full voter turnout, for example—we can explore the interaction of the other two components and how they coproduce outcomes.[6]

The default number of voters used in the results in this chapter and chapter 7 is 1,000; this is also a tunable parameter, limited only by computational constraints.[7] Voters' ideal points are fixed in a given simulation. Several distributions of voters' ideal points may be chosen, including the uniform, the normal, and evenly spaced voters (ideal points evenly spaced on an interval)[8]; any of these may be in one or two dimensions. To focus on the impact of varying multiple model components at once rather than the effects of varying voter distribution, in this chapter we assume evenly spaced voters in one dimension. Table 6.1 summarizes default values of all voter-related and general parameters.

We consider two parties, R and D. Parties in the computational model are defined by their positions and by how they change these policies over time. They are purely office-motivated, as in chapter 3. As there, they satisfice, and only challengers search for new platforms. There are five options for adjusting these platforms over time. The first turns off party search. This permits a comparison with models that have static parties and allows us to study how turnout and vote choice interact without the added complexity of party dynamics.

---

[6] The program also provides options to fix turnout and vote propensities at any of the initial conditions available to them, and to adjust turnout or vote propensities via the equal-adjustment dynamic mentioned in remark 5.4. See appendix B for details.

[7] As of this writing, our posted program cannot go much beyond 50,000 voters. We believe that our results will change little with additional voters, but we will continue trying to increase this limit and will post new versions as we overcome technical hurdles.

[8] The uniform and the evenly spaced distributions are related. With the former, the computer draws a sample of n voters from the uniform distribution; under the latter, it is guaranteed that the realized ideal points will be evenly spaced. Thus, for large n, one could regard the evenly spaced case as a discrete approximation of a continuous, uniform distribution.

TABLE 6.1
Default simulation and voter parameters.

Parameter	Value
Number of simulations	1,000
Number of voters (n)	1,000
Elections	500
Voter distribution	Evenly spaced in $[-3, 3]$
Voter utility	Quadratic loss
Voting cost (c)	0.2
Shock term ($\epsilon_{i,t}$)	$\sim N(0, 0.1)$
Action adjustment (λ)	0.1
Initial turnout propensity distribution	All 0.5
Aspiration adjustment and payoffs	Linear with stochastic quadratic payoffs
Aspiration adjustment (ν)	0.1
Initial aspiration distribution ($a_{i,1}$)	Center of payoff distribution
Initial vote propensity distribution	All 0.5

The other four options are adaptive and are as described in chapter 3. They dictate that losing parties search for new platforms stochastically, either globally (ignoring the old platform) or locally (centered on the old platform). Search is either uniform, putting equal weight on all policies within some adjustable range, or normal, placing higher weight on centrally located policies, per a normal distribution with an adjustable mean and standard deviation. We also allow parties to be sophisticated in varying degrees: a tunable parameter allows search to be biased toward the mean of the voter distribution. Table 6.2 summarizes default values of all party-related parameters.

This covers the actors. They interact in the model in a very simple context, a plurality-rule election. The time line in each period of the model, which parallels that of chapter 5, is as follows.

1. An election occurs and a winner is chosen.[9]
2. Voters receive payoffs from incumbents.
3. Propensities for both vote choice and turnout adjust based on these payoffs and the previous period's aspirations.
4. Aspirations adjust.
5. Parties may search for new platforms.
6. Simulation outcomes are recorded.

[9] The first election is thus randomly determined, given initial propensities.

TABLE 6.2
Default party parameters.

Party search rule	Local ~ $N(0, 0.3)$
Party distribution	Two-party competition
D-party position	−1
R-party position	1
Party sophistication	Naïve (0)

TABLE 6.3
Basic results of the integrated model.

Average distance of winning policy from median voter	0.574
Average turnout	29%
Average percentage voting correctly	63%

The model repeats these periods, either indefinitely or to some predetermined ending point. In the results below we use 500 elections as a stopping point—though in many cases the process seems to have reached its limiting distribution well before this date—and display outcomes from this final period. We call each such a series of elections a *history*; each history begins with initial distributions of voters and parties.

A systematic analysis of the model would involve averaging the simulation data from multiple histories at each parameter value. Sweeping the parameter space would provide a picture of the model similar to that obtained via comparative statics in standard equilibrium analyses (Siegel 2009). Though, as noted above, the parameter space is simply too large to do this for all combinations of parameters, we do apply the same level of rigor to the regions of the parameter space that we choose to explore. All results discussed in this chapter and the next were derived by averaging the outcomes of 1,000 histories of the model.

6.2 Some Results of the Basic Integrated Model

The preceding section describes a rather rich set of possible models. Here we focus on this chapter's basic model, which presumes the default values listed in tables 6.1 and 6.2.

Let us inspect the endogenous variables after 500 elections averaged over 1,000 histories. Table 6.3 and figure 6.1 provide an

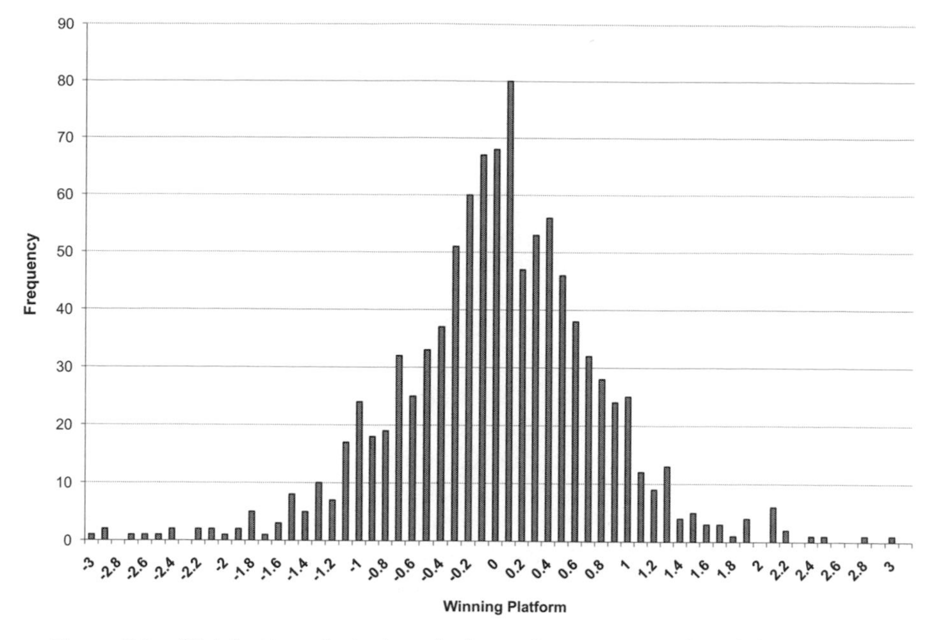

Figure 6.1. Distribution of winning platforms, basic integrated model.

overview. Figure 6.1 shows that although the parties started out at -1 and 1, winning platforms are usually fairly close to the median voter. The centrist tendencies identified in the simple party competition model in chapter 3 are present in this more complex model.[10]

Now turn to the voters. Table 6.3 reveals that participation is substantial. As to vote choice, although citizens start off neutral, they learn—albeit quite imperfectly—which party better serves their interests, picking the candidate whose platform is closer to theirs 63 percent of the time on average. (Doing so is difficult because the parties are moving around; we will investigate this issue below.)

[10] The average winning policy is almost exactly the median voter's ideal point. This is not, however, reported in table 6.3 for two reasons. First, it is an artifact of the model's symmetry. Second, and more importantly, if voters have satiable preferences—their utility functions have ideal points—the average policy is not an informative statistic. What matters is how far the winning policies are from the median voter's ideal point (Bendor and Meirowitz 2004). For example, suppose that in the limit the winning platform is either 3 or -3, with equal likelihood; hence, the average policy is exactly at the median voter's bliss point. Obviously, however, such a system is much less responsive to the desires of this voter than is one with a limiting distribution of -1 and 1.2 with equal likelihood. The latter's payoffs to the median voter first-order stochastically dominate the former's.

Even this modest degree of accuracy yields the centrist tendencies of winning policies described in the preceding paragraph.

Overall, then, the picture is of a crude stochastic electoral system that performs "reasonably" well on average, although of course that conclusion depends partly on the appraiser's aspiration level. A nonnegligible subset of the electorate participates; of those who do, many vote for the side they would select if they were fully informed Downsian voters; the parties respond to this environment by moving stochastically toward the center of the voter distribution.[11]

This overview leaves much unexplained. Let us now see whether we can get a better understanding of the guts of this electoral system. To do this, it is helpful to fix one and sometimes even two of the computational model's key processes. For example, to grasp how adaptive parties respond to the selection environment produced by voters, it is useful to temporarily transform the latter into perfect Downsian automata, who in any given election always vote for the side that is closer to their ideal points. By providing a benchmark with a deterministic component—unerring vote choice—it is easier to comprehend the more complex model in which all the actors are imperfect and stochastically so.

It is convenient to have terms for model variants with fixed components. Models which have two active elements will be (unimaginatively) called two-component models. If we need to identify which element is fixed, we will name it: for example, a model in which parties and vote choice are active is called a two-component model with fixed turnout. The simplest models—those with only one active element—are named by their active component. Thus, something called a *vote choice model* has static parties and turnout fixed at complete participation.

Where to start analyzing an adaptive dynamic system in which all the endogenous processes affect each other is somewhat arbitrary. Clearly, however, the selection environment is vital. Hence, we start with vote choice.

---

[11] One way to measure how much the process moves toward the median voter is to compare what happens under the default assumptions to what would happen in a zero-intelligence process, where challengers search blindly and citizens vote randomly. It is easy to prove, given any exogenously fixed probability distribution of turning out, that the zero-intelligence process converges to a unique limiting distribution which puts probability of $1/m$ on each of the m policies. Since the policy space is $[-3, 3]$, the average distance of the winning policy from the center of the distribution of ideal points would be 1.5 in the zero-intelligence process. Thus, by adaptively adjusting their vote propensities, voters reduce the average distance to the median voter from 1.5 to 0.57.

6.3 The Choices of Voters

In the basic integrated model, parties are purely office-oriented. They have no intrinsic attachment to any policy; a platform is merely a means to winning office. This differs sharply from the voting choice model in chapter 5, where parties are represented by fixed platforms. This can be interpreted as a model of parties with such strong policy preferences that they always advocate the same platform; opportunistically espousing a policy in order to win office is ruled out. We saw in the latter model (e.g., proposition 5.2) that voters develop partisan tendencies: they learn to support the side that will better serve their interests. With opportunistic parties, completely stable partisan identification will not emerge; the parties move around too much for that to happen.[12] For example, a D-challenger, seeking a platform that would return him to office, might take up a policy to the right of the incumbent R. As we shall see shortly, this occurs not infrequently with several search rules.

Nevertheless, the notion of correct voting is still meaningful in a short-run sense in the integrated model: since winning parties—despite their opportunism—implement their platforms with complete fidelity and since citizens have symmetric loss functions, voting correctly in any election implies backing the side whose platform is closer to one's ideal point. Hence, apart from the special circumstance of R and D's platforms being equidistant from the median voter, typically one of the parties is better for the majority of the electorate than the other in a given election. The electoral mechanism works.

More precisely, it works if citizens learn to vote correctly in the above sense. As several scholars—pointedly, Achen and Bartels (2004)—have warned, voting correctly is not a trivial task for at least some kinds of adaptive retrospective voting. This is certainly the case for the rather stark class of rules considered in this book: citizens guided by these rules do not directly compare incumbents to challengers, relying instead on assessments of the performance of incumbents. Hence, for example, if a majority of voters have established a habit of supporting the incumbent,[13] then they might continue doing so for several elections even though the challenger is espousing a new policy that would make most of them better off.

[12] Indeed, given that the parties are completely opportunistic, it would be odd if voters developed completely stable partisan identification. Such predispositions would reflect mistaken beliefs.

[13] A habit might loosely be defined as a high propensity to vote one way.

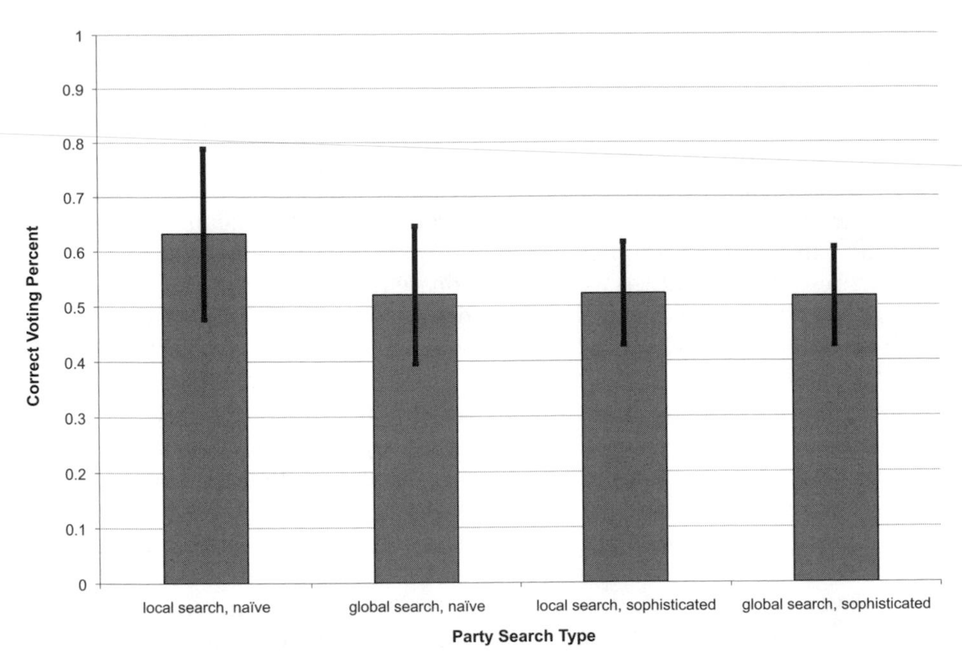

Figure 6.2. Correct voting percent, basic integrated model.

It may take awhile for dissatisfaction toward the incumbent to set in among such voters. Meanwhile, of course, the challenger, who is continuing to lose, might impatiently discard the superior policy; hence, by the time a majority of voters are dissatisfied enough to vote against the incumbent, they may unwittingly embrace an inferior new policy—a kind of coordination failure. In short, both type 1 and type 2 errors abound in feedback-driven processes with multiple agents who can get out of synch with each other.

Given these difficulties, figure 6.2, which reports voters' average accuracy for four different party search rules, may not be shocking. The bars correspond to the mean correct voting percent; the error bars bound a change of one standard deviation in either direction. This figure reveals that accuracy under global-naïve search and two kinds of sophisticated search is only a tad above the baseline of a fair coin; it is highest for local-naïve search. Let us first try to explain why all the rates are low and then why the local-naïve rate exceeds the others.

We have suggested that the task facing adaptive voters in the integrated model is more difficult than the one confronting adaptive voters in chapter 5's model because here the parties are themselves adaptive and so their platforms are moving targets. Intuitively, orienting to dynamic platforms is harder than orienting toward fixed ones. We check this intuition by running a two-component model with fixed platforms. Turnout and vote choice stay activated. Figure 6.3 shows that the intuitive guess is on target: correct voting is much more common when platforms are fixed. Further, the more they differ from each other—here, the further they (symmetrically) are from the median voter—the more accurate is voting. (The horizontal axis gives a measure, x_α, of the distance of each (symmetric) party from the mean of the voter distribution, or equivalently the platform extremity. The higher x_α, the further the parties are from the center and the more in line with extremist voters' preferences on each side.) This makes sense: bigger spatial differences make it easier for our adaptive voters to extract the deterministic signal (the incumbent's policy) from the payoff lottery generated by that policy.[14] (And, of course, in this two-component model, correct voting is equivalent to the endogenous emergence of party identification: since the parties are fixed, the criterion of "correct voting" is constant over time.)

Now consider the second question: why does local-naïve search produce more accurate voting than the other three rules? The explanation has two parts. First, since the parties are initially quite different—they begin at -1 and 1—the sluggish nature of local-naïve search means that they will remain different for quite a long time. And we know from figure 6.3 that the more distinct party platforms are, the easier it is for adaptive voters to figure out which side to support. So the sluggish local-naïve rule is a dynamic, though ultimately transient, analogue to the simple case of fixed platforms. At the opposite extreme, the two sophisticated rules generate platforms that resemble each other relatively quickly.

The second part concerns parties that flip-flop. This behavior increases voter error. Consider, for example, voter j, who has a liberal ideal point and who has learned to vote D after a history of that party's implementing platforms to the left of those implemented by R. Abruptly, however, a D-challenger searches globally, winds up to the right of R, and wins. This new right-leaning D-incumbent then gives a bad payoff to j, but because this voter has built up a high propensity to vote D, his chance of voting for R doesn't rise

[14]It is easy to jump to the following incorrect explanation of the effect: If $\tilde{x} = x + \epsilon$ and $\tilde{y} = y + \epsilon$, then obviously the closer x and y are, the easier it is to rank-order the estimated values incorrectly. But our adaptively retrospective voters don't directly compare the two parties' platforms; this straightforward model of perception with additive error is not what is going on here. Instead, voters are reacting sequentially to different streams of payoffs.

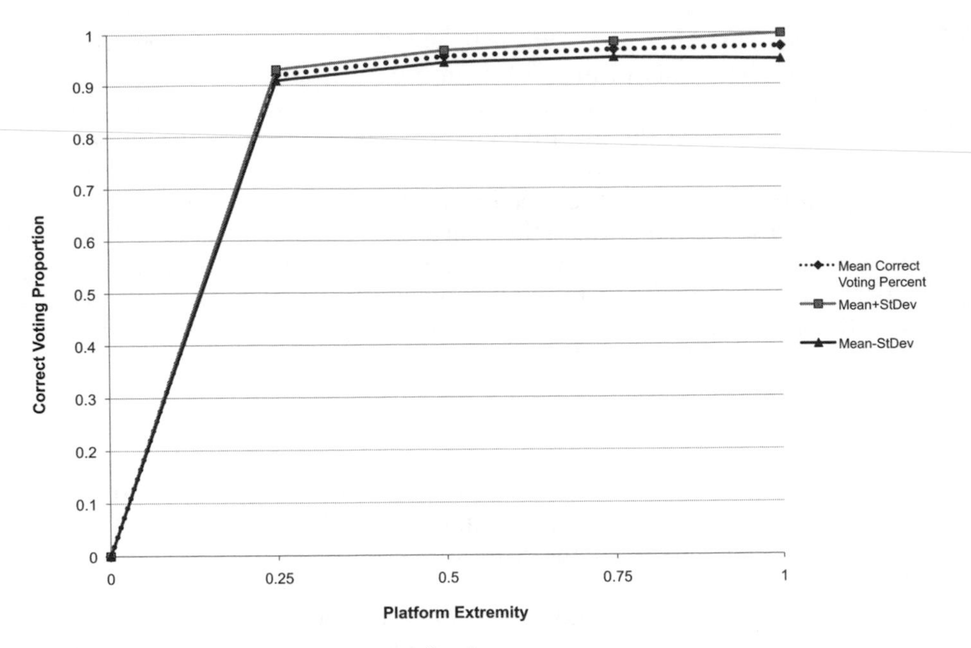

Figure 6.3. Correct voting, parties fixed.

much, and in fact *j* supports D in the current election. Given D's new position, *j*'s choice is a mistake. Parties that often flip-flop confuse habit-driven voters, and we suspect that the global-naïve search rule generates quite a bit of flip-flopping.[15]

It follows that anything that reduces flip-flopping increases the accuracy of voters. Hence, factors that induce parties to search in a specific part of the policy space—a strategic concern for consistency, the influence of ideologically inclined activists, policy preferences of candidates, and the like—will probably make voters look more competent. Their increased accuracy would, however, result not from increased sophistication but from *their choice problem becoming easier.*[16]

[15] Flip-flopping is an inherently dynamic property. Hence, the output reported in figure 6.3 is not relevant here; the underlying model presumes static platforms, so flip-flopping cannot occur.

[16] Several scholars (Pomper 1972; Abramowitz and Saunders 1998; Levendusky 2009) have argued that the apparent increase in ideological coherence among American voters in the 1960s, above the levels of the 1950s, was mainly due to the parties being further apart in the 1960s. Hence discriminating between them got easier. We believe this holds whether people vote prospectively (e.g., as in the perception-with-error model in footnote 14), retrospectively, or by a combination of the two.

6.4 Party Location

As figure 6.1 revealed, the distribution of winning policies is almost single-peaked. Thus, the closer a platform is to the median voter's ideal point, the more likely it is that it will win. Further, one can see that the distribution is packed rather tightly around that centrist voter: the average distance is 0.57; the parties started at a distance of 1.0. (The challenger, of course, moves around indefinitely, looking for something that will beat the incumbent. This echoes proposition 3.4.) Clearly, however, the winning policy does not lock onto this central location, whereas this would occur in chapter 3's simple model of party competition. Indeed, a few of the winning policies are considerably further from the median voter than are the parties' initial platforms, even though the policy space is unidimensional and the electoral process has a true center of gravity—the median voter. In electoral environments such as this, the trajectory of winning policies cannot move away from the median voter in the simple model of party competition (proposition 3.1).

There are two reasons for these differences between this chapter's model and its stripped-down predecessor. Naturally, these involve the features—active vote choice and turnout—that distinguish the full model from chapter 3's one-element model. We first consider voters' choices.

In the party competition model, citizens are Downsian: they vote for the candidate whose platform is closer to their bliss points. And for the main results in chapter 3, they do so with complete fidelity. Thus, because the voters are myopically infallible (and because turnout is always 100 percent), the median voter is always decisive, whence the trajectory of winning platforms can never move away from that voter's ideal point. In the integrated model, however, voters can err: they only have propensities to support one or the other candidate, and as remarks 5.2 and 5.3 showed, adaptive retrospective rules can lead voters astray. They can even mistakenly throw out of office an incumbent who has implemented the median voter's bliss point. And although these errors and the ensuing dispersion of winning platforms are dampened in large electorates, as illustrated in table 6.4, they are not eliminated by sheer size.

One might think that unrealistically high aspirations are the culprit, and indeed they can intensify this problem. As we warned earlier, however, realistic aspirations do not eliminate it. To see why, consider the median voter's situation. Suppose, counterfactually, that the winning platform settles down at her ideal point, z_{MV}. Under

TABLE 6.4
Centrality of winning platforms.

Population	Average distance from median voter
10	0.989
100	0.740
1,000	0.568
10,000	0.508

many adjustment rules, this voter's aspiration level will eventually be in a neighborhood of her maximal deterministic payoff. But given the random payoff shocks, the outcome will disappoint the median voter with a probability of roughly $\frac{1}{2}$. Hence, her propensity to vote for the incumbent will fall. The same logic affects the other voters. Consequently, even an incumbent who implements the most centrist policy will lose eventually.[17]

One might also believe that the benchmark of Downsian voters would be irrelevant as a guide to the integrated model: whereas such voters never make mistakes, our adaptively retrospective citizens are little better than fair coins, given several party search rules. But here the model's endogenous logic assets itself. As long as the parties are far apart, the choice problem is easy, so citizens often vote correctly. When they do, the movement of winning policies toward the median voter is strong. But this movement toward the center is self-limiting: the closer the platforms, the more the voters err, which inhibits and sometimes reverses the policy trajectory.

Now let us turn to the second key difference between chapter 3's model and this chapter's: turnout. In the former, nobody shirks: all citizens vote in every election. Here, they can choose to stay home. The forces producing centrist outcomes are clearly stronger under universal participation by a law of large numbers. To see this concretely, consider the following example. Suppose voters' bliss points are uniformly distributed on $[-1, 1]$. Assume that the incumbent in a given period is D. She is camped at 0.5 and has won several elections in a row, allowing aspirations to adjust. Then, in a future period the voters throw out D; the new incumbent, R, implements -0.3. Since aspirations had adjusted to payoffs generated by a status quo policy of 0.5, those produced by a policy of -0.3, which is closer to the median voter, are often better than many citizens' aspiration levels,

[17] In this benchmark setting the median voter is also the mean voter. So there is no ambiguity here: this is the central value of the voter distribution.

which is promising news for R. However, an increase in citizen satisfaction is more likely to matter if many people turn out. If many stay home, then just by chance—unlucky realizations of underlying vote propensities, for example—R could be defeated. Put simply, the process is noisier when fewer people vote. Hence, the universal turnout of chapter 3's party competition model should ensure that centrist outcomes happen more reliably.

And so they do. We check this in two ways. First, while maintaining adaptive parties and vote choice, we fix turnout so that all individuals vote. Reducing the electorate's size in this two-component model allows us to explore one aspect of reduced turnout—increased noise in the process, because fewer people vote—while keeping the distribution of voters symmetric. These results were reported in table 6.4, and strongly suggest that turnout affects party location via a sample-size effect. The smaller the electorate, the more spread out incumbents' platforms.

Second, we examine a one-element model with adaptive party competition. Adaptive turnout is replaced by two simple kinds of participation: (1) full turnout and (2) stochastic turnout in which everyone votes half the time. Adaptive vote choice is replaced by the flawless Downsian rule. The results are reported in figure 6.4, which plots the mean incumbent location. Error bars on each mean display the range of positions within one standard deviation of the mean in the simulation output. As one can plainly see, just making turnout uncertain is sufficient to substantially increase the spread of winning policies. This is true for all search rules, even the more sophisticated ones that yield tighter distributions of platforms under both turnout regimes. Note that, with Downsian voters, it is not the case that decreasing the number of voters leads to unlucky realizations of underlying vote propensities. Rather, with stochastic turnout it is possible that the effective median voter shifts with each election, altering the set of winning platforms. This leads to greater divergence from the true median than under full turnout.[18]

[18] Because adaptive turnout produces sampling effects, proposition 3.1 does not hold: the trajectory of winning policies can move away from the median voter. However, sampling theory suggests that if those who do turn out vote accurately, then adaptive turnout will not influence the winner's location very much in good-sized electorates. We see this in figure 6.4; the increased variance in incumbent platform induced by stochastic turnout is comparatively small. As a further check, we did runs (unreported here) of two-element models with adaptive turnout but Downsian voters. Here too the distribution of winning policies is packed quite tightly around the median voter. (Results available upon request.)

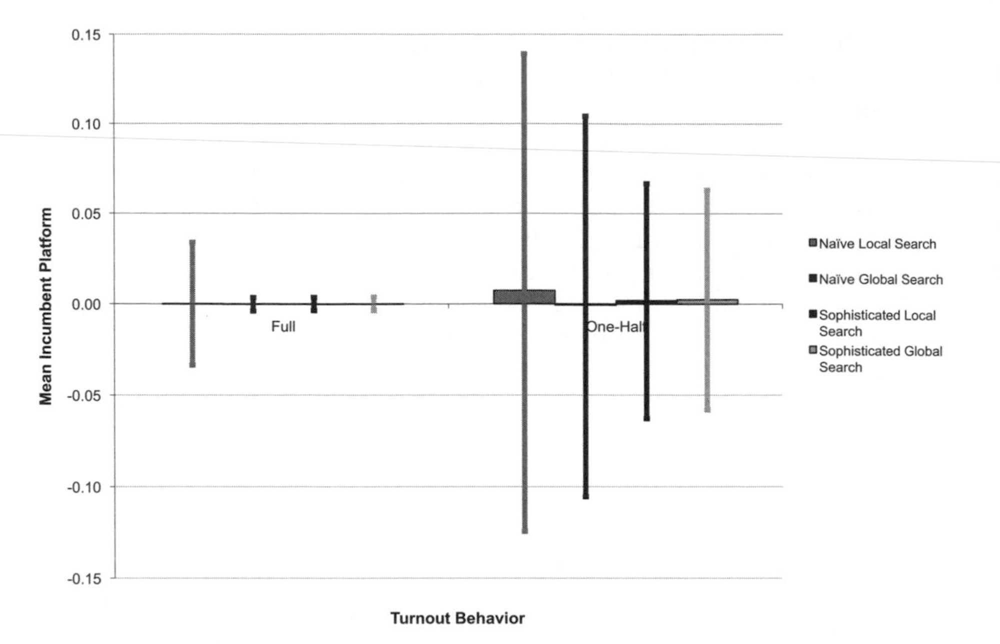

Figure 6.4. Winning platforms by fixed turnout behavior, vote choice fixed.

6.5 Turnout

The third and final endogenous component is participation. Average turnout settles down around the neighborhood of 30 percent in the integrated model with default parameter settings: somewhat lower than in chapter 4's one-element turnout model but still substantial. Turnout is not destroyed by parties' changing their platforms, though it is reduced somewhat. If we start the model at a state of near-universal apathy, figure 6.5 reveals the same dynamics—the "breakout of participation"—described in chapter 4. Further, key comparative statics are similar in the two models: as shown in table 6.5, turnout in the integrated model is smaller the larger the electorate and the higher the costs of voting, just as it was in the model in chapter 4. Qualitatively, then, the integrated model produces the same turnout picture as did its simpler component.

Why is this so? After all, the integrated model differs in two key ways from the turnout model—there are no fixed factions (every voter can support either party) and parties' positions are dynamic rather than fixed—and a priori one might be concerned that either difference could destabilize robust turnout. But this does not happen.

TABLE 6.5
Effects of population and voting cost on turnout.

Population	Average turnout
10	0.471
50	0.378
100	0.356
1,000	0.301
Cost	**Average turnout**
0.1	0.373
0.2	0.301
0.3	0.251

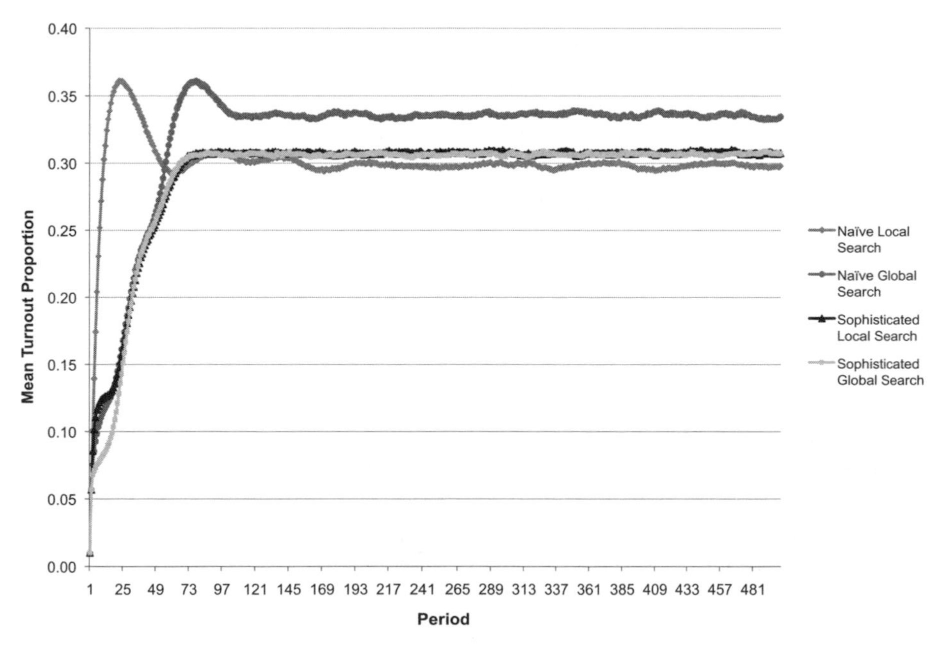

Figure 6.5. Breakout of participation, basic integrated model.

We can quickly address the possibility that dynamic voting blocs depress turnout. This occurs when citizens have three options—vote for D, vote for R, stay home—instead of the binary choice in chapter 4. Consider voter i. Suppose she votes for D in t and is dissatisfied with her payoff. In the simple turnout model she

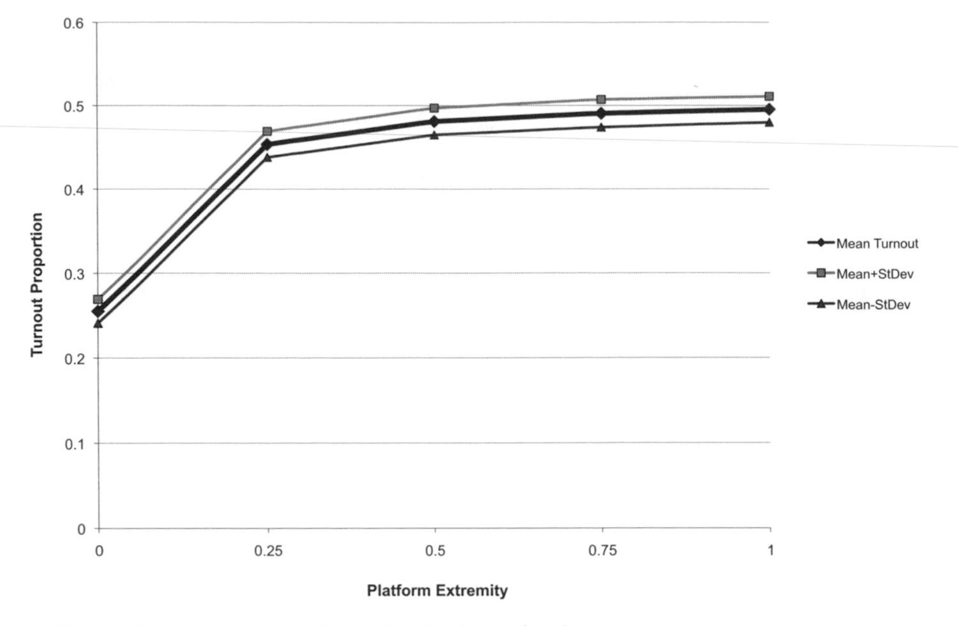

Figure 6.6. Turnout, parties and vote choice fixed.

has only one recourse: don't vote.[19] In contrast, in the integrated model she has two options: stay home or vote for R. Switching parties involves remaining politically active. Intuitively, then, allowing a choice between parties will not reduce average turnout.

We can check this guess by comparing average turnout in two variants of the basic integrated model. In the first, platforms are fixed and voters are Downsian; only participation adapts dynamically. The second model also has fixed platforms, but it allows voters a genuine choice between parties: they adjust their propensities to support either side, as well as their propensity to turn out. The results are reported in figures 6.6 and 6.7, respectively: average turnout is very similar. Our guess is confirmed: allowing voters to switch parties does not by itself suppress turnout.

Hence, the quantitative change in participation, as we go from chapter 4's one-element model to the integrated one, is probably driven by the difference between fixed versus adaptively adjusting platforms. We already know that the selection environment of two-party races drives adaptive parties closer together when the policy space is unidimensional. Perhaps when the parties' policies are

[19] We state this crudely for expositional reasons. More precisely, her propensity to vote D would fall and her propensity to shirk would rise.

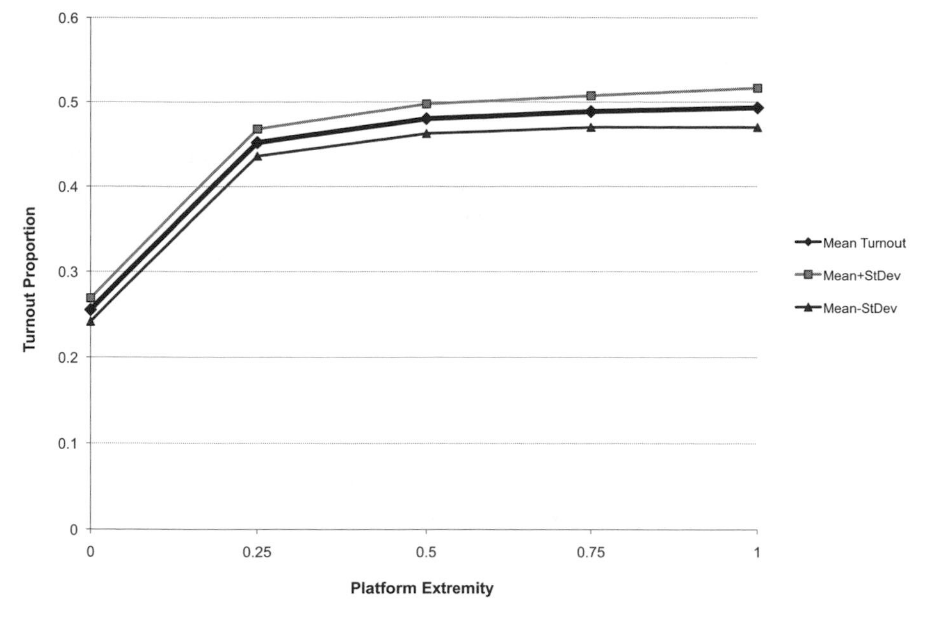

Figure 6.7. Turnout, parties fixed.

similar, turnout falls: elections don't matter much when candidates are Tweedledum and Tweedledee. Proposition 4.2 did give some analytical assurance that if the costs of voting were small, then participation would not collapse even when parties offered identical platforms. But this result presumed fixed aspirations and flawless vote choice, which are unrealistic assumptions. Hence, we reexamine this question via the computational model, which allows aspirations to adjust and voters to err. We first examine the effect of policy similarity on turnout via a two-component model with fixed platforms; varying the parties' positions allows us to assess the validity of the intuitive conjecture that apathy results from parties being similar. Figure 6.7 shows that the conjecture holds: average participation is monotonically increasing in the difference between the parties. Most of the damage to participation occurs at very high degrees of similarity: when parties are identical, turnout is under 30 percent; it rises to more than 45 percent at the relatively modest x_α of 0.25, rising gradually thereafter. Thus, some of the turnout difference between chapter 4's fixed-platform model and this chapter's formulation of endogenous platforms is indeed the result of parties converging in the full computational model.

This is not the whole story, however. Convergence of platforms to the mean is aided in decreasing turnout by the combination of stochastic behavior and the nonlinearity of decreasing turnout as parties converge. To see how this works, consider two examples. In the first, the parties adopt fixed platforms, $\pm x_\alpha$, which are near the middle of the voter distribution. In the second, each moves in an unbiased, random fashion around the same $\pm x_\alpha$. Because turnout decreases nonlinearly as the parties get closer to each other, each convergent move decreases turnout more than each divergent move increases it. As these moves happen randomly in an unbiased fashion, over time turnout will be lower when parties move than when they do not, even when the parties' platforms have the same mean over time.

The above pieces form a consistent picture. Once again, overwhelming apathy is unstable: some losing shirkers are disappointed with their payoffs and start turning out. When they do, they learn to vote more often for the party that has better served their interests. This implies that the electoral mechanism works (albeit crudely and stochastically): it tends to select parties that better serve majoritarian interests, giving a centrist thrust to the trajectory of winning platforms. This thrust is stronger the higher the level of turnout.

This process never ends because citizens can always be disappointed, but because the underlying adaptive mechanisms are always present for both citizens and parties, the resulting outcomes exhibit clear stochastic patterns.

So much for the relations among the endogenous variables. Our basic computational model can also address several new questions that the previous chapters did not investigate at all.

6.6 New Questions

6.6.1 Who Votes?

The first new question is, Who votes? Do extremists participate more, or do more moderate citizens shoulder the burden of democracy? Because there are data on this matter—they tend to support the former conclusion (e.g., Converse 1965, p. 323)—the answer to this question affects our model's evidential standing. Hence, if our rather simple model of behavior yields this empirical regularity as an implication—which it was not designed to do—we will gain additional confidence in our model's plausibility and problem-solving power (Laudan 1977).

To address the question Who votes? we need a measure of the correlation between realized turnout and voters' degree of extremism.

The former is an output variable of the model. The latter must be constructed, however. If the mean of the voter distribution is taken as the definition of "moderate," then the farther away a voter is from this statistic the more extreme she is. The most extreme citizen is the one at the edge of the distribution of voters; we set the extremism measures of such voters to 1.[20] Voters between the mean and the most extreme position have values of extremism equal to the distance from their bliss points to the mean divided by the distance from the most extreme position to the mean. We then calculate the correlation coefficient between these two series. A positive coefficient would imply that voters far from the mean vote more often than moderates, while a negative value would imply that they vote less often.

Figure 6.8 displays results for a two-component model with fixed parties, given initial turnout propensities of 0.5 for all citizens. As in previous figures, the center line corresponds to the mean correlation of turnout with voter interests (i.e., extremism); the outer two bound a change of one standard deviation in either direction. We choose to fix parties to make the analysis as transparent as possible. As we will see, the logic underlying the results depends on the parties' positions, and freezing the platforms clarifies this logic.

As figure 6.8 shows, the correlation of turnout with interests is almost always positive: extremists vote more often than moderates. This happens because extremists have a bigger stake in elections than do moderates. There are, in turn, two reasons why they do. Naturally, both are related to properties of voters' utility functions. First, consider an election in which the parties' platforms, x_D and x_R, differ significantly from the median voter's bliss point; for simplicity, assume that they bracket this centrist point symmetrically, say at $(-1, 1)$. Now compare the perspectives of a voter who is on the wing, say -2, and of a centrist, at -0.5. For the liberal voter, the difference between how far x_D versus x_R are from her ideal point is the full distance of the platforms from each other: 2. For the moderate, however, some of this distance is eliminated because her ideal point is between the platforms: the distances are 0.5 and 1.5, so the difference is only 1.0—just a half of the liberal's stake.[21] Hence, because

[20] For a bounded distribution, such as the uniform, the most extreme citizens are those on the boundaries. For an unbounded distribution, we define the most extreme citizens as those located at least three standard deviations from the mean: all such voters have an extremism measure of 1.

[21] This is roughly equivalent to a low b in the turnout model in chapter 4. (Recall that that model has homogeneous factions, so it does not examine turnout differences among people in the same faction.)

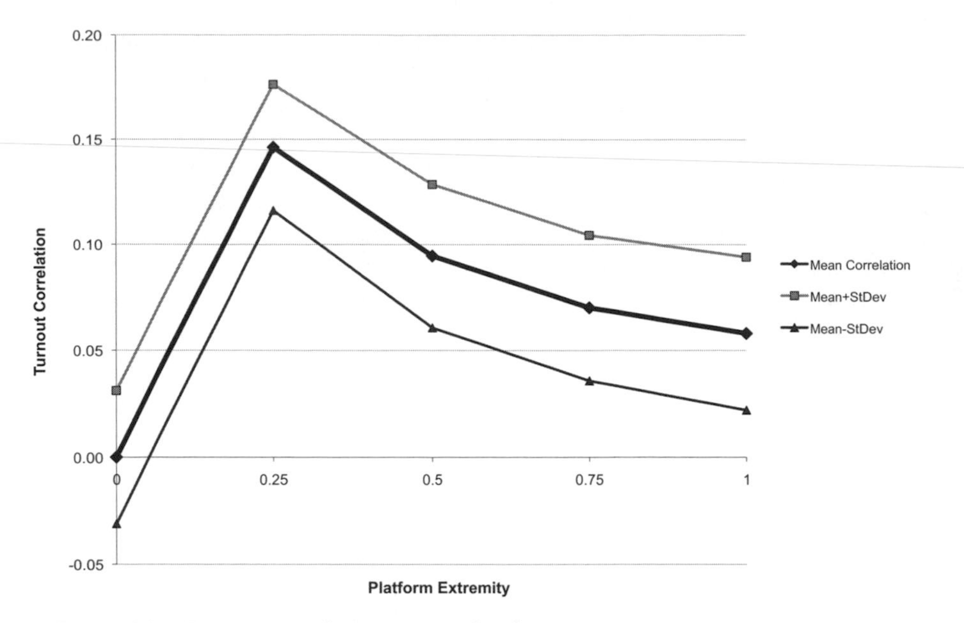

Figure 6.8. Turnout correlation, parties fixed.

the ideal points of most moderates are between the platforms of significantly divergent parties whereas those of extremists are outside $[x_D, x_R]$, extremists have a bigger stake in such elections.[22]

Second, consider an election in which the parties are (symmetrically) close to the median voter, say at -0.25 and 0.25. Now the ideal points of most citizens are outside $[x_D, x_R]$; nonetheless, extremists still participate more. (Indeed, the correlation between extremism and turnout is stronger here than it is when the parties are farther apart.) The reason is that extremists still have a bigger stake in the election than moderates because of the concavity of the (common) utility function. Compare the same two voters: the liberal of -2 and the moderate of -0.5. True, x_D is closer than x_R to both voters' ideal points and by exactly the same amount: 0.5. But the concavity of the quadratic loss function ensures that small differences in platforms have big payoff implications for voters who are far away from both

[22] One should keep in mind that citizens in our model vote retrospectively. They do not directly compare the parties' platforms, as the text's terse explanation might seem to suggest. But having bliss points inside or outside the $[x_D, x_R]$ interval affects the turnout of prospective and retrospective voters similarly: in both cases the key is how much the election matters to different citizens.

parties: that same policy difference of 0.5 hurts the liberal more than it hurts the moderate.[23]

6.6.2 *Who Votes Correctly?*

We already know that in the aggregate, people more often vote correctly the more the parties' platforms differ: recall figure 6.3, which reported this effect for a two-element model with parties exogenously fixed at different distances from the median voter. But because the computational model allows voters on the same side to be heterogeneous, we can also investigate whether extremists or moderates are more likely to vote correctly, holding party heterogeneity constant.

The analysis here mirrors that for the question Who votes? and we can see the same pattern in figure 6.9. The logic that explains turnout variation—how much the election matters for different people—holds for differences in voting accuracy, so we should expect the same patterns. This expectation is borne out. In all cases, extremists vote correctly more often than do moderates, with the most gain observed when the parties are the closest together and so the least differentiated.[24]

6.6.3 *Dynamics*

Thus far we have focused mostly on static, mean behavior. We have done so in order to compare our models to game-theoretic models, which concentrate on equilibrium behavior—hence, statics. Yet this focus obscures a strength of adaptive modeling: it can describe not only behavior in (probabilistic) equilibrium but also the dynamics that lead to that equilibrium. We have seen this throughout this book, in how parties climb up the chain of policies, in how turnout spirals up or collapses, and in how an electorate polarizes. Given that our computational modeling tool is well suited for analyzing dynamics, we would be remiss if we did not address this aspect of our full model at least briefly here. Figure 6.5 gave a taste of this by showing the full model's breakout of participation; much more can be done.

[23] We can test this intuition by explicitly varying voters' payoff functions. A linear loss term neither reduces small differences nor magnifies big ones; thus, if this were the utility function, then we would expect the correlation between interests and turnout to decrease. This is indeed the case, with correlation dropping by a factor of 10, from 0.14 to 0.014, upon switching to linear loss with parties closely spaced.

[24] As with turnout, this result is in part dependent on the shape of the utility function. When voters instead posses piecewise-linear utility loss functions, extremists vote appreciably more accurately only when parties are far apart.

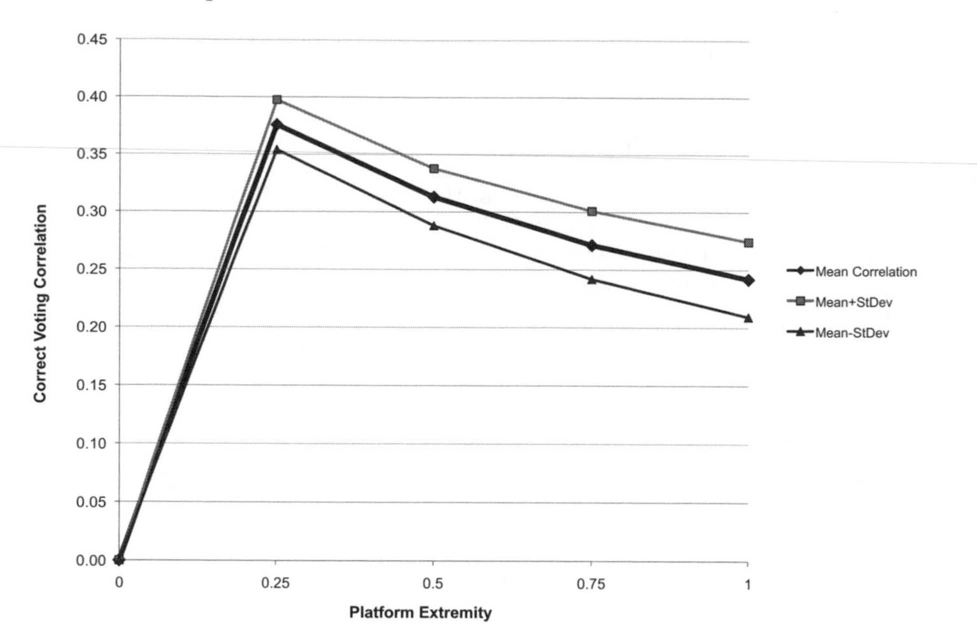

Figure 6.9. Correct voting correlation, parties fixed.

The graphical model is an especially good tool for such analyses because it provides multiple visual displays of electoral dynamics.[25] Figures 6.10–6.12 give a taste of this. Each presents multiple snapshots, taken after different elections, of both parties and voters. The horizontal line represents the ideal points of citizens. Those on the left have bliss points in the liberal part of the political spectrum; those on the right, conservative. Each rectangle contains one or more citizens, with those of similar interests grouped together.[26] The color of each rectangle indicates vote choice: the darker color (blue) represents votes for D; the lighter color (red), votes for R. Shades between the two (purple) represent rectangles where citizens voted for both parties in various proportions. A rectangle's degree of faintness symbolizes turnout: in transparent rectangles voters stay home; in opaque ones they turn out. Different degrees of opacity represent mixed turnout behavior.

[25] Readers have an extra incentive to replicate results via the provided executable computer model here—it produces color figures. For convenience, we have placed color versions of the book's figures on the book's website. (See http://press.princeton.edu/titles/9352.html for links to this site.)

[26] The grouping is solely for display purposes; it has no substantive import. "World Size" parameters allow users to change the coarseness of the grouping to preference.

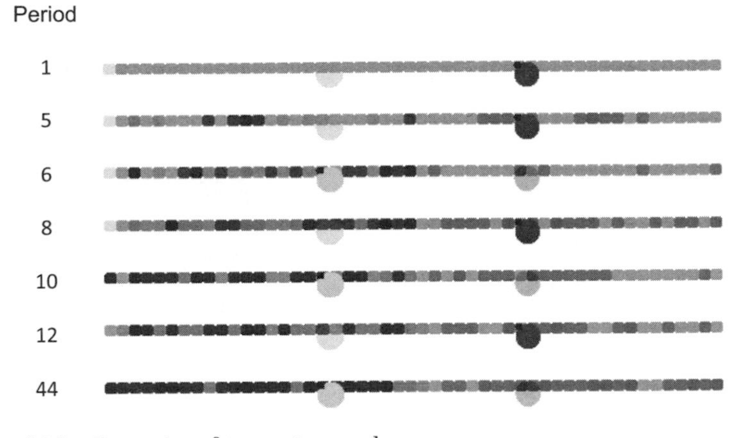

Figure 6.10. Dynamics of turnout spread.

Parties are the big (green) circles; the lighter-colored one represents party D. Each circle is located at the corresponding party's position, i.e., x_R and x_D. Transparent parties are challengers, opaque ones are incumbents. (The model produces graphs and histograms representing other variables of interest regarding the electorate; for reasons of space we do not show them here.)

Figure 6.10 displays how turnout changes in a system with 100 Downsian voters and static parties.[27] The transparent electorate symbol in period 1 indicates that initially everyone stays home. By period 5, however, turnout begins to grow, reaching nearly 20 percent. Because the distribution of turnout in this sample path happens to favor R, R wins the election. This yields poor payoffs to liberal citizens, who begin to think that staying home might be undesirable if it results in such a poor incumbent. This makes liberal turnout increase in period 6. At the same time, those closer to the incumbent are generally satisfied with their payoffs. Since turnout propensities are still low in general, fewer conservatives wind up voting in period 6. Together, these processes flip the election to D.

By period 8, this dynamic of loser-driven mobilization hands the election back to R. By period 10 it has helped turnout to reach 32 percent. Because the process is stochastic, however, turnout does not always increase in every history, and in this particular one it drops from 36 percent in period 11 to 29 percent in period 12. This too is temporary, though, and well before the period 44 electorate

[27] This drop in the number of voters is to make transparency clearer on the page, not for any substantive reason.

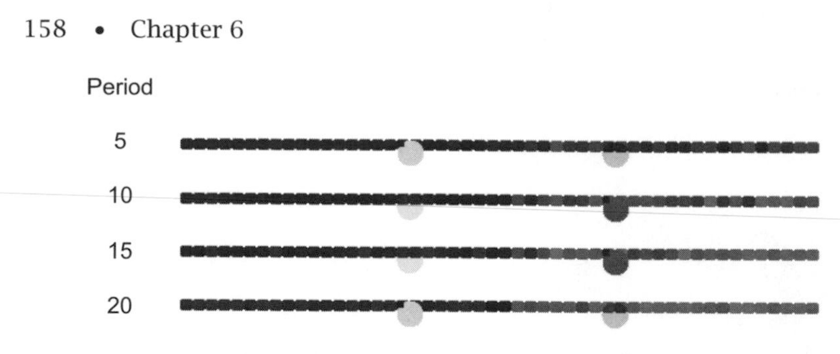

Figure 6.11. Dynamics of polarization.

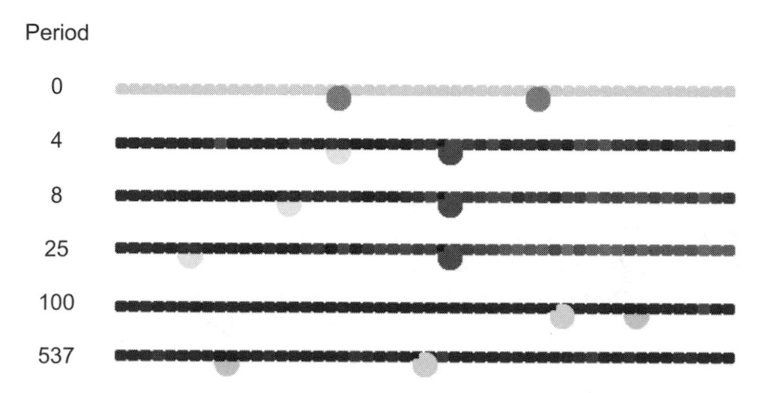

Figure 6.12. Dynamics of party movement.

shown, participation has begun to hover around its steady state of 50 percent.

Next turn to figure 6.11. Here we keep adaptive turnout but focus on how adaptive voting creates electoral sorting. We return to 1,000 voters. The picture tells the story clearly. Early on, the electorate is largely an in-between shade (purple), indicating that voters with varied interests are similarly likely to vote for both D and R. In only a few periods, however, the citizens begin to sort themselves out, and voting factions are fairly discernible by period 10. By period 15, it is pretty clear who tends to vote for whom. The distribution bears this out: 90 percent of the citizens vote for one party or the other at least 80 percent of the time. By period 20 polarization is nearly complete: 90 percent of the population votes for one party or the other more than 90 percent of the time. As expected, centrists are the last to sort correctly.

Finally, consider the dynamics of party movement with fully adaptive voters shown in figure 6.12. Parties use local naïve search. We can follow in detail how the combination of incrementalism and naïvety often produces nonmedian outcomes. Start at period 1, when the parties are located at their initial platforms. After only four periods, R manages to find a platform close to the mean (0.127). This has three effects. First, because aspirations adjust relatively slowly and because R is implementing a centrist policy, many citizens get satisfactory payoffs for a substantial period. Hence, the hapless D loses for a long, long time. Because winners satisfice, this means that the process of party competition is not putting any pressure on the incumbent to move closer to the mean. Further, by chance the challenger often ends up quite far away from the incumbent, as in period 25.

Second, long periods of one-party rule lead to more accurate sorting, which is easily seen in period 25. It also results in lower turnout, though this is harder to see with the larger population of 1,000 citizens. Aggregate numbers corroborate this visual impression, with 85 percent correct voting and 35 percent turnout in period 25. This state of affairs does not last, however. Eventually the challenger gets lucky and wins. Turnout then spikes, while voting becomes error-ridden as people keep voting habitually for the party that had been good for them. For example, at period 537 the party platforms have flipped and the electorate is a confused in-between shade (purple).

Third, because both turnout and vote choice are stochastic, sometimes the party closer to the mean of the voter distribution loses (which never happens in chapter 3's simple model of party competition). A sequence of such events can produce outcomes like that of period 100, where both incumbent and challenger are far from the mean, and on its same side.

6.7 Conclusion

A key task of this chapter has been to examine the robustness of the basic models in chapters 3–5. They have fared quite well: most of their core results have stood up even when the theory has grown substantially more complex. The few that have not—polarization and, to a lesser extent, 50 percent turnout, both in the context of party search—had to be adjusted for intuitive reasons.

Of course, we have not varied all possible parameters, so speculations about variations that might materially alter our results are in order. In many cases we have not explicitly varied parameters because the effects are apparent from the analyses of this chapter and previous ones. For example, making vote propensities adjust more quickly (λ) is likely to speed up polarization when parties are static. This is indeed what happens; raising λ to 0.5 makes the electorate almost completely polarized in a handful of periods.[28]

Much remains to be explored. We offer the computational model to readers who want to go further along with us, hoping it proves fruitful. Avenues beyond those the model is designed to address beckon as well; we plan to add a demographic component that will allow us to explore generational change in party affiliation and turnout.

There is one road, however, that we cannot pass up taking right now. In the next chapter we turn our attention to multiparty competition and explore how adding a third party affects electoral dynamics.

---

[28] It also increases the average percentage of correct voting under local naïve search, as citizens more quickly figure out the parties' relative benefit to them before the parties switch places and ruin what voters have learned.

CHAPTER SEVEN

Elections with Multiple Parties

THUS FAR WE HAVE studied two-party elections. That is a natural place to start, but there is no need to restrict attention to two-party systems. Indeed, previous work in formal theory (e.g., Cox 1997) suggests that multiparty elections are strategically far more complex than two-party ones. Hence, cognitive constraints are more likely to bind, especially on voters.[1] This makes multiparty competition a particularly promising area for behavioral models, not only for voters but also for candidates who must contend with multiple rivals.

Thus, in this chapter we study multiparty systems using tools provided in earlier chapters. First, we will examine the module models in chapters 3 and 4 to see what modifications are required in order to extend the framework to multiple candidates and to see what analytical results carry over to this context. (Because vote choice is a central focus of the present chapter, it is unnecessary to cover chapter 5 here.) Second, we will provide a computational model for one of the most well-known problems in the study of multiparty elections: voter coordination in plurality-rule elections and Duverger's Law.

7.1 Extending Our Results to Multiple Parties

7.1.1 Turnout

The turnout model in chapter 4 holds, as is, for $m > 2$ parties. To see why, consider the following sketch of a multiparty extension of the two-party model. As in the original context, we assume fixed factions. Hence, for any given citizen the choice is binary: either shirk or turn out and vote for one's exogenously determined faction. Therefore, we can use the Bush-Mosteller reinforcement rule exactly as it is specified in chapter 4. Regarding payoffs, we again divide them

[1] Sniderman and his coauthors have persuasively argued that it is the institution of two-party competition that does most of the "heavy lifting" (Sniderman and Bullock 2004, p. 346); i.e., it is this institution that enables voters to choose in relatively sensible, consistent ways.

into a deterministic and a random component. As before, the former is represented by a quadratic utility function defined over a unidimensional policy space. Party platforms are fixed at $x_1^*, \ldots, x_m^*$. One can recover the Palfrey-Rosenthal assumption that the (deterministic) benefits of winning exceed the private cost of voting (i.e., $b_i > c$ for all i) by assuming that the party platforms and clusters of voters' ideal points are sufficiently far apart so that for every voter the deterministic payoff from winning and voting exceeds that of shirking plus having one's second-best party elected.

Thus, neither the setting—a Palfrey-Rosenthal game of factions competing for a fixed indivisible prize, with the winner taking all—nor the individual-level decision rules are affected whatsoever by the number of groups competing for the prize. It follows immediately that the process is ergodic for $m > 2$: i.e., theorem 2.3 holds, so there is a unique limiting distribution of turnout. Of course, since we could not analytically characterize average turnout in this limiting distribution when there were only two parties, we cannot do so when there are many. But as figure 7.1 illustrates, the turnout results are qualitatively similar. This figure plots average turnout over 1,000 simulations and 1,000 periods, with starting turnout propensities set at the two-party steady state of 50 percent. Compared to the two-party case, the simulation settles at lower turnout (40 percent), but we otherwise see the same rapid adjustment to the average long-run turnout level.

Moreover, the explanation for this breakout of participation is the same as in the two-party context: the analysis provided by remarks 4.1–4.3 and proposition 4.1 holds almost without modification for $m > 2$. The only change that is required is in remark 4.3. The key change here is that we must add the assumption that less than half the electorate has voted in t. Substantively, this addition is innocuous because we are trying to explain why a level of low turnout is unstable; hence, assuming that more citizens stayed home than voted in the current election is unproblematic.

7.1.2 Party Competition

As in chapter 3, we assume that winners satisfice and losers search. Voters are sincere and error-free Downsians who always turn out. In the game-theoretic literature this case has been analyzed by Cox (1987a). The assumption of sincere voting, however, is not innocuous: voters may have incentives to vote strategically. For example, to avoid wasting their votes, citizens may not want to vote for trailing candidates (e.g., Cox 1997; Myerson 2000). We will return to this

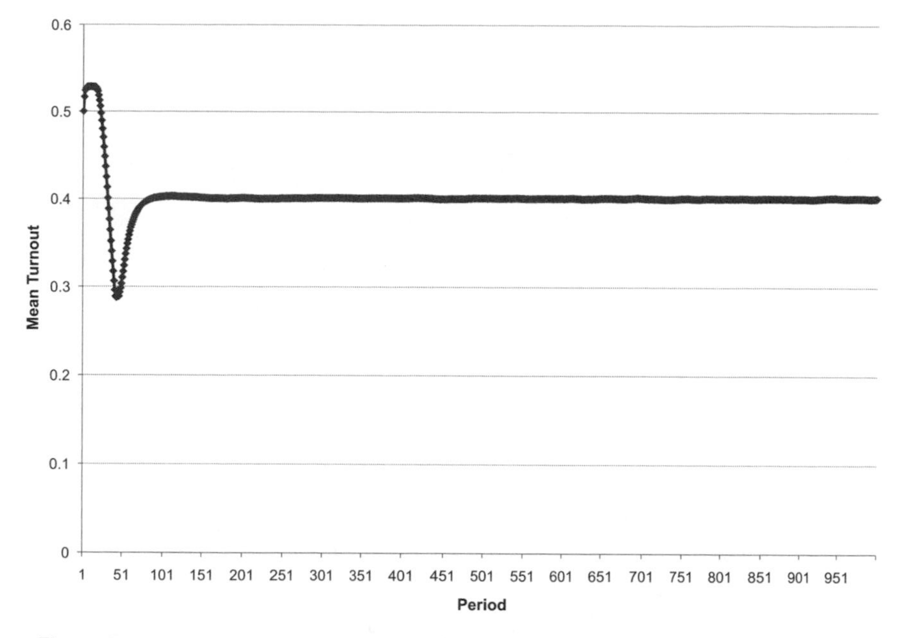

Figure 7.1. Average turnout over time for three parties.

case below. Here we first want to consider the case where voters vote sincerely and do not abstain. We consider two benchmark cases in which challengers search blindly (uniformly) over the policy space. In the first case, there are three parties. The results are provided by figure 7.2, which plots the kernel density of winning platforms at $t = 500$ over 1,000 simulations.

The distribution of winning platforms is packed rather tightly around the median voter's ideal point, with a mean distance of 0.1375. This does not hold for game-theoretically rational candidates (Cox 1987c). Indeed, for an odd number of candidates no pure strategy Nash equilibrium exists. Cox (1987a, theorem 1) shows that in equilibrium at least one candidate must be located on the border or outside the interquartile interval of the electorate's distribution of ideal points.

We can also compare the results of our simulation model directly to Cox's (1987a) predictions under an even number of parties. Here a unique pure strategy Nash equilibrium exists, but it is not centrist. With a uniform distribution of voters on $[0, 1]$ and four parties, the unique equilibrium has two parties each locating at $\frac{1}{4}$ and $\frac{3}{4}$, resulting in a tie. Analogously to figure 7.2, figure 7.3 plots the kernel density of winning platforms at $t = 500$ over 1,000 simulations.

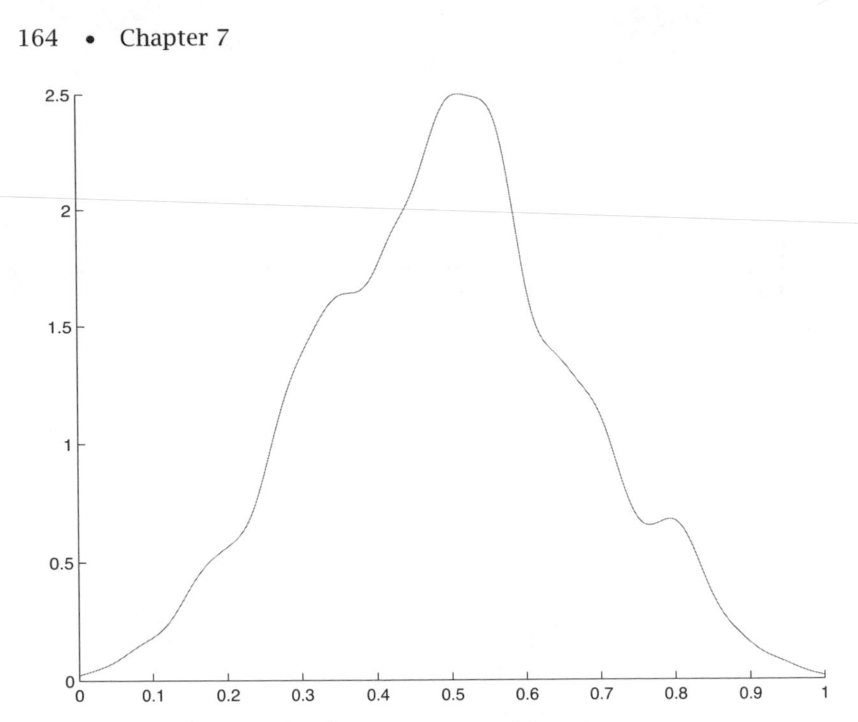

Figure 7.2. Platforms under three-party competition: sincere voters.

Here the parties are approximately bimodally and symmetrically distributed around the median. Platforms, however, are more centrist—somewhat contrary to the Cox prediction—with a mean distance from the median of 0.1760 rather than 0.25. While we do not plot the distribution of vote shares, each party does receive roughly 25 percent most of the time.

In our adaptive model, parties don't calculate mixed-strategy equilibria; they produce varying choice probabilities as a consequence of their responses to winning and losing. These probabilities typically differ: the naive parties of our benchmark model put more probability on centrist platforms than do game-theoretically rational parties—another testable prediction.

The models differ in a second, more subtle way. Although satisficing by winners and search by losers produce stochastic patterns, these are not equivalent to game-theoretic randomization: the former typically yields a trajectory of winning platforms that exhibit serial correlation; the latter do not. This matters substantively. Fully rational agents understand that rivals can exploit serial correlation in one's behavior; hence, although the same randomizing procedure is used consistently in the stylized repeated models, draws are

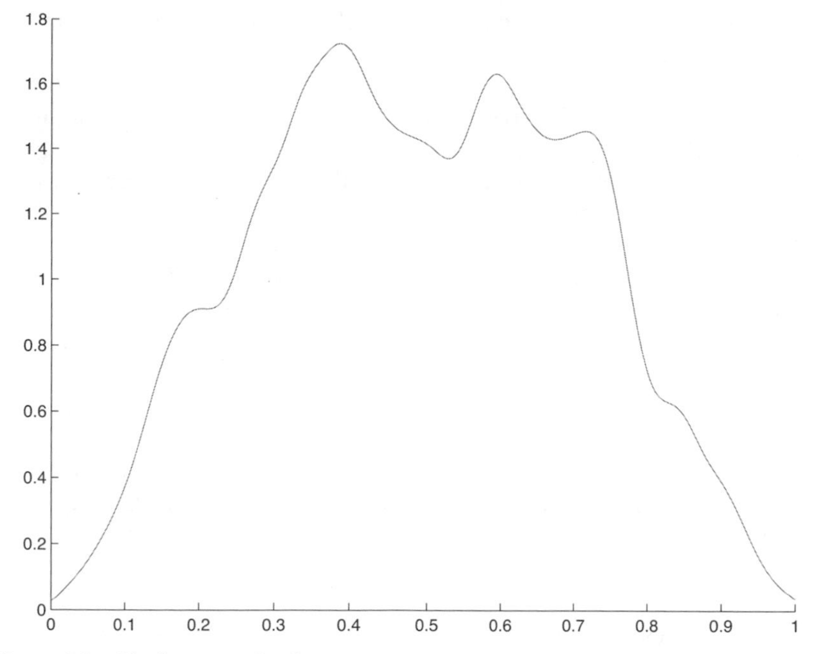

Figure 7.3. Platforms under four-party competition: sincere voters.

independent over time. Boundedly rational agents may not grasp this idea.[2] This difference can be tested empirically.[3]

Finally, the probabilistic behavior of our adaptive agents differs from true mixed strategies in a third way (Bendor, Diermeier, and Ting 2003b, pp. 240–241). The comparative statics of mixed-strategy equilibria have a notoriously counterintuitive property. For example, in a two-person game, the row player's mixing probability does not respond to changes in her payoffs; it responds instead to changes in her *partner's* payoffs. This seems counterintuitive, even to some game theorists. The actions of decision makers guided by ABARs are markedly different: as we have often seen in this book, they

[2] Since challengers in our benchmark model search blindly in every election, their behavior is statistically independent across elections. It is the satisficing of winners that generates serial correlation in the trajectory of winning platforms. In general, however, the behavior of boundedly rational challengers will also contribute to serial correlation in this state variable: e.g., if challenger's search is incremental—they usually try platforms that are close to their previous one—then this will intensify the serial correlation of the trajectory of winning policies.

[3] In their study of penalty kicks by elite soccer players, Chiappori, Levitt, and Groseclose (2002, p. 1147) found no evidence of serial correlation. However, Rosenthal, Shachat and Walker found evidence of (puzzlingly) strong positive serial correlation (2003, p. 274).

respond to changes in their own payoffs (mediated, of course, by their aspiration levels).

Thus, for all three reasons one should not mistake the probabilistic tendencies of these adaptive agents for the mixed strategies of game-theoretically rational players.

Of course, the above simulation results come from a benchmark model with completely naive challengers who search blindly. More sophisticated, though still boundedly rational, challengers might learn to squeeze centrist incumbents by moving toward the middle of the distribution of voters' ideal points. (This could be implemented by assuming that parties adjust their propensities to try different platforms in accord with the fundamental axioms of positive and negative feedback specified in chapter 2. Thus, platforms associated with winning office in the past would be more likely to be tried again; those associated with losing would be less likely.) The long-run implications of such behavior are an open question and await research.

7.2 Multicandidate Competition and Duverger's Law

As we pointed out above, multiparty competition introduces new strategic complexities in the study of elections. Perhaps the best known of these puzzles is called *Duverger's Law* (Duverger 1954). William Riker, in an influential article (Riker 1982), argued that it constitutes one of the few true laws in political science. Duverger's Law pertains to plurality-rule elections.[4] In a plurality-rule election, sometimes called the "first-past-the-post" rule, the electorate is assigned to regional districts equal to the number of seats in the legislature. Each voter casts a single vote for one candidate. The candidate with the most votes is elected. If a tie occurs, a tie-breaking rule is invoked. (In the United Kingdom, for example, ties are resolved by a coin flip by an election office.) Simply put, Duverger's Law says that plurality-rule electoral systems favor two-party competition. Duverger proposed two arguments for this prediction: a "mechanical effect" and a "psychological effect." The mechanical effect concerns the translation of votes into seats. In plurality-rule elections the party

[4] Duverger's hypothesis, which states that other voting systems (e.g., proportional representation) promote multiparty competition, will not concern us here. A generalization of Duverger's Law to the single nontransferable vote (used, e.g., in Japan until recently) is known as *Reed's Law*. It states that in an electoral rule where the M top vote getters are elected, only $M + 1$ candidates will be competitive (Reed 1991; Cox 1994).

that wins the most votes often gets disproportionately many seats. In the extreme case a party that wins a bare majority in all districts could thus capture all the seats in the legislature. The strength of the mechanical effect therefore depends on the alignment between geographic districts and voters' preferences for political parties. In the United States the mechanical effect has received much attention in the context of *gerrymandering*—the redesign of electoral districts by the governing party in order to maximize the expected number of seats (e.g., Cox and Katz 2002).

Our focus in this chapter will be on the second factor identified by Duverger, the psychological effect: voters' tendency to desert parties with a small chance of winning to avoid wasting their votes. Duverger explains this effect as follows:

> In cases where there are three parties operating under the simple-majority single ballot system, the electors soon realize that their votes are wasted if they continue to give them to the third party: whence their natural tendency to transfer their vote to the less evil of its two adversaries in order to prevent the success of the greater evil.
>
> (Duverger 1954, p. 226)

It is this tendency for voters to abandon parties with a small chance of winning that has been the research focus subsequently. Although Duverger was the first one to state this regularity as a law, the idea of simple-plurality elections leading to a two-party system goes back as far as 1869, when Droop, an English barrister and inventor of Droop's quota, wrote

> Each elector has practically only a choice between two candidates or sets of candidates. As success depends upon obtaining a majority of the aggregate votes of all the electors, an election is usually reduced to a contest between the two most popular candidates or sets of candidates. Even if other candidates go to the poll, the electors usually find out that their votes will be thrown away, unless given in favour of one or other of the parties between whom the election really lies.
>
> (Droop cited in Riker 1982)

Notice that Droop's analysis is about candidates, whereas Duverger's is about parties. This has led to some confusion in the literature. We need to distinguish district-level effects from national ones. For example, coordination of two parties at the district level does not imply coordination at the national level. That is, suppose there are districts 1, 2, and 3 with parties A, B, and C that field a candidate in each district. At the district level, Duverger's Law simply states that at most two parties will be competitive, with the third receiving only a very small share. But this could be parties A and B in district 1, B and C in district 2, and A and C in district 3. So, two-party dominance at the district level does not imply two-party dominance at the national level. Indeed, there are well-known counterexamples to national two-party dominance such as in Canada and India.[5]

Much of the empirical and theoretical work on Duverger's Law has concentrated exclusively on the district-level phenomenon, and this will be our focus in this chapter. Specifically, we will investigate the canonical model of this literature: a single district with three candidates who have fixed policy positions. Notice that this model considers only voting behavior; that is, parties maintain fixed platforms. The assumption of fixed parties is more reasonable in the non-U.S. context as party activists play a much bigger role in shaping party platforms. As in previous chapters, voters are policy-oriented; they care only about the outcome of an election. Despite its simplicity the model is rich in strategic complexity. The reason is that the wasted vote issue makes it rational to vote sophisticatedly (Riker 1982). Voters who prefer a candidate who is badly trailing his rivals and is therefore expected to lose may have an incentive to vote for their second-best candidate who still has a chance of winning. In short, voting sophisticatedly, which takes into account the *probabilities* of different outcomes, maximizes expected utility; voting sincerely, which ignores probabilities, does not. The standard account of Duverger's Law states that this process can create a bandwagon effect (Simon 1954), which will lead to only two candidates receiving a significant vote share.

Note that this argument assumes that voters form expectations about the likelihood that their candidate will win and then use these expectations to vote for the alternative that maximizes their expected utility. However, these expectations themselves depend on the expected vote choices of the entire electorate. In recent years rational choice theorists have modeled this problem as a noncooperative game. In equilibrium all voters play best responses given their expectations, which in turn are based on the equilibrium choices of

---

[5] For some work on Duverger's Law at the national level in India and the United States, consider, e.g., Chhibber and Kollman (1998). They emphasize the role of national government in local politics and local economies. As centralization increases, voters develop national policy preferences and local candidates associate themselves with national party labels. These processes lead to national two-party systems.

others. As is obvious from this brief exposition, voting in multicandidate elections is a highly complex decision problem. One may therefore be tempted to simply assume that citizens vote sincerely, always choosing their preferred party. The problem with this view that it cannot account for empirical regularities such as Duverger's Law.[6] So, assuming universal sincere voting will not do. On the other hand, the cognitive demands of the fully rational approach are formidable, as a brief overview of the rational choice literature on Duverger's Law will demonstrate.

A warning to the reader: the following brief tour of existing models may seem overly complicated, but it is important for two reasons. First, what does Duverger's Law imply? What testable predictions does it generate? As we will discuss below, this is less obvious than commonly thought. Second, Duverger's Law seems to rely on a bandwagon effect. A thorough investigation of this intuition, however, demonstrates that the compelling logic of the bandwagon cannot account for the data, which leaves us with a fresh puzzle.

7.2.1 An Intuition Formalized—Game-Theoretic Models of the Bandwagon Effect

Despite its apparent simplicity, the problem of providing a satisfactory model of Duverger's Law (at the district level) has occupied formal theorists for the last 25 years. One challenge is that the regularity as stated by Duverger is somewhat vague. What exactly does it mean to say that plurality rule "favors" two-party competition? Game theorists have reformulated Duverger's Law in terms of *Duvergerian equilibria*, equilibria where only two candidates receive votes. The question then becomes, When do Duvergerian equilibria exist, and when they are unique? There are various models that yield Duvergerian equilibria (e.g., Palfrey 1989; Feddersen 1992; Myerson and Weber 1993; Myerson 2002). All of these are formal representations of the informal bandwagon effect. Voters abandon their preferred candidate and vote for their second choice when they believe, e.g., on the basis of polling information, that their first choice is very unlikely to win. Observers of U.S. presidential primaries are well aware of this phenomenon. Cox (1994) and Myerson (2002) point out that existing models also allow for non-Duvergerian equilibria, in which all three parties get votes. But these equilibria require precise coordination among voters and are not dynamically stable (Fey 1997, Myatt 2007).

[6] For other evidence of sophisticated voting in multicandidate elections, see Cox (1997).

TABLE 7.1
New York senatorial election 1970.

Candidate	Share
Richard L. Ottinger	37%
Charles E. Goodell	24%
James R. Buckley	39%

TABLE 7.2
United Kingdom general elections 1997.

Candidate party	Folkestone-Hythe	Enfield Southgate
Labour	25%	44%
Liberal	27%	11%
Conservative	39%	41%

Here are two examples of non-Duvergerian outcomes. The first is the 1970 New York senatorial election (e.g., Riker 1982). The two liberal candidates, Richard Ottinger and Charles Goodell, competed against the conservative, James Buckley. Goodell was the Republican Party nominee; because of his liberal stance on the Vietnam War, he was also supported by the Liberal Party. Ottinger was the Democratic Party nominee. The liberal candidates had a total support of about 60 percent, but their votes were split in such a way that Buckley won the election (table 7.1).

The second example is the 1997 U.K. general election (e.g., Myatt and Fisher 2002a). The incumbent Conservative Party, which was unpopular at that time, faced challenges from the Liberal and the Labour parties. The Conservative Party polled between one-half and one-third in more than half of the constituencies. With less than half the total votes, it was theoretically possible the incumbent would lose the elections; but with the support of over one-third of the electorate, it could lose only if the anti-Conservative voters successfully coordinated behind one of the challengers. In some constituencies they were able to coordinate; in others they were not. For example, in Folkestone-Hythe, the anti-Conservative votes were split equally between the Liberal and Labour candidates, while in Enfield Southgate they successfully coordinated behind the Labour candidate, who just edged out the Conservative (table 7.2; Myatt and Fisher 2002a).

Note, however, that these examples are not inconsistent with the formal models, as they may constitute non-Duvergerian equilibria as in Cox (1994). But then one may ask, What is the explanatory power of rational choice models given that they are consistent with both Duvergerian and non-Duvergerian equilibria? Moreover, since the models do not predict whether Duvergian or non-Duvergian equilibria are more common, do they indeed imply a tendency toward Duvergerian outcomes?

Closer inspection (Cox 1994, 1997) reveals that the existing formal models *do* make a sharp prediction, though it is not Duverger's Law. Cox pointed out that despite the multiple equilibria, game-theoretic models of multicandidate competition make precise predictions about the ratio of the second to the first loser's vote total (SF ratio). In a Duvergerian equilibrium, the SF ratio should be close to 0; in a non-Duvergerian equilibrium it should be close to 1. Plotting the distribution of SF ratios across districts, the bandwagon models therefore predict a bimodal distribution with one spike at 0 and another at 1. It is important to note that this prediction is logically independent of Duverger's Law. Whereas the latter implies that the spike at 0 should be the larger of the two, bandwagon models—absent an auxiliary argument about equilibrium selection—give only the weaker prediction of bimodality. Thus, strictly speaking, they do not imply Duverger's Law.

Surprisingly, the evidence for the bimodality hypothesis is quite weak. Although Cox (1997) finds some support for it, Myatt and Fisher (2002a,b) argue that the data that Cox analyzed (English constituencies in the 1992 election) indicate that the SF ratio is *single-peaked* at around 0.4. Thus, third-party candidates consistently get more votes than are predicted by Duvergerian equilibria. Coordination under plurality rule is only partial.

Notice, however, that a unimodal distribution at around 0.4 may very well be consistent with Duverger's Law, even though the bimodality hypothesis is violated. In this case one would need to develop a different theoretical account.

This is a complicated story, and a short summary may be helpful.

1. There is broad evidence that Duverger's Law holds at the district level (e.g., Cox 1994, 1997).

2. The most common theoretical intuition for Duverger's Law is based on a bandwagon effect: voters abandon sure losers to avoid wasting their votes.

3. Game-theoretic formalizations of the bandwagon effect usually exhibit Duvergerian equilibria (coordination on two candidates), which are consistent with a strict interpretation of Duverger's Law, and non-Duvergerian equilibria (coordination on three candidates), which are not.

4. Bandwagon models imply bimodality (Cox 1994): the distribution of the ratios of the second loser's vote total to the first's should have two spikes, at 0 and 1. However, absent an equilibrium selection argument, they do not yield the stronger implication of Duverger's Law.
5. Recent evidence supports a weak version of Duverger's Law (interpreted as a statement about the mean of the distribution of SF ratios) but not the bimodality hypothesis.

7.2.2 A New Approach—Partial Coordination and Uncertainty

Where does this leave us? The compelling bandwagon intuition as formalized by game-theoretic models seems flawed. Can it be replaced? Myatt and Fisher (2002b) and Myatt (2007) have proposed an alternative framework to account for the major empirical findings. Following Fey (1997) they model the problem as a "beat-the-incumbent" game, a simplification of the three-candidate game discussed above. Here an incumbent competes against two challengers. The incumbent enjoys a fixed level of support, between one-third and one-half of the total votes. Anti-incumbent voters may have different preferences over the two challengers but they prefer either challenger over the incumbent. The question then is whether the two anti-incumbent factions can coordinate on the same candidate. Of course, this setup does not represent all three-party races, but it is a reasonable fit for the 1992 U.K. elections where the Liberal and Labour parties competed to replace the incumbent Conservatives. The key innovation in the Myatt-Fisher model is the particular use of uncertainty, known as the global games framework (Carlsson and van Damme 1993). Voters receive both a public signal (e.g., an opinion poll) and private signals (e.g., discussion with their neighbors) about the distribution of preferences for the two challengers. Myatt (2007) shows the existence of an equilibrium where voters only partially coordinate. That equilibrium has some novel and possibly counterintuitive properties. For example, there is *no* bandwagon effect. Rather, when voters anticipate strategic voting by others, they become more cautious in their decisions and reduce incentives to vote strategically. Strategic voting exhibits negative feedback, which prevents a fully coordinated outcome.

As in game-theoretic treatments that are more standard, the Myatt-Fisher model represents voters as confronting complex, cognitively demanding choice problems. It is thus a promising target for bounded rationality approaches, especially ABAR-based models. As we now know, the logic of these models is very different from that of game-theoretic ones. Voters do not form expectations about pivot ratios but simply adjust their votes in response to feedback. To be sure, our behavioral model was not intended to analyze coordination among voters. But if it yields useful insights on this problem, we would gain confidence in the basic framework.

7.3 The Model and Simulation Results

To facilitate comparisons with existing models, we focus on the game form proposed by Fey (1997), Myatt and Fisher (2002b), and Myatt (2007). There are three candidates labeled A, B, and C, and n voters. Voters are divided into three types: *AB*-type, *BA*-type and *C*-type. *AB*-type voters prefer A to B to C; *BA*-type voters prefer B to A to C; *C*-type voters prefer C to A to B.

We refer to *AB*- and *BA*-types as the majority factions, and the *C*-type as the minority faction. Coordination is deemed successful (from the perspective of the majority factions) if either A or B is elected.

In order to focus on the voters' coordination problem, we assume that party positions are fixed, there are no voting costs ($c = 0$), and all voters turn out. As always, we allow voters to adapt their behavior through evolving voting propensities and aspirations. Voting propensities adjust according to the Bush-Mosteller rule; aspirations, according to the Cyert-March rule.[7]

We will use the same computational model as in chapter 6 and therefore place party A at $(0, -1)$, party B at $(0, 1)$, and party C at $(x_C, 0)$, where x_C is a parameter to be set in simulations. Placing the voters on the same triangle, with *AB*-types at $(0, -1)$, *BA*-types at $(0, 1)$, and *C*-types at $(x_C, 0)$, we construct a symmetric three-party model. For example, if we set $x_C = 5$, the payoffs (the deterministic component) of the three types based on spatial considerations are $u_{AB} = \{0, -2, -13\}$, $u_{BA} = \{-2, 0, -13\}$, and $u_C = \{-13, -13, 0\}$.

The payoff of an arbitrary voter with ideal point $z = (z_1, z_2)$ for electing a party at location $x = (x_1, x_2)$ is given by

$$-\frac{(x_1 - z_1)^2 + (x_2 - z_2)^2}{2}.$$

To facilitate comparison with game-theoretic models [e.g., Fey (1997)], we renormalize the utilities so that the largest payoff corresponds to 1 while the lowest corresponds to 0. The renormalized

[7] The vector of vote propensities is renormalized after each adjustment to ensure that all propensities add to 1.

TABLE 7.3
Default simulation and voter parameters.

Parameter	Value
Number of simulations	100
Number of voters (n)	1,000
Elections	2,000
Voting cost (c)	0
Shock term ($\epsilon_{i,t}$)	$\sim U[-\omega/2, \omega/2]$ ($\omega = 2.4$)
Action adjustment (λ)	0.1
Initial turnout propensity distribution	All 1.0
Aspiration adjustment and payoffs	Linear with stochastic quadratic payoffs
Aspiration adjustment (ν)	0.05
Initial aspiration distribution ($a_{i,1}$)	Center of payoff distribution
Initial vote propensity distribution	All one-third
x_C	5 (implies $v = 0.85$)

TABLE 7.4
Benchmark cases.

	N_{AB}	N_{BA}	N_C	A's share	B's share	C's share	A winner	B winner	C winner
Case 1	30%	30%	40%	37.67%	36.97%	25.34%	50.97%	48.97%	0.05%
Case 2	45%	45%	10%	37.74%	37.73%	24.52%	49.97%	49.97%	0.05%
Case 3	40%	20%	40%	41.91%	32.80%	25.27%	69.92%	30.01%	0.06%
Case 4	45%	35%	20%	46.59%	28.65%	24.75%	89.88%	10.06%	0.05%

payoffs are then $u_{AB} = \{1, v, 0\}$, $u_{BA} = \{v, 1, 0\}$, and $u_C = \{0, 0, 1\}$, where, for the example, we have $v = 0.85$. Aspirations are similarly renormalized.

7.3.1 Benchmark Case

As a benchmark, we set the values for the parameters listed in table 7.3.

Later we will vary the parameters to gain additional insights. Each run is replicated 100 times to yield average values of the simulation data. The simulation results for the benchmark cases, in which we vary the proportion of each type of voter, are presented in table 7.4.

Our results yield partial coordination. Vote shares are concentrated among A and B, yet C obtains a substantial share of the vote. Despite this appreciable vote share, however, C rarely wins the

TABLE 7.5
Lower noise.

	N_{AB}	N_{BA}	N_C	A's share	B's share	C's share	A winner	B winner	C winner
Case 1	30%	30%	40%	37.26%	37.26%	25.47%	49.98%	49.98%	0.03%
Case 2	45%	45%	10%	37.88%	33.67%	28.43%	57.82%	42.12%	0.04%
Case 3	40%	20%	40%	37.49%	37.07%	25.42%	50.97%	48.97%	0.04%
Case 4	45%	35%	20%	47.63%	26.86%	25.49%	94.79%	5.13%	0.07%

TABLE 7.6
Higher speed of adjustment.

	N_{AB}	N_{BA}	N_C	A's share	B's share	C's share	A winner	B winner	C winner
Case 1	30%	30%	40%	36.51%	36.63%	26.84%	48.98%	50.97%	0.04%
Case 2	45%	45%	10%	37.83%	37.92%	24.23%	51.98%	47.97%	0.04%
Case 3	40%	20%	40%	38.64%	34.30%	27.05%	60.82%	39.13%	0.04%
Case 4	45%	35%	20%	41.20%	33.13%	25.65%	76.94%	23.01%	0.04%

election. Finally, as factions for A and B become more unequal, so do their respective vote shares and winning percentages, but not in a linear fashion. The larger faction (here the one for A) gets somewhat more votes as it becomes larger, but it becomes substantially more successful in winning elections. So, our model implies both partial coordination on vote shares, consistent with Duverger's Law, and successful coordination: the probability that C wins is negligible.

We now vary some of the model's parameters to check whether the basic insights are robust.

7.3.2 Variations

First, we decrease the noise spread, ω, to 0.3. Everything else remains unchanged. The simulation results are presented in table 7.5.

Next, we increase the speed of adjustment for both propensities and aspirations; now $\lambda = 0.4$ and $\nu = 0.4$. The simulation results are presented in table 7.6.

As we can see from the tables, the model's main insights remain unchanged. The only discernible effect concerns the relative winning percentages between factions for A and B; importantly, however, the winning percentages for C remain unchanged. Thus, factions for A and B are just as successful in achieving coordination, but whether they coordinate on A or on B changes.

TABLE 7.7
Intermediate v.

	N_{AB}	N_{BA}	N_C	A's share	B's share	C's share	A winner	B winner	C winner
Case 1	30%	30%	40%	38.49%	36.60%	24.89%	53.91%	45.91%	0.17%
Case 2	45%	45%	10%	38.07%	37.22%	24.70%	52.94%	46.99%	0.06%
Case 3	40%	20%	40%	46.56%	28.01%	25.42%	89.86%	10.03%	0.10%
Case 4	45%	35%	20%	47.25%	27.55%	25.19%	93.82%	6.11%	0.06%

TABLE 7.8
Lower v.

	N_{AB}	N_{BA}	N_C	A's share	B's share	C's share	A winner	B winner	C winner
Case 1	30%	30%	40%	25.89%	25.50%	48.60%	0.33%	0.35%	99.30%
Case 2	45%	45%	10%	38.46%	34.94%	26.59%	56.83%	43.09%	0.06%
Case 3	40%	20%	40%	48.58%	27.08%	24.33%	99.38%	0.11%	0.49%
Case 4	45%	35%	20%	48.80%	25.57%	25.62%	99.64%	0.23%	0.12%

Next, we set $x_C = 4$. This implies $v = 0.76$. Note that decreasing v lowers the cost of miscoordination; this effect is quite intuitive. All other parameters are unchanged. The simulation results are presented in table 7.7.

Again, the results are similar to the benchmark case. Finally, we set $x_C = 2$. This implies $v = 0.2$, significantly reducing incentives to coordinate. All other parameters are unchanged. The simulation results are presented in table 7.8.

Now we see that coordination can break down. This happens when C-types are the largest faction. Also, notice that the winning percentages are now substantially skewed toward the largest faction. Only when there is no unique largest faction do we observe consistently alternating winners.

7.3.3 Coordination Among Majority Factions

The results of the benchmark model and its variants are encouraging. We consistently observe partial coordination among voters. Moreover, the majority factions successfully coordinate as long as the incentives for coordination are sufficiently high. Yet, even the losing candidates receive substantial vote shares. In this section we investigate the simulation results in more detail. One important question is the extent of coordination. Note that in our simulations we always report averages over 100 runs. This is appropriate for most applications, but it is problematic for multicandidate elections, especially if we want to compare our findings to the game-theoretic results. Recall that the standard game-theoretic models predict precise coordination either on Duvergerian (two-candidate) or non-Duvergerian (three-candidate) equilibria. On closer examination, we can see that our results may still be consistent with the game-theoretic predictions. How? Consider the following case. Suppose in each run there is perfect coordination on Duvergerian or non-Duvergerian equilibrium vote shares in roughly equal proportions. But, if we average over a sample of runs, we may observe something similar to our simulation results. That would mean that our model, like its fully rational predecessors, could be consistent with perfect coordination.

To address this concern, we henceforth set the number of runs to 1 and focus on the case where *AB*-types and *BA*-types are the same fraction of the electorate, for example, 30 percent. When we restrict ourselves to single runs we find that in some cases, roughly 50 percent vote for A, 25 percent for B, and 25 percent for C; in other cases we have 25 percent for A, 50 percent for B, and 25 percent for C. Taking averages we obtain 37 percent for A, 37 percent for B, and 25 percent for C, which recovers the original averages. This yields an interesting insight. By the last election of any given run, voters have coordinated on *one of the candidates*, thereby yielding a clear winner. Importantly, the observed vote shares do not resemble the game-theoretic predictions. Indeed, voters may vote for choices that are strictly dominated. As we discussed elsewhere, choosing dominated actions is not unusual in aspiration-based adaptive models. It can be observed, e.g., in the Prisoner's Dilemma (Karandikar et al. 1998).

To check whether this insight is robust, we conduct additional simulations, again varying various parameters but now focusing on the single-run case. First, we vary the noise spread from $\omega = 0.3$ to $\omega = 2.76$. The results are presented in table 7.9. Different levels of noise hardly impact the coordination levels. Notice the consistent coordination on one of the majority factions at around 50 percent, yielding a clear plurality winner each time.

Next we vary the speed of adjustment for both propensities and aspirations. The results are presented in table 7.10. (Recall that ν and λ are the speeds of adjustment for aspirations and propensities, respectively.) Again we set the number of runs to 1. We see that lower speeds of adjustment yield higher levels of coordination. This finding is consistent with other results about the negative impact of rapid adjustment. For example, Karandikar et. al (1998) find that

TABLE 7.9
Varying noise spread with voter distribution 30%, 30%, and 40%.

ω	A's share	B's share	C's share
0.3	47.9%	27.5%	24.6%
0.54	27.3%	50.1%	22.6%
0.84	50.9%	22.6%	26.5%
1.08	26.3%	50.1%	23.6%
1.38	48.2%	26.6%	25.2%
1.62	48.9%	26.8%	24.3%
1.92	48.4%	27.3%	24.3%
2.22	29.4%	48.4%	22.2%
2.46	49.9%	24.8%	25.3%
2.76	52.1%	24.2%	23.7%

TABLE 7.10
Varying speed of adjustment with voter distribution 30%, 30%, and 40%.

	A's share	B's share	C's share
$v = 0.1; \lambda = 0.1$	27.2%	48.1%	24.7%
$v = 0.1; \lambda = 0.2$	43.9%	27.1%	29.0%
$v = 0.1; \lambda = 0.3$	31.0%	48.6%	20.4%
$v = 0.1; \lambda = 0.4$	28.8%	45.2%	26.0%
$v = 0.2; \lambda = 0.1$	26.2%	44.9%	28.9%
$v = 0.2; \lambda = 0.2$	27.7%	48.1%	24.2%
$v = 0.2; \lambda = 0.3$	47.4%	30.1%	22.5%
$v = 0.2; \lambda = 0.4$	41.8%	28.9%	29.3%
$v = 0.3; \lambda = 0.1$	24.9%	50.6%	24.5%
$v = 0.3; \lambda = 0.2$	25.2%	49.7%	25.1%
$v = 0.3; \lambda = 0.3$	28.1%	44.9%	27.0%
$v = 0.3; \lambda = 0.4$	43.7%	29.3%	27.0%
$v = 0.4; \lambda = 0.1$	26.8%	46.4%	26.8%
$v = 0.4; \lambda = 0.2$	27.1%	47.3%	25.6%
$v = 0.4; \lambda = 0.3$	48.8%	25.9%	25.3%
$v = 0.4; \lambda = 0.4$	27.4%	44.9%	27.7%
$v = 0.5; \lambda = 0.1$	47.7%	25.2%	27.1%
$v = 0.5; \lambda = 0.2$	28.0%	45.1%	26.9%
$v = 0.5; \lambda = 0.3$	46.9%	24.4%	28.7%
$v = 0.5; \lambda = 0.4$	29.9%	42.4%	27.7%

players in a repeated Prisoner's Dilemma cooperate most of the time if aspirations are updated sufficiently slowly.

Finally, we vary x_C, which determines the value of v and therefore the incentives to coordinate. Specifically, we increase x_C from

TABLE 7.11
Letting v vary with voter distribution 30%, 30%, and 40%.

v	A's share	B's share	C's share
0.05	26.8%	25.3%	47.9%
0.13	22.6%	27.3%	50.1%
0.20	25.0%	23.2%	51.8%
0.26	25.7%	26.4%	47.9%
0.31	22.5%	27.7%	49.8%
0.36	24.2%	26.4%	49.4%
0.41	31.7%	47.6%	20.7%
0.49	48.1%	30.0%	21.9%
0.60	49.3%	28.9%	21.8%
0.70	49.3%	29.2%	21.5%
0.76	52.9%	26.1%	21.0%
0.81	24.9%	49.9%	25.2%
0.85	49.6%	27.1%	23.3%
0.87	24.8%	50.2%	25.0%
0.89	47.4%	28.3%	24.3%
0.91	25.6%	48.2%	26.2%
0.92	25.7%	49.4%	24.9%

1.8 to 7. Again we focus on the single-run case. The results are presented in tables 7.11–7.14. Note first that if the C-types form the largest faction, then low levels of v yield wins for C: the majority faction is unable to coordinate on a candidate. For higher levels of v coordination always occurs. These results illustrate the idea of viewing v as the cost of miscoordination. In the extreme case of $v = 1$, the two factions are completely indifferent between A and B. This is a case of pure coordination. On the other hand, if $v = 0$, then the AB-types, for example, are solely interested in A winning: they are indifferent between B or C winning because in either event they receive a payoff of 0.

Miscoordination occurs in our simulation only if C-types are among the largest factions. This is illustrated in the next example where C-types are the smallest faction, here 10 percent. Varying v has no impact in this case.

If C-types are one of the largest factions, then miscoordination occurs only when v is very small, as illustrated in table 7.13.

These simulations clearly show that our model's implications differ significantly from standard game-theoretic ones. The distribution of vote shares resembles neither Duvergerian equilibria (only two candidates receive any votes) nor non-Duvergerian equilibria (votes shares are balanced between the three candidates). Rather, provided the incentives for coordination are sufficiently high, one

TABLE 7.12
Letting v vary with voter distribution 45%, 45%, and 10%.

v	A's share	B's share	C's share
0.05	50.3%	23.5%	26.2%
0.13	24.8%	46.5%	28.7%
0.20	25.2%	47.5%	27.3%
0.26	48.0%	25.2%	26.8%
0.31	25.4%	47.4%	27.2%
0.36	48.4%	25.4%	26.2%
0.41	47.0%	26.4%	26.6%
0.49	48.2%	25.2%	26.6%
0.60	25.2%	50.2%	24.6%
0.70	53.4%	23.8%	22.8%
0.76	29.1%	47.5%	23.4%
0.81	26.8%	46.9%	26.3%
0.85	48.7%	27.7%	23.6%
0.87	48.8%	25.9%	25.3%
0.89	45.7%	29.0%	25.3%
0.91	25.6%	50.0%	24.4%
0.92	27.8%	48.2%	24.0%

of the majority factions will win a plurality of votes by a substantial margin, yet all candidates will receive substantial votes shares, even when they lose for sure, in sharp contrast to the game-theoretic equilibria. Particularly striking, voters may chose dominated voting strategies. Notice also that majority voters usually coordinate on the largest faction's preferred candidate (here A). For large v, however, they may also coordinate on the other candidate, i.e., B. The reason is that as v increases, the two factions (*AB* and *BA*) become more homogeneous. In the extreme case of $v = 1$, they have the same preferences and coordinating on A or B yields the same payoff.

7.4 An Intuition

To explore these insights in more depth we investigate an extreme example. This example was not chosen for verisimilitude or plausibility. Indeed, it probably has never and will never occur in any real election. The purpose is rather to reveal, in a stark setting, the inner workings of our behavioral model.

Presume the model just described. Assume further, for the parameter values of the benchmark case, that all voters are *C*-types, all located at (25,0). Running the model, we get the following results

TABLE 7.13
Letting v vary with voter distribution 40%, 20%, and 40%.

v	A's share	B's share	C's share
0.05	26.4%	26.2%	47.4%
0.13	48.1%	29.2%	22.7%
0.20	48.5%	31.0%	20.5%
0.26	50.6%	26.8%	22.6%
0.31	49.0%	27.3%	23.7%
0.36	47.4%	26.9%	25.7%
0.41	49.2%	24.8%	26.0%
0.49	50.5%	27.3%	22.2%
0.60	48.8%	25.9%	25.3%
0.70	48.9%	25.8%	25.3%
0.76	51.1%	25.2%	23.7%
0.81	47.7%	27.1%	25.2%
0.85	49.0%	26.0%	25.0%
0.87	26.8%	49.7%	23.5%
0.89	48.8%	23.7%	27.5%
0.91	47.9%	28.2%	23.9%
0.92	23.5%	47.9%	28.6%

at $t = 500$: A gets 25.3 percent, B gets 25.9 percent, and C gets 48.8 percent.

Why do we get these results? Shouldn't an electorate composed only of C-types vote 100 percent for C? The answer is no, not if they adjust their behavior via aspiration-based adaptive rules.[8] To see why, we walk through a few periods, beginning with the first election. All voters start with neutral vote propensities: every citizen initially has a $\frac{1}{3}$ chance of voting for each party. Their initial aspirations are set at the average payoff arising from each party. (There are only C-types here, so initial aspirations are $\frac{1}{3}$ for all voters.) Suppose that C wins. Then all voters will get a payoff around 1. On average, this payoff will be viewed as a success by more than half of the voters and as a failure by less than the other half; hence they will increase the same average level of likelihood to vote for C. On the other hand, if either A or B wins, all voters will get a very small payoff. Because

[8] For an analytical result along these lines, recall proposition 2.1. Both the proposition and this chapter's simulations are driven by the combination of endogenous aspirations and stochastic payoffs. As we explained in chapter 2, this combination makes even an optimal alternative inevitably disappointing. Hence it is impossible for agents who adapt via stationary Markovian ABARs to settle down on their best option. Because this happens even when $n = 1$, it should not surprise us that an electorate composed only of C-types does not always vote for C: even in the limit, some voters will sometimes find C's performance unsatisfactory.

TABLE 7.14
Letting v vary with voter distribution 45%, 35%, and 20%.

v	A's share	B's share	C's share
0.05	47.7%	25.9%	26.4%
0.13	50.4%	22.7%	26.9%
0.20	50.8%	26.5%	22.7%
0.26	48.9%	26.7%	24.4%
0.31	50.4%	22.7%	26.9%
0.36	51.0%	25.8%	23.2%
0.41	50.0%	27.6%	22.4%
0.49	47.4%	24.9%	27.7%
0.60	48.1%	26.8%	25.1%
0.70	46.0%	27.0%	27.0%
0.76	46.7%	26.0%	27.3%
0.81	49.5%	25.2%	25.3%
0.85	48.6%	26.6%	24.8%
0.87	26.2%	47.7%	26.1%
0.89	48.4%	27.7%	23.9%
0.91	47.4%	26.3%	26.3%
0.92	28.2%	49.6%	22.2%

this will be well below their aspiration levels, voters will substantially decrease their propensities of voting for A or for B. Meanwhile, aspirations will be driven downward whenever A and B are elected, increasing the likelihood that C yields payoffs that are regarded as satisfactory. Thus, in the beginning at least, positive probabilities of electing A or B and C result in a gradual increase in the propensity of voting for C.

This process will continue for a while; e.g., in our simulation we see that at $t = 70$ C's vote share has risen to 85 percent, which indicates a high propensity of voting for C. But as p_C increases and C is elected consistently, everybody receives the maximum deterministic payoff in each period. This drives up aspiration levels, and they approach the maximum deterministic payoff. Once aspirations are very close to 1, half of the voters are no longer satisfied with their payoffs (remember that the payoff equals $1 + \epsilon$, where ϵ is normally distributed with mean 0). Voters who are happy with their payoffs will increase their propensities to vote for C, but since that propensity is close to 1, that increase must be small. On other hand, about as many voters will be dissatisfied with their payoffs, so they will reduce their p_C. Furthermore, because their prior propensity to vote for C was quite high and because they adjust via the Bush-Mosteller rule, which generates changes that increase linearly in the amount of adjustable probability, dissatisfied voters will change their propensities by substantial amounts. Therefore, the average propensity to vote for C will fall. This is reflected in simulation results: starting around $t = 70$, C's vote share drops from 85 percent to around 50 percent and remains at this level until the end. A vote split of 25 percent for A, 25 percent for B, and 50 percent for C corresponds, roughly, to average propensities to vote for A, B, and C of 0.25, 0.25, and 0.5, respectively. With this propensity distribution, C wins the election with high probability, and thus everybody's expected payoff is around 1. Again, since aspiration levels are themselves close to 1, half of the voters will be satisfied; the other half, dissatisfied. The happy ones will increase their propensities to vote for C; the disgruntled will reduce them. But now, with an average propensity to vote for C near 0.5 and with an adaptive rule that responds symmetrically to positive and negative feedback, the increase and decrease will balance out. Hence the average propensity to vote for C remains at 0.5. In short, an outcome of 25 percent votes for A, 25 percent for B, and 50 percent for C is a stationary (i.e., invariant) distribution.

This intuition applies more generally. The dynamic unfolds as follows. First, one faction quickly attains a plurality. At first, those in the faction receive higher payoffs from their party than they were used to; hence, aspirations are satisfied, which increases the average propensity to vote for that faction. Thus, a positive feedback loop—bigger pluralities, higher propensities—ensues, until propensities and aspirations are close to one. But then we are back at the above case, with C as the winning faction, so we know what happens next: many voters will be disappointed by payoffs below the (now high) aspirations. Hence propensities and aspirations will drop, leveling off once vote shares reach the neighborhood of 0.25, 0.25 and 0.5. Note that this also explains the importance of relative faction size discussed above. Recall that the largest faction was likely to end up as the winner. This was true even for C, provided the coordination incentive v is sufficiently low. We can now see that a larger relative faction size bestows this critical advantage, as it is more likely to snatch the first win, which then triggers the positive feedback loop illustrated in the extreme example.

7.5 ABARs and Dynamic Stability

Our results show that the logic of our behavioral model of multicandidate elections yields very different predictions and insights than the game-theoretic formulations. What about alternative dynamic models? To the best of our knowledge, only one paper—Fey (1997)—presents a dynamic model of multicandidate elections. Fey uses the same majority coordination model as discussed above. Following Palfrey (1989), he then shows that there are three equilibria. Two are Duvergian: in one, all *AB*- and *BA*-types vote for A, and *C*-types for C; in the other, all *AB*- and *BA*-types vote for B, and *C*-types for C. In the non-Duvergerian equilibrium, on the other hand, we have a tie between the first and second losers. For example, Fey (1997) finds a non-Duvergerian equilibrium in which C receives 40 percent of the vote, A and B 30 percent each. This may look similar to our results, e.g., a typical simulation outcome of (50 percent, 25 percent, 25 percent). The underlying logic, however, is completely different. In our results, the vote share of 50 percent allocated to the winner is made up of votes from all three types. Suppose A is the winner and receives 50 percent. Then, on average, 50 percent of *AB*-types vote for A, 50 percent of *BA*-types vote for A, and 50 percent of *C*-types also vote for A. Thus, some agents use dominated strategies, in stark contrast to the equilibrium strategies in Fey (1997).

Fey then posits an adjustment dynamic that eliminates the non-Duvergerian equilibrium. His model uses a belief-based adjustment process (based on opinion polls) that defines a best response for each *AB*-voter. The goal is then to identify the fixed points of this adjustment process. Fey shows that only the Duvergerian equilibria are dynamically stable; the non-Duvergerian one is unstable. This result formally captures the intuition that non-Duvergerian equilibria are knife-edge phenomena, requiring an implausible amount of coordination.

We can now compare our model to Fey's. Suppose *AB*- and *BA*-types each comprise 30 percent of the electorate, with *C*-types the remaining 40 percent. Then for sufficiently high values of v (in the simulations above this would be true for $v > 0.4$), either A or B captures a little less than one-half of the votes and the other two parties get about one-fourth each. This prediction is very different from Fey's. Thus, once again we can see that the solutions of ABAR-based models are not refinements of Nash equilibria: they do not select from the set of Nash equilibria. Instead, they are an alternative formalization of behavior in strategic interactions.

7.6 Model Meets Data

It is now clear that our behavioral model is governed by a very different logic than are standard game-theoretic models of multicandidate elections. But can it account for the data? Our first results were quite promising. The model yielded partial coordination provided the benefits from coordinating were sufficiently high. Voters in the majority faction were able to coordinate their behavior on A (or B); yet both B and C (or A and C) received substantial vote shares, just not enough to win.

Careful data analysis will be required to assess the empirical success of our model. Yet providing some initial observations may be useful. To do so, we apply our model to the 1997 U.K. general elections.[9] This case is suitable because three main parties competed in most districts: the Labour, Liberal Democrat, and Conservative parties. Moreover, the incumbent Conservative Party was confronted by rivals—Labour and Liberal—whose supporters generally ranked the Conservatives last. More precisely, we can use data from the British Election Survey to reveal the various faction sizes in each constituency. Following Myatt and Fisher (2002a) we have identified 143 constituencies for which we have survey data. One of the survey questions was, "Generally speaking, do you think of yourself as [name of the party]?" The respondents could choose from the following answers:

0 none/no

1 Conservative

2 Labour

3 Liberal Democrat

4 Scottish National Party (SNP)

5 Plaid Cymru

6 Green Party

7 other

We note that in English districts the shares of SNP, Plaid Cymru, and Green Party are close to 0 percent, so we can compute the share support of the Conservative, Labour, and Liberal Democrat parties based on the above question and ignore the answers that indicate SNP, Plaid Cymru, or Green Party as the most preferred party. Putting this electoral situation in the context of our model, we identify the

[9] This case was extensively discussed by Myatt and Fisher (2002a,b). The data are due to Heath et al. (1997–2000). In interpreting these data the reader should keep in mind that this analysis is intended to be suggestive rather than conclusive. For example, many districts have about 10 to 15 observations, which is an unreliable estimate of the district's representative preferences over parties.

Labour Party as party A, the Liberal Democrats as B, and the Conservatives as C. The *AB*-voters are those that prefer Labour to Liberal Democrat to Conservative; *BA*-types prefer Liberal Democrat to Labour to Conservative; *C*-types prefer Conservative to Labour and Liberal Democrat. We assume that voters who listed themselves as Labour supporters prefer the Labour candidate to the Liberal Democrat to the Conservative; those that listed themselves as Liberal Democrats prefer the Liberal Democrat candidate to the Labour to the Conservative; and Conservative voters prefer the Conservative candidate and equally dislike the Labour and the Liberal Democrat candidates. (Of course, these claims may not hold exactly, but they are probably a serviceable approximation.)

Now we can run our behavioral model on each constituency using the survey data as inputs. (All the model's parameters are set as in the benchmark case with v at 0.85.)

To compare data and predictions we compute some summary statistics. We first consider the winner-to-first-loser (WF) ratio.[10] Our simulations yield a mean of 1.8, which is quite close to the sample mean of 2.19, as we see by comparing figures 7.4 and 7.5.

The results for the second-to-first-loser (SF) ratio, introduced by Cox, are less promising. While the data bear little resemblance to the bimodality prediction of the game-theoretic models, the SF ratio of the simulations does not stand up well either as we see by comparing figures 7.6 and 7.7. The overall ratio is too high; our simulations predict more support for second losers than the data report. Notice also that the high SF ratio is a consequence of the balancing property induced by the specific version of aspiration-based adjustment we are using here. Recall that dissatisfied voters are assumed to vote for one of the other candidates with equal probability. This seems like an innocuous assumption, but other variants, e.g., with payoff-dependent choice probabilities, should be considered in future research.

Where does this leave us? First, the simulations can account for partial coordination. Second, the results perform well in predicting WF ratios. Third, they overstate the support for second losers. Of course, all this is highly preliminary and should be viewed with much caution. For example, our simulations are based on survey data that

---

[10] Game-theoretic models do not have a clear implication for the WF ratio. In Duvergerian equilibria the ratio would be given by the size of the *AB*-faction over the *C*-faction. So, for the case of 30 percent A supporters, 30 percent B supporters, and 40 percent C supporters, the ratio would be $60/40 = 1.5$, while for non-Duvergerian equilibria the ratio would be $40/30 \approx 1.33$.

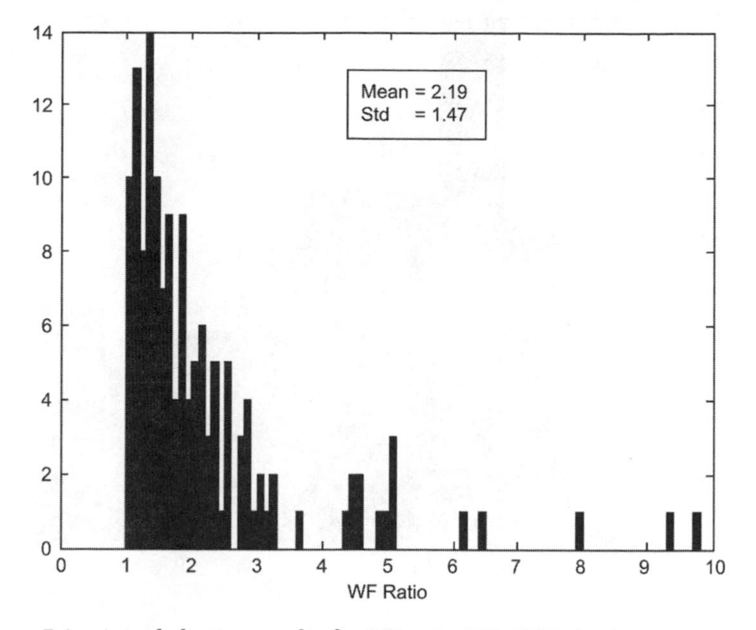

Figure 7.4. Actual election results for WF ratio, U.K. 1997 elections.

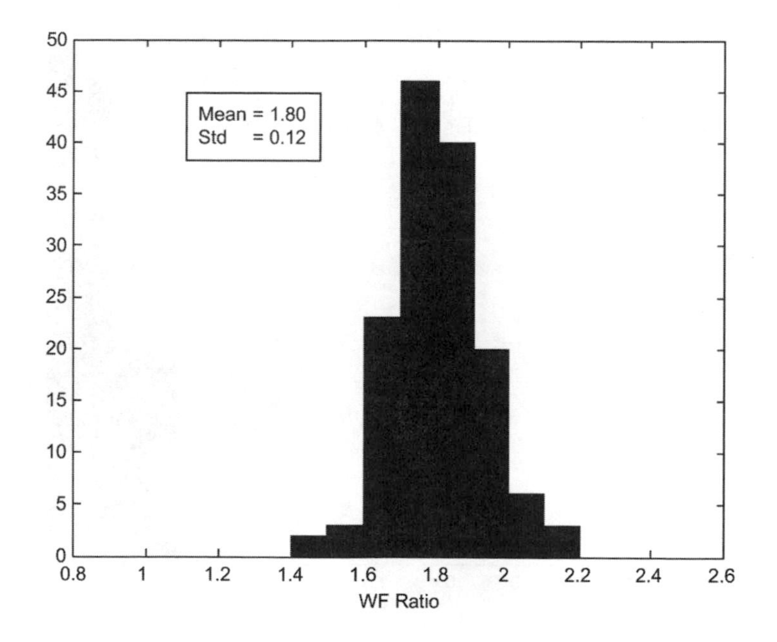

Figure 7.5. WF ratio calculated on simulation results, U.K. 1997 elections.

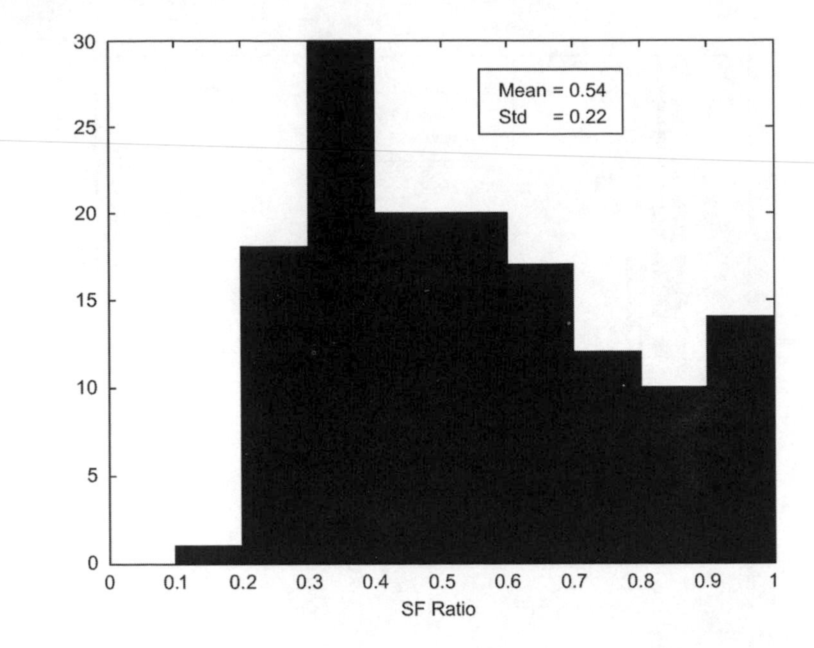

Figure 7.6. Actual election results for SF ratio, U.K. 1997 elections.

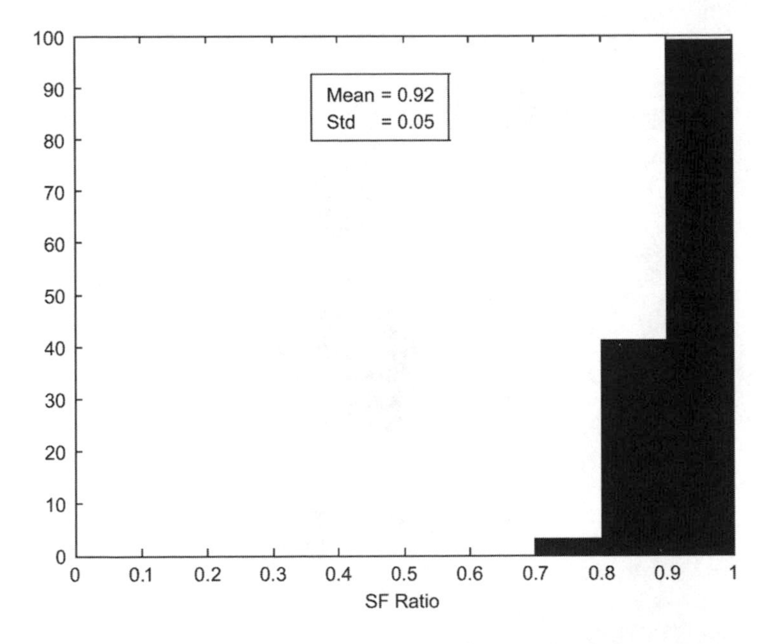

Figure 7.7. SF ratio calculated on simulation results, U.K. 1997 elections.

may or may not accurately capture faction sizes. Only careful empirical analysis will resolve these issues. Nevertheless, the preliminary empirical support for our model is encouraging.

But what about the more puzzling implications, e.g., the prediction of voting for dominated candidates? Unfortunately, field data cannot be easily used to test these implications. Yet, we do find some support in experimental data. Forsythe et al. (1993) conducted a series of experiments using the same preference structure as in our model but without random trembles. First, voters are able to coordinate on the Condorcet winner using shared histories even if polls are unavailable. Moreover, a closer inspection of the data shows increases in voting propensities after successful outcomes.[11] Finally, voters do vote for dominated choices, e.g., *AB*-types voting for C, and so forth. The experimental data also show that *AB*/*BA*-types have a tendency to coordinate on the candidate first listed on the ballot. In an ABAR model this may mean that ballot order leads to the first win for one of the candidates from one of the larger parties, which then reinforces voting propensities until coordination occurs. Recall from our model that this happens in the first phase of the adjustment process. Suppose A is the first listed candidate and wins, which reinforces the propensities of *AB*/*BA*-types to vote for A and for *C*-types to vote for C, and so forth until *AB*/*BA*-types as well as *C*-types are (almost) perfectly coordinated. But, as we discussed above, in a model with endogenous aspirations this is not the end of the story. Given that A is now winning consistently, aspirations for *AB*/*BA*-types have to rise. This eventually leads to disappointment and the balanced distribution with A receiving a little more than 50 percent of the votes and B and C splitting the rest equally. The experimental results support the first part of the process (coordination on A and reinforced propensities) but not the second part (increasing aspirations leading to balancing). This is likely due to the fact that the experimental design used deterministic payoffs. Thus, the majority faction will never be dissatisfied, and the process will never get to the balanced outcome of 50 percent, 25 percent, 25 percent. To properly test that implication of the model one would need to include payoff trembles. In addition, it is important that the experimental sessions last long enough for the second phase to kick in. This is particularly true if aspirations adjust slowly, as may be the case in an environment where actual payoffs are low. Notice that if this intuition is correct, a similar argument may resolve the issue of overpredicting support for second losers (a too high SF ratio) observed in the U.K. simulations.

[11] We wish to thank Thomas Rietz for sharing the experimental data with us.

This brief review suggests promising future research not only empirically but also theoretically. For example, a natural next step would be to combine an ABAR model with a prospective model where voters pay attention to polls and (at least crudely) estimate pivot probabilities. Such an extension would be reminiscent of the treatment in chapter 5. As other next steps, one may want to consider more sophisticated parties, as in chapters 3 and 6. We intend to pursue this topic in future work.

CHAPTER EIGHT

Conclusions
Bounded Rationality and Elections

WE HAVE EXPLORED how boundedly rational candidates and voters try to make their way in a confusing world. The properties of these decision makers are broadly consistent with empirical work by political psychologists and foundational ideas of cognitive psychologists about how people process, store, and retrieve information. Our agents perform no heroic feats of computation. Instead, they adapt by aspiration-based trial and error. These models can analyze both statics (i.e., the limiting distribution of the stochastic process) and dynamics. Some of the most important and robust findings are as follows.

- *Party location.* The simple party competition model in chapter 3 implies that in unidimensional policy spaces, satisficing by winners plus search by losers produces a string of governmental policies that converges to the median voter's ideal point when citizens always vote for the party that will better serve their interests. The mechanism is simple. With the incumbent cleaving to the platform that won him office in $t - 1$, the pivotal decision maker—the median voter—can do no worse than the status quo policy. Hence, either the challenger finds something better for the median voter or not. If so, the challenger wins and her platform becomes the new government's policy; if not, nothing changes. Hence the trajectory of winning policies cannot move away from the median voter and can move closer.

  Our adaptively retrospective citizens can err, but as we have seen, they learn to get it right more than half the time. This is enough voting accuracy to give the trajectory of winning platforms an impulse toward the median voter, though naturally this tendency is less reliable than when voters are flawless Downsians.[1] Hence, the distribution of winning policies in chapter 6's integrated model is packed fairly tightly around the median voter.

[1] Less than universal turnout also adds variety due to sampling effects.

However, the distribution of winning policies never collapses onto the median voter's bliss point no matter how long the process is simulated. This holds despite the fact that parties in almost all our models are purely office seeking. Rather than policy motivation, the cause of the persistent dispersion of winning platforms is partly mistakes made by our adaptively retrospective voters. Consider, for example, a moderate citizen who has lucked out and received a series of good payoffs from a liberal incumbent. This voter will be inclined to support the incumbent even if the challenger's platform is closer to his ideal point. A flawless Downsian voter would support the latter and so would help pull triumphant policies closer to the median voter. Party divergence is a real phenomenon (Stokes 1999; Ansolabehere, Snyder, and Stewart 2001). So is voter error (Bartels 1996; Lau and Redlawsk 1997). Our models suggest that the latter helps to make the former a persistent pattern.

To be sure, there are well-known rational choice models that also predict divergent policy locations of office-seeking candidates (Wittman 1983; Calvert 1985). In these models uncertainty about the median voter's location is critical to the generation of nonconvergence. However, this is not the proper comparison to our most general model (chapter 6), which also allows for abstention. In a rational choice model with abstention, both candidates locate at the center and nobody votes (Ledyard 1984). So our model not only proposes an entirely different theory of voter and candidate behavior, but also has different empirical implications, predicting nonconvergence and positive turnout even when citizens can abstain and candidates are motivated only by the perquisites of office.

- *Turnout.* No 'paradox of voting' plagues these models. Turnout is always nonnegligible; in some variants it is in the empirical ballpark for large electorates. Though these aggregate patterns are descriptively reasonable, at the individual level this is suboptimal behavior in a well-defined sense. In all our models the chance that a single voter will be pivotal is miniscule. Hence, any given citizen could free-ride on the efforts of her peers and save the cost of participating in politics. But our citizens are not fully rational: they don't think about the chance of being pivotal, taken exogenously, as in decision-theoretic models, or endogenously, as in game-theoretic ones. Aspiration-based adaptation generates loser-driven mobilization: staying home and losing is often dissatisfying, so near-universal apathy is unstable.

Turnout responds in intuitive ways to changes in parameter values. Average participation is higher the further apart the parties, in both two-component models with fixed platforms and in the simple turnout model in chapter 4. Further, turnout is lower the larger the electorate, the farther apart the rival factions are in size, and the higher the cost of voting, in both chapter 4's simple model as well as in chapter 6's integrated one. These implications are well supported by empirical research on turnout.

- *Voters' choices.* Voters in these models learn to support parties that better serve their interests. As in real elections, their learning is quite imperfect. Naturally, it is achieved more often the less parties move around. Because the learning environment is easiest when parties never change platforms, voters learn to vote correctly most often in this setting. Furthermore, average vote accuracy is increasing in the difference between the parties' platforms. These tendencies are amplified when vote choice combines retrospection and prospection. Hence, voters will appear more ideological when the parties offer more distinct alternatives (e.g., Fiorina 2005; Levendusky 2009). This kind of elite behavior makes the choices of ordinary citizens easier (Lau, Andersen and Redlawsk 2008). We would expect to see similar differences between polities that have parties with obviously distinct ideologies versus those that are more fluid or more person-centered.
- *Voter coordination.* The model can also be used to study multiparty competition. When applied to the classic coordination problem of multiparty competition under plurality rule—i.e., Duverger's Law—the model yields implications that differ sharply from those of standard rational choice formulations. Moreover, it performs surprisingly well. First, coordination is usually successful: the Condorcet loser is almost never selected. Second, the results are surprisingly consistent with the data, though they overstate the support for second losers.

These results are very encouraging—especially in light of the fact that our model was not designed to account for coordination problems.

8.1 Testing the Theory

In contrast to rational choice models, our theory is formulated in the languages of dynamic systems and stochastic processes. While these formalisms require some initial investment, their mathematics is well understood. However, the probabilistic nature of our theory may cause some concerns about how to test its predictions. In this context it is vital to remember that the long-run tendencies of our stochastic models typically are described by nondegenerate limiting distributions. Individual sample paths are not static; what stabilizes is a *population* of sample paths. Put less technically, this means that a single electoral system never settles down to a specific state. This property is not a modeling artifact; it follows directly from the combination of aspiration-based adaptation and stochastic payoffs. To see this, suppose for the sake of the argument that the parties and voters do settle down: the former stabilize at a pair of platforms, and the latter at a vector of actions in which some citizens vote D, some vote R, and the rest stay home. It is easy to see that this situation is, in fact, unstable. There are two main reasons. First, the losing party, disgruntled by its defeat, might try a new platform: inertia is possible but not inevitable. Second, citizens may become discontented with their lot. Supporters of the majority party, dissatisfied with current payoffs, may stay home in the next election. Some of the current shirkers will get bad payoffs today; they may vote for the challenger tomorrow. This restless dynamic must arise when individual agents have endogenous aspirations and stochastic payoffs: today's good payoffs drive up aspirations, setting the stage for tomorrow's disappointment. A system peopled by such fickle decision makers cannot settle down. But *populations* of such systems will exhibit stable probabilistic patterns. (This property of ergodic Markov processes was explained in some detail in chapter 2; as a simple reminder, imagine a single satisficing voter switching indefinitely between two parties that offer fixed platforms, either of which can deliver disappointing payoffs.) In other words, our predictions are best understood as applying to populations or samples of elections, not individual cases. But this does not make the model any less testable. All one must do is compare the model's implied distribution to the empirical distribution. Well-known statistical methods, e.g., Kolmogoroff-Smirnov tests, do exactly this.

Although particular sample paths never become static, our models' best-understood variants—finite ergodic Markov chains—have two features that give even a single sample path a measure of stability. First, a path produced by such a process has intuitive long-run temporal properties: the percentage of periods that it spends in a given state will converge to its limiting probability by a law of large numbers. Suppose, for example, that there are 10 centrist platforms, $x_1, \ldots, x_{10}$. With a little hand-waving, we can say that the limiting probability of the system having these centrist platforms as the government's policy is $\tilde{p}_{x_1}, \ldots, \tilde{p}_{x_{10}}$, respectively. Thus, in the long run, the fraction of the time that this particular system will have one of these centrist platforms as the government's policy will converge to $\tilde{p}_{x_1} + \cdots + \tilde{p}_{x_{10}}$. Therefore, although a particular sample path will not settle down into a unique state, it will acquire long-run probabilistic tendencies. In empirical terms one can think of this as follows. Suppose we take snapshots of a particular sample path at random intervals. The underlying stochastic process has n states, numbered (labeled) so that $\tilde{p}_{x_1} > \tilde{p}_{x_2} > \cdots > \tilde{p}_{x_n}$. Then a snapshot is most likely to be a picture of x_1 and least likely to be a picture of x_n.

Second, finite ergodic Markov chains converge to their limiting distributions at geometric speed. This implies, inter alia, that if a particular system's initial conditions are far from the limiting distribution, then we can expect big changes early on. More generally, *the more a sample path currently differs from its underlying limiting distribution, the faster we can expect that system to change.* Consider the following example. Suppose the citizens in an electorate adjust their propensities to vote D or R and to shirk or turn out via the Bush-Mosteller rule; meanwhile, the winning party satisfices while the loser searches blindly. Further, the initial incumbent, D, starts at the far left of the policy spectrum. Most citizens initially are apathetic; few voters are highly disposed toward D. Although we don't know the exact trajectory of this individual system, we can offer some conjectures about several of its tendencies. First, on average at least one of the system's endogenous variables will change a lot from t_0 to t_1. For example, suppose that the citizens' aspirations are close to those at the limit. Then many are likely to be dissatisfied by current payoffs produced by an incumbent who is so extreme. Hence, their propensity to vote for the incumbent will fall, and sharply so, given the properties of the Bush-Mosteller rule.[2]

Alternatively, suppose that aspirations start out far from their average limiting value; in particular, they begin at very low levels,

[2] Recall that the Bush-Mosteller rule is a weighted-average equation. Therefore, if a citizen's intial propensity to vote D equals 1, then a dissatisfying payoff makes her propensity to vote for the incumbent fall by the largest possible amount.

so that most people are content with the status quo and, hence, with the incumbent. In this case the movement of the government's policy will be initially slow, but aspirations will adjust swiftly.[3] And once citizens have gotten used to the payoffs produced by a far left governmental policy, the rest of the system will start to change more rapidly as the number of voters displeased by current payoffs starts to rise.

In sum, working with behavioral models requires a taste for probabilistic predictions. These predictions are no less testable than their rational choice counterparts, but they require that empiricists appreciate that the predictions are distributions, not states or outcomes. That said, in contrast to many game-theoretic models which are plagued by multiple equilibria, the implied distributions of our theory are unique. This increases their predictive power.

8.2 Normative Considerations: Voter Error and Systemic Performance

Agents who use aspiration-based adaptive rules make mistakes—persistently and sometimes often. (Recall, for example, that the voting accuracy in the default versions of the integrated model ranged between 0.52, for three of the party search rules, and 0.63, for the local-naive rule.) Individual performance is not, however, the end of the story (Bendor and Bullock 2008). How do *systems* composed of such actors perform?

A first-pass answer to this question could be based on the idea encoded in Condorcet's Jury Theorem (CJT): under majority rule, many inaccurate agents might collectively generate an accurate decision, provided that the individuals choose independently.[4] There are, however, two problems with this answer. The first is obvious:

[3] With conventional weighted-average aspiration adjustment, people will rapidly approach the aspiration distribution based on the government's putatively stable far left policy. Once that happens, half the citizens will be discontent with current payoffs, and the incumbent will probably be thrown out of office within a few elections.

[4] In addition to independent errors, Condorcet's original theorem assumed that the decision makers are homogeneously competent and have the same preferences. Extensions of the Jury Theorem have relaxed all three assumptions. In particular, Nicholas Miller (1986) reformulated it for electoral contexts. In discarding the common-interest setting of the Jury Theorem, he proposed a new definition of "correct" choice: it is the party that would be elected by fully informed rational voters. This is now the standard criterion in election-related Condorcet theorems. See also the extensive literature on information aggregation in elections with strategic voters following Feddersen and Pesendorfer (1996, 1997).

the CJT examines collective choice problems with fixed alternatives, such as a defendant who is, in fact, either guilty or innocent. But in elections, the options—the policies offered by the candidates—are endogenous. Of course, this problem also applies to the game-theoretic models. And if the parties are office seeking and adapt via ABARs, at least the losing side will adjust indefinitely. This introduces another source of error into the system—e.g., even if a median voter exists, the challenger may not locate there even in the limit—and *this* source of error is not controlled by the large-n mechanism of the CJT as the number of parties or candidates is likely to be small.

By itself, this problem might not create systemic difficulties. As we saw in chapter 3, if voters were flawless Downsians, then the trajectory of the winning policy would converge to the median voter (given a unidimensional policy space) even if the challenger searched blindly while the incumbent satisficed. Further, this will hold for imperfect Downsian voters; if there are infinitely many of them, their errors are independent and their (homogeneous) competency exceeds $\frac{1}{2}$ (Miller 1986, p. 180).

What makes this a systemic problem is the adaptive behavior of voters. Downsian voters, imperfect or not, compare parties only to each other. Their mental representations don't include aspiration levels; therefore, they don't compare available alternatives to an internal standard. But because voters who adjust via ABARs make exactly this comparison, they can be dissatisfied by any alternative, even the optimal one. And by the basic axiom of negative feedback, dissatisfaction can trigger search.[5] In short, the dynamics implied by voter behavior governed by endogenous aspirations is very different from the rational choice–based models underlying the CJT in all its variants. Hence, having large numbers of (adaptive) voters is not a sure-fire remedy, even if they all have the same preferences (see remark 5.4).

Nevertheless, the results from the integrated model reported in chapter 6 indicate that a system is likely to spend more time near the ideal point of the median voter the larger the electorate. Large numbers still have a benign effect in our models, reminiscent of the Condorcet Jury Theorem, though it is somewhat muted by the irrepressible tendencies of aspiration-driven behavior.

[5] It is easy to show that dissatisfaction-based search is a robust phenomenon: it occurs in complex choice processes in which alternatives are compared to each other as well as to an aspiration level.

8.3 Extensions

To use the gentle language of modelers, the present formulations are rather stylized. Fortunately, most of the stark assumptions can be relaxed, thus generating a variety of extensions.

8.3.1 Multidimensional Policy Spaces

It is well known—notorious, in fact—that models of two-party competition with fully rational agents are qualitatively different in multidimensional versus unidimensional policy spaces (e.g., Plott 1967; McKelvey 1976; Schofield 1977; Patty, Snyder, and Ting 2009). In the latter, the median voter theorem often obtains: office-seeking parties, striving for the approval of the pivotal voter, converge to the ideal point of that citizen, and that policy is the unique equilibrium of the party competition game. Because multidimensional policy spaces generically lack a political center of gravity, many game-theoretic models in this context have no pure strategy equilibria at all. Although this is not the methodological disaster that some have seen,[6] there is nonetheless a sharp difference between electoral competition in one dimension versus higher ones—for fully rational players.

If, however, the agents are only adaptively rational, as in the present models, the dimensionality of the policy space is less important. Most importantly, our solution concept, the limiting distribution of the adaptive process, exists in multidimensional spaces, in sharp contrast to game-theoretic solution concepts, i.e., the generic absence of a pure strategy equilibrium and of the core. Moreover, the integrated model, like its component models, is continuous in its parameters. Hence, the closer the voter distribution is to having a generalized median in a multidimensional policy space, the more tightly packed the limiting distribution (Ferejohn, Fiorina, and Packel 1980; Ferejohn, McKelvey, and Packel 1984).

8.3.2 Parties with Policy Objectives

Wittman (1983), Calvert (1985), and other rational choice scholars have investigated the effects of alternative assumptions about the objectives of parties. chapter 3's simple model of party competition

[6] Thus, following the arguments given in chapter 3, we emphatically depart from the "anything can happen" interpretation of the McKelvey-Schofield-Cohen chaos theorems. For a detailed criticism of these interpretations of the so-called chaos theorems, see Diermeier and Krehbiel (2003).

took some small steps in this direction (proposition 3.5), but our integrated model kept to the straight and narrow path, investigating only parties that seek office and desire nothing else. As a modeling strategy, this is a sensible place to start, but it is empirically unsatisfactory. Politicians and party activists spend their entire careers immersed in policy debates. It would be strange indeed if they cared not a whit about which policies get implemented apart from the effects on their careers. Fortunately, it is quite easy to extend the integrated model in this direction.

A somewhat deeper analysis would decompose parties into factions, possibly of pragmatists and ideologues (Clark and Wilson 1961; Eldersveld 1982). Pragmatists would push for platforms that they think would win elections; ideologues would have policy goals. A party would be a coalition of these factions (Cyert and March 1963); its objective function would reflect the relative power of each faction (March 1966). A faction's power would wax and wane with the party's electoral performance and with actors' blame-credit attributions.[7] A central modeling problem here would be to figure out a plausible representation of this process of attribution, i.e., of the actors' causal inferences.

Based on the results of two-element models with fixed platforms, we anticipate higher turnout and more accurate voting when the ideologues dominate. When opportunistic factions dominate in both parties, platforms change more and also will probably be closer together. These features make it harder for voters to vote accurately; they also dampen turnout.

8.3.3 Comparative Analysis

Our work has focused on the paradigmatic case of two-candidate competition under majority rule. Fortunately, the model can easily be extended to study other electoral contexts, such as multiparty competition under plurality rule (the focus of chapter 7). Primary elections, which are important in weak-party systems such as the

[7] The aftermath of the 2008 presidential election provided many examples of factional debate among American conservatives. For example, Jonah Goldberg, an editor at the *National Review*, asked, "Was George W. Bush a conservative president?" ("GOP Looking Glass," *National Review Online*, November 12, 2008, http://article.nationalreview.com/?q=NjIxMTJkOTZmMTY0YTExYzRjNWNhNGMzZDZkY2I2ODg=, accessed January 6, 2009) and argued in response to critics of the Republican party's failure to moderate that "The GOP would simply cease to exist as a viable party without the support of social and religious conservatives." ("Keep Right," *National Review Online*, November 14, 2008, http://article.nationalreview.com/?q=MjRlMDEyZDcyYTNlODliYmRhZWRkNjc2OGE2YjViOWI=, accessed January 6, 2009).

United States, are another natural extension. While many activists participate in these elections, these are often low-information settings. Since party labels don't help voters in primaries, it has been suggested that these voters frequently use simple heuristics such as familiarity (name recognition) (Key 1984; Lau and Redlawsk 2006). Some work will be required in order to represent such heuristics in an extended model. Of course, for primaries where the incumbent is running, adaptive retrospective voting can be presumed.

Other applications include the comparison of electoral rules. This has been a major area of research for rational choice models (e.g., Cox 1987c; Myerson 2002). State-of-the-art rational choice models assume strategic voting by the electorate. This assumption is, of course, consistent with the research program's core premises, but empirical considerations also matter: there is evidence of voter coordination under various electoral rules that cannot be explained by sincere voting (e.g., Cox 1997). Many of the existing models, however, presume that voters reason in ways (e.g., comparing pivot ratios) that are implausibly sophisticated. Thus, these are very promising venues for future applications of adaptive models which combine strategic interaction with more plausible behavioral assumptions.

8.3.4 Institutionalism Reconsidered

The comparative study of electoral rules is but one instance of marrying an institutionalist approach to a behavioral model. Rational choice models have been particularly successful in modeling political institutions, as noted by Diermeier and Krehbiel (2003), who listed the following postulates for an institutional theory (2003, p. 127; emphasis in the original):

1. Define and hold fixed *behavioral postulates* for political actors within the collective choice setting to be studied.
2. Characterize formally the *institutions* in effect (…).
3. Deduce the *behavior* that arises within the institutional setting given the behavioral postulate and characterize the *outcome* that results from the behavior.
4. Compare the derived implications with empirical regularities and *data*.

Noncooperative game theory, which has Nash Equilibrium as its main solution concept, certainly satisfies these postulates. So, however, could other behavioral postulates, as long as they remain constant across different institutional settings.[8] Our aspiration-based approach is one such alternative. It can capture the same institutional richness as normal form games, and it generates clear empirical predictions regarding both outcomes and behavior. Indeed, one can argue that this adaptive approach provides additional methodological advantages as its prediction—i.e., the limiting distribution—is necessarily unique, if theorem 2.3 holds (the adjustment process is Markovian, and so forth). Of course, as we have noted before, there is a subtlety here. Although the solution concept makes a unique prediction, it is probabilistic. The model will usually predict a distribution over outcomes, not a particular outcome.

In short, by replacing (1) the behavioral postulates of rational choice theory with those of bounded rationality theories and (2) the solution concept of Nash equilibrium with the limiting distribution of adaptive behavioral dynamics, we can pursue an institutional research program in the same way as rational choice theory.

In addition to explaining empirical regularities, we can also pose normative questions. For example, we can ask how likely it is that a given electoral rule will lead to the election's Condorcet winner, or how different electoral rules or degrees of voter error affect the ideological congruence between citizens and their government. These and other normative criteria can then be used to compare and evaluate electoral rules.

8.3.5 Correlated Payoff Shocks and Overlapping Generations of Voters

After the stock market crash of 2008, triggered by the collapse of the housing bubble, Roemer's suggestion (2001) to build models with correlated payoff shocks has acquired special force. The reality underlying this recommendation is impossible to deny. And as Roemer pointed out, there are also important theoretical issues to explore here: for example, the benign effects of large electorates are reduced when payoff shocks are positively correlated.

This extension would fruitfully interact with another one: assuming overlapping generations of (finitely lived) voters.[9] This second

[8] To quote Diermeier and Krehbiel (2003, p. 128): "Although institutional analysis can be conducted using any such postulate (or more specific postulates within these families), if the focus is on how institutions affect collective choices, it is crucial that behavioral postulates remain fixed and consistent within and across studies."

[9] Implementing this extension would not be difficult: imagine that children inherit their parents' estimates of the payoffs generated by the two parties plus a random shock, or alternatively, a weighted average of their parents' estimates and the societal average (Achen 1992, p. 201). Aspirations would be inherited in a similar manner.

move has obvious empirical appeal. Moreover, when combined with correlated payoff shocks and plausibly nonstationary adaptive voting rules that adjust less as a person ages, this formulation would yield interesting and testable implications about cohorts with correlated voting tendencies.[10]

8.3.6 Complex Choice Processes

As we suggested in chapter 1, in some situations it is easy for decision makers to compare alternatives directly to each other, as required by classical decision theory. It is also plausible that actors confronting complex choices first use noncompensatory rules, in which options are independently compared only to standards of evaluation; only after the feasible set has been reduced to manageable proportions would alternatives be compared to each other via compensatory decision rules that can deal with trade-offs. More subtly, the latter phase could involve both aspiration-based and classical comparisons.[11] Consider, for example, an ordinary voter in a presidential election with an incumbent in the race. In a primary election simple noncompensatory rules might eliminate certain possibilities: if, e.g., a voter had strong views on abortion, then he or she might not support any candidate who advocated an unpalatable position. In the general election this voter might directly compare the platforms of both candidates, but the incumbent's prior performance, measured against the voter's aspiration level, would also matter: it could predispose the voter to be more, or less, sympathetic to the incumbent's campaign pitch. This hypothesis might generate testable implications. Survey questions could be used to see whether aspiration-related processes are more salient than between-party comparisons during most of an incumbent's time in office and whether the salience of the latter rises in the general election.

8.3.7 Deeper Microprocesses

Although there is substantial evidence for the hypothesis that aspiration-based adaptation is common in human affairs, it must

[10] Absent correlated payoff shocks, one would not expect sharp differences between models with a single generation of infinitely lived agents and those with overlapping generations of finitely lived ones. Indeed, that was one of the main points of the latter models with overlapping generations: they showed that by itself, the assumption of infinitely lived actors was not exacting a high cost regarding the plausibility of conclusions relative to the more realistic but less tractable assumption of finite lives (Cremer 1986).

[11] Other formulations of bounded rationality such as Prospect Theory already represent complex choice processes (Munro and Sugden 2003).

be acknowledged that it is not tightly connected to cognitive or neuropsychological microtheories. This is, of course, an advantage for social scientists, at least in the early phases of a research program. But hopefully scholarly aspirations will rise as the bounded rationality program progresses. If this happens, then we might hanker for electoral models that are more closely tied to basic cognitive processes. For example, we could study how voters categorize political objects (Collins 2008). How do they come to see certain candidates as being similar and others as different? Judgments of similarity are probably fundamental to cognition (Goldstone and Son 2005) in politics as well as in the rest of life. We cannot claim to understand voters at a deep level until we have a good grasp of how they make similarity judgments.

Politicians face difficult problems in campaigns. How should one allocate resources, for example, in a 50-state race? What themes should one pursue? What are good reasons for discarding one theme and taking up another? These are complex questions. However, unlike voters, most politicians are professionals who have repeatedly tackled such problems. Hence a plausible candidate for a psychologically deeper theory would be one that explores how specialists work on hard problems—a branch of the growing field of expertise (Ericsson and Lehmann 1996). If this path were followed, we would expect to see the appearance of micromodels of problem solving in political domains (e.g., Newell and Simon 1972). Because the basic ideas would take a relatively fine-grained view of cognition, formalizations would probably be computational models for the most part.

Overall, we suspect that extensions focusing on alternative institutions (multiparty races, primaries) are pretty easy to do. Those that allow actors to be more sophisticated, such as the hybrid adaptive-Downsian voter represented by proposition 5.7, are not difficult either, especially if the formulation is of a reduced form, e.g., weighted-average decision rules or probabilistic combinations of a naive process and a sophisticated one (e.g., the sophisticated challengers in chapter 3). We believe that the most challenging kind of extension of the present models will involve deeper microprocesses of thought and emotions.

If these predictions are correct, then historical institutionalists should take heart. Adaptive models of elections will be able to handle concerns central to these scholars: such formulations are preadapted to study dynamics and dynamic properties such as path dependence (Page 2006). From this perspective, the unfolding of a particular historical trajectory is the identification of a sample path of an underlying stochastic process. Hence, we look forward to fruitful collaboration between political historians and formal theorists who study politics as stochastic processes generated by adaptively rational agents.

This kind of collaboration will work better if different specialists understand each other's basic ideas. So we hope that basic training in stochastic modeling, especially Markov chains, becomes standard fare in graduate programs in political science. This should include both analytical (e.g., Taylor and Karlin 1998) and computational (e.g., Kollman and Page 2006) methods. As we have argued repeatedly in this book, mathematical analysis and computation complement each other. Unified by formal theories of stochastic processes and substantive ones of bounded rationality, they would constitute a significant addition to our toolkit.

Proofs

IN THIS APPENDIX we follow the convention of using "with positive probability" (wpp) as a shorter way of saying "with strictly positive probability."

Proof of proposition 2.1. Consider the class of states in which the propensity to play the optimal action, α^*, is exactly 1. Call this class C^*.

The following fact about states not in C^* is very useful. Consider any state $s \notin C^*$. If the process is in s, the probability that α^* is not selected is some strictly positive number. If the process visits any state not in C^* infinitely often with probability 1, then there exists an infinite sequence of action choices wherein suboptimal actions are selected with positive probabilities that are bounded away from zero uniformly in t. Given this sequence, the realizations of the action choices are independent events. Hence, the second Borel-Cantelli lemma (Feller 1950, pp. 201–202) can be applied, and it implies that a suboptimal action is selected infinitely often with probability 1.

Therefore, it suffices to show that C^* is not a closed class of states. (A class of states is *closed* if no state outside the class is accessible from any state in the class.) We do this by examining the following cases.

Case 1: none of the states in C^* are recurrent.

If all states in C^* are transient, then it follows immediately that C^* is not closed.

Case 2: some of the states in C^* are recurrent.

In this case it will suffice to show that for any recurrent $s \in C^*$, there exists a state $s' \notin C^*$ which is accessible from s. We do this in two steps.

First, we show that that there is a state in C^*, s^*, which is accessible from all other states in C^* that are recurrent. (This is trivially true if s^* is the only recurrent state in C^*, so we move immediately to examining the other possibility, i.e., s^* is not the only recurrent state in C^*.) For s^*, we nominate the state which puts probability 1.0 on α^* and in which the aspiration level equals $\overline{\pi}(\alpha^*)$, the maximum payoff produced by α^*. Any state in C^* in which the aspiration level exceeds $\overline{\pi}(\alpha^*)$ is transient, by (A2.4). Hence we need to consider only states for which $a < \overline{\pi}(\alpha^*)$. Because in any such state the propensity to try α^* is 1, the agent gets $\overline{\pi}(\alpha^*)$ wpp. So a sequence of such payoff realizations occurs wpp. Such a sequence would, by (A2.4) and the finiteness of the state space, drive the process up to s^*. Hence, since the process visits recurrent states infinitely often with probability 1, we can again use the second Borel-Cantelli lemma to show that starting from any recurrent $s \in C^*$, the process must transition to s^* infinitely often with probability 1.

Second, now consider what can happen if the process has reached s^*. Since the aspiration level in this state is $\overline{\pi}(\alpha^*)$, if the agent gets any payoff less than this, she will be dissatisfied, whence by (A2.2) she will reduce her propensity on α^*. Thus, the process reaches some $s' \notin C^*$. Hence, C^* is not a closed class of states. □

Proof of theorem 2.3. By Theorem 2.2, we need to establish aperiodicity and that all recurrent states communicate. Aperiodicity is ensured by our assumption that agents are inertial with positive probability at every state. Hence, it only remains to show, for every case [i.e., for parts (i)–(iv) of the theorem], that all recurrent states communicate. To show this, the following lemma is very useful.

Lemma A.1. *In any stationary Markov chain with finitely many states, if there is a state which is accessible from all states, then all recurrent states communicate.*

Proof. Call such a state s^*. Since s^* is accessible from all other states, it must be recurrent. Now partition all other states into those which are accessible from s^* (S_1) and those which are not (S_2). By definition, therefore, states in S_1 communicate with s^*. Further, since accessibility is a class property, all the states in S_1 are accessible from all other states. Therefore, the process must eventually get inside the union of S_1 and s^*. But this union must be closed since no state in S_2 is accessible from s^*. Hence the states in S_2 must be transient. Hence all recurrent states communicate with s^*. □

We now return to the proof of the main result. [For parts (i), (ii), and (iv), these proofs apply to payoffs with degenerate distributions for a given vector of actions. Extending them to cover nondegenerate distributions is straightforward.] Parts (i)–(iii) exploit the lemma by identifying a state s^*, which we will also call a *distinguished state*. This, together with the aperiodicity provided by inertia, ensures ergodicity.

(i) and (ii) By assumption there is at least one outcome, say o^*, in which everyone's payoff strictly exceeds their minimal payoff, i.e., $\pi_i(o^*) > \underline{\pi}_i$ for all i. Now consider the following state of the Markov process.

Associated with o^* is a state in the Markov process, s^*, in which all players put maximal propensity on the action corresponding to o^* and have an aspiration equal to the payoff they get from o^*. That is, $s^* := (p^*_{i,t}; a^*_{i,t})_i$ such that for all i and some t: $p^*_{i,t}(\alpha_i(o^*)) = \overline{p}_i$ and $a^*_{i,t} = \pi_i(o^*)$. We nominate s^* as a distinguished state, in the sense of lemma A.1. Hence we must show that given any arbitrary starting state, the process can reach s^* wpp.

The assumption in both parts (i) and (ii) ensures that each agent in every period can play any action wpp, and hence also every outcome can occur wpp in every period. Hence, every finite string of outcomes can occur wpp.

Consider an arbitrary starting state s. Now construct an arbitrarily long but finite string of outcomes in which player 1 gets his minimal payoff $\underline{\pi}_1$. Such a string must occur wpp. For some finite t we must then have $a_{1,t} = \underline{\pi}_1$. To see why such a state must exist, note that because of (A2.3) and (A2.4), $|\underline{\pi}_1 - a_{1,t}|$ is decreasing in t. Equality is ensured by the fact that there are only finitely many aspiration levels and that there exists an aspiration level for each individual payoff level. Call such a state s_1. Now consider a second string of outcomes, commencing at s_1, where player 2 receives $\underline{\pi}_2$ and where player 1 is inert with respect to his aspiration level. Since the event where player 1 is inert occurs wpp and is independent of the updating process of other players, there must exist some t where $a_{2,t} = \underline{\pi}_2$ and (by inertia) $a_{1,t} = \underline{\pi}_1$. Repeat this procedure for all n players until we reach state s_N at some t where for all i, $a_{i,t} = \underline{\pi}_i$.

Next, consider an outcome o^* and state transition where all i are inertial with respect to their aspiration level, i.e., where we continue to have $a_{i,t} = \underline{\pi}_i$ for all i. Such a state must be reached wpp. Then, we have $\pi_i(o^*) > \underline{\pi}_i = a_{i,t}$ for all i. Hence, by (A2.1), $p_{i,t+1}(\alpha_i(o^*)) > p_{i,t}(\alpha_i(o^*))$. Repeat this outcome until for all i, $p_{i,t}(\alpha_i(o^*)) = \overline{p}_i$ while maintaining $a_{i,t} = \underline{\pi}_i$ for all i. Then apply an analogous process for each i's aspiration level. That is, consider a sequence of states with outcome o^* where agents are inert with respect to their propensity; i.e., each agent's propensity is frozen at $p_{i,t}(\alpha_i(o^*)) = \overline{p}_i$. Since for all i, $\pi_i(o^*) > a_{i,t}$, (A2.3) implies that $\underline{\pi}_i < a_{i,t+1} \leqslant \pi_i(o^*)$. By an analogous argument, consider a finite sequence of states until for some t we have $a_{i,t} = \pi_i(o^*)$ for all i. But this is exactly the distinguished state, s^*.

(iii) Here we will show that the state in which everyone puts maximal propensity on some action α_i^* and in which everyone's aspiration is their minimal possible payoff from the outcome produced by $(\alpha_1^*, \alpha_2^*, \ldots, \alpha_n^*)$ is a distinguished state. That is, there exists a profile of actions $(\alpha_1^*, \alpha_2^*, \ldots, \alpha_n^*)$ with $o^* := \Omega(\alpha_1^*, \alpha_2^*, \ldots, \alpha_n^*)$ such that $s^* := (p_{i,t}^*; a_{i,t}^*)_i^t$, where for all i and t we have $p_{i,t}^*(\alpha_i^*(o^*)) = \overline{p}_i$ and $a_{i,t}^* = \underline{\pi}_i(o^*)$.

From any state s in period t_0, consider some agent i and action α_i.

Case (a): Suppose $p_{i,t_0}(\alpha_i) > 0$. Then, construct an arbitrarily long but finite string of states where in each state (1) every agent's propensity is frozen; in particular i's propensity is constant at $p_{i,t_0}(\alpha_i)$ (this occurs wpp by inertia); (2) player i's realized action is α_i [this must occur wpp by (1)]; (3) the realized outcome is some fixed o [this must occur wpp by (1)]; and (4) agent i's realized payoff is minimal, i.e., $\underline{\pi}_i(o)$ (this occurs wpp given random payoffs). Such a string must occur wpp. For some finite t_1 we then must have $a_{i,t_1} = \underline{\pi}_i(o)$. Then construct a second string of states with (1) every agent j's (including i's) aspiration level frozen at $a_{j,t_1}(\alpha_i)$ (again this occurs wpp by inertia); (2) agent i's realized payoff is maximal, i.e., $\overline{\pi}_i(o)$; since $\overline{\pi}_i(o) > a_{i,t} = \underline{\pi}_i(o)$ for all $t > t_1$, $p_{i,t}(\alpha_i)$ is strictly increasing until $\overline{p}_{i,t}(\alpha_i)$ [by (A2.4)]; (3) the realized outcome is some fixed o [this must occur wpp by (2)]; and (4) player i's realized action is α_i [this must occur wpp by (2)]. Thus, at some t_2 we must have $p_{i,t_2}(\alpha_i(o)) = \overline{p}_i$ and $a_{i,t_2} = \underline{\pi}_i(o)$. These are the desired α_i and o^*.

Case (b): Suppose instead that $p_{i,t_0}(\alpha_i) = 0$. Then for some other action, α_i', we must have $p_{i,t_0}(\alpha_i') > 0$. Now construct an arbitrarily long but finite string of states where in each state (1) every agent j's (including i's) propensity is frozen; in particular i's propensity is frozen at $p_{i,t_0}(\alpha_i')$ (this occurs wpp by inertia); (2) player i's realized action is α_i' [this must occur wpp by (1)]; (3) the realized outcome is some fixed o' [this must occur wpp by (1)]; and (4) agent i's realized payoff is maximal, i.e., $\overline{\pi}_i(o')$ (this occurs wpp given random payoffs). Such a string must occur wpp. For some finite t_1 we then must have $a_{i,t_1} = \overline{\pi}_i(o')$. Now consider a state at $t_1 + 1$ where (1)–(3) hold but where agent i's realized payoff is minimal, i.e., $\underline{\pi}_i(o')$. But since $\underline{\pi}_i(o') < a_{i,t_1} = \overline{\pi}_i(o')$, agent i is dissatisfied. Hence, (A2.3) implies that wpp i reaches a propensity vector in which $p_{i,t_2+2}(\alpha_i) > 0$. But then we are back at case (a).

Hence in both cases there must be some t where $p_{i,t}(\alpha_i(o)) = \overline{p}_i$ and $a_{i,t_2} = \underline{\pi}_i(o)$. But because this holds for all i and because each i's aspiration and propensity can be frozen by inertia, we must eventually reach s^*.

(iv) By assumption every player can tremble wpp to any neighboring state. Hence, all states communicate. Since we also have aperiodicity (via inertia), ergodicity follows immediately. □

Proof of proposition 2.3. First observe that because there is a one-to-one correspondence between p values and q values and there are finitely many of the former, there must also be finitely many of the latter. Hence, we are again examining a stationary Markov chain with finitely many states. Therefore, it again suffices to consider C^*, the class of states in which $p(\alpha^*)$ is 1, where α^* denotes the optimal action.

As in the proof of proposition 2.1, it suffices to show that C^* is not closed. For this, the corresponding part of the proof of proposition 2.1 can be used without modification. □

Proof of proposition 4.2. Given that $b = 0$, a citizen's payoff does not depend on which party wins the election. Instead, it is based only on whether a citizen turns out or shirks. Hence, we have n separate choice problems that can be analyzed in isolation. We study an arbitrary citizen, i.

It is important to establish that the process is well-behaved (ergodic). The ABAR is Markovian and stationary, and it has finitely propensity values; this, together with an exogenous aspiration level, means that it is a finite Markov chain. Further, the process exhibits inertia. Finally, it is given that both arms fail wpp. Hence, it is easy to see that the stochastic process satisfies the hypotheses of a simple extension of theorem 2.3 (i.e., one assuming exogenously fixed aspirations and failure on every action wpp); hence, it is ergodic.

The rest of the proof is in two steps.

(1) Suppose that $c = 0$. In this case the payoff distributions for voting and shirking are identical. Given this symmetry, it follows that in the limit citizen i turns out with an expected probability of $\frac{1}{2}$. We will prove this by showing that if $c = 0$, then the (unique) limiting probability distribution over the action propensities is symmetric about $\frac{1}{2}$. First, however, we show that the state space (the action propensities) is itself symmetric about $\frac{1}{2}$ under conditions satisfied by proposition 4.2.

Lemma A.2. *Consider an agent playing a two-armed bandit. Payoffs are stationary, the aspiration level is exogenously fixed, and* $\Pr(a > \max\{\underline{\pi_L}, \underline{\pi_R}\}) > 0$. *He uses a stationary Markovian ABAR that is action-invariant; he is inertial regarding propensity adjustment wpp. If there are finitely many propensity values, then the set of nontransient propensities is symmetrically distributed about* $\frac{1}{2}$.

Proof. First we show that the set of nontransient propensities must include both 0 and 1. Consider any interior propensity p. (Recall that propensities are defined as the probability of choosing L in the two-armed bandit.) Since p is in $(0, 1)$, the agent must be able to choose either L or R wpp. Let him choose R. Since it is given that $\Pr(a > \underline{\pi}_R) > 0$, he can be disappointed by the payoff generated by R, whence by (A2.2) his propensity to select R must fall, so the propensity to choose L rises. Since there are finitely many propensity values and (A2.2) holds, this process can be repeated until his propensity to choose R (L) reaches 0 (1). The same argument holds for reaching a propensity of 0 on L.

Now consider the set of propensities that are descendants of 0 and 1, i.e., can be reached in one step wpp. Recalling that we consider only deterministic ABARs here, there is only one new propensity value that can be reached from an L propensity of zero: that produced by negative feedback (NF) on R. [Positive feedback on R just reproduces a propensity of 1 on R, and L cannot be used when $p(L) = 0$.] Let p_1 denote the (unique) descendant of 0, given NF on R. If the current propensity to use L is 1, then by action invariance its descendant (given NF on L) must equal $1 - p_1$.

Now we can repeat this argument for p_1 and $1 - p_1$. The only new consideration is that these state values can have more descendants than can 0 or 1: they can have (at most) four descendants. But the logic of the preceding argument, which turns on action invariance, holds exactly as before.

We then repeat this argument for any descendants of p_1 and $1 - p_1$ that are new, i.e., not in the set $\{0, 1, p_1, 1 - p_1\}$. Since the set of propensity values is finite, this procedure must terminate. Hence we have shown by construction that the set of nontransient propensity values must be symmetric about $\frac{1}{2}$. □

With this lemma in hand, we need only to show that the probability distribution over the symmetric set of nontransient propensity values is itself symmetric. To see why this must be so, consider the following thought experiment.

In this thought experiment, each arm activates a corresponding random device (RD), which actually does the work of generating payoffs. In the standard bandit problem, arm L always activates RD1 and arm R always activates RD2. But here we introduce a twist: with probability $q \in [0, 1]$ L activates RD1, as before, but with probability $1 - q$ it triggers RD2, and the parallel relation holds for R and RD2.

All the agent observes, however, are arms and payoffs. He doesn't observe the random devices nor does he have any information about them. As far as he knows, the arms themselves generate realized payoffs directly.

Of course, for $b > 0$, the value of q will affect the agent's payoffs and, hence, the trajectory of his actions and their underlying propensities. In our setting, however, $b = 0$, so the two random devices generate identically distributed payoffs when $c = 0$. Hence, q has no effect whatsoever on the agent's payoffs; hence, it cannot affect his actions or propensities. But this means that he reaches the same limiting distribution (over actions) no matter what q is. In particular, that distribution is the same for $q = 1$ as for $q = 0$. And since $q = 0$ implies that he really is taking the *opposite* action—he is unwittingly selecting RD2, not RD1—the probability distribution over the action propensities must be symmetric, whence $E[p(L)] = E[p(R)] = \frac{1}{2}$.

(2) Now consider $c > 0$ but small. Since i's payoff shock, ϵ_i, has a continuous density, so does i's payoff, $\epsilon_i - c$. Hence, $\Pr(a_i > \epsilon_i - c) - \Pr(a_i > \epsilon_i)$ must be small for small c; i.e., the difference gets arbitrarily close to zero as c falls to zero. Because the probability of dissatisfaction varies continuously with c, the transition probabilities vary continuously in c. Further, because the limiting probabilities vary continuously in the transition probabilities, the former vary continuously in c. Hence, for c small but positive the limiting probabilities are close to what they are when c is exactly zero. Finally, because the expected probability of turning out is a continuous function of the limiting probabilities over the propensities to turn out, it follows that the expected probability of turning out must be close to $\frac{1}{2}$ when c is sufficiently close to zero. □

Proof of proposition 5.1. We prove a more general version of proposition 5.1. The version in chapter 5 can be recovered by assuming only two possible payoffs, l and h, and replacing $\underline{\pi}$ with l and $\overline{\pi}$ with h. For the following proposition, assume that the voter's payoff set, $\{\underline{\pi}, \ldots, \overline{\pi}\}$, is a subset of her feasible aspiration set, A_i. Specifically, A_i is a compact set, $[\underline{a}_i, \overline{a}_i]$, with $\underline{a}_i \leqslant \underline{\pi}_i$ and $\overline{a}_i \geqslant \overline{\pi}_i$. □

The more general proposition is as follows.

Proposition A.1. *Suppose that (A5.1) holds.*

(i) *(a) If $a_{t'} \in (\underline{\pi}, \overline{\pi})$, then with probability* 1 *$a_t \in (\underline{\pi}, \overline{\pi})$ for all $t > t'$. (b) If in addition payoffs are stochastic, then* $\Pr(\lim_{t\to\infty} a_t = \underline{\pi}) = \Pr(\lim_{t\to\infty} a_t = \overline{\pi}) = 0$.

(ii) *(a) If either $a_0 < \underline{\pi}$ or $a_0 > \overline{\pi}$, then a_t moves monotonically toward $[\underline{\pi}, \overline{\pi}]$ and is absorbed into that interval with probability* 1 *as $t \to \infty$. (b) If in addition payoffs are stochastic, then a_t is absorbed into $(\underline{\pi}, \overline{\pi})$.*

Proof. (i) (a) This proof is by induction. Suppose that $a_t \in (\underline{\pi}, \overline{\pi})$. The payoff must be in $\{\underline{\pi}, \ldots, \overline{\pi}\}$. By part (1) of (A5.1), if $\pi_t > a_t$, then a_{t+1} must be in (a_t, π_t), whence it is in $(a_t, \overline{\pi})$. If $\pi_t = a_t$, then a_{t+1} must equal a_t. And if $\pi_t < a_t$, then (A5.1) implies that a_{t+1} must be in $(\pi_t, a_t) \subseteq (\underline{\pi}, a_t)$. Hence, $a_t \in (\underline{\pi}, \overline{\pi}) \Rightarrow a_{t+1} \in (\underline{\pi}, \overline{\pi})$, so by induction $a_{t'}$ is in that open interval for all $t' > t$. Finally, it is given that the hypothesis of the induction holds at t.

(b) Consider $\underline{\pi}$ as a possible limit, given stochastic payoffs. Given that $a_{t'} \in (\underline{\pi}, \overline{\pi})$ for all $t' > t$, (A5.1) implies that $a_t \to \underline{\pi}$ in the limit only if there is an infinite consecutive run of $\underline{\pi}$ as the payoff. But as we assume here that payoffs are stochastic, and since the environment is stationary, a run of k straight $\underline{\pi}$ payoffs occurs with probability p^k, for some p in $(0, 1)$, and that probability goes to zero as $k \to \infty$. Hence, the probability that $\underline{\pi}$ is the limit is zero. The same logic applies to $\overline{\pi}$.

(ii) (a) We analyze the case of $a_0 < \underline{\pi}$; the proof for $a_0 > \overline{\pi}$ parallels it exactly. That a_t's movement toward $[\underline{\pi}, \overline{\pi}]$ is monotonic is easily shown by induction: if $a_t < \underline{\pi}$, then (A5.1) implies immediately that $a_t < a_{t+1}$. Therefore, for all $a_t < \underline{\pi}$, the a_t's form a strictly increasing sequence.

The proof for a_t's absorption into $[\underline{\pi}, \overline{\pi}]$ is based on two facts. First, consider the right boundary. It is easily shown, via the inductive reasoning of (i)(a)'s proof, that if $a_0 < \overline{\pi}$, then $a_t < \overline{\pi}$ for all $t > 0$. Second, consider the left boundary. Take the deterministic sequence, $a_0, a_0 + \epsilon(\underline{\pi} - a_0), \ldots$, which, as the ordinary geometric series, converges to $\underline{\pi}$. Further, given that (A5.1) requires that aspirations move at least a fraction ϵ of the way to the realized payoff and given that $\underline{\pi}$ is the smallest payoff the agent can get, that deterministic sequence is a lower bound, at every date, for the real a_t's. Hence, since $a_t < \overline{\pi}$ for all t and since the sequence of a_t's is bounded below by a sequence that converges with probability 1 to $\underline{\pi}$, it follows that a_t goes into $[\underline{\pi}, \overline{\pi}]$ with probability 1 as $t \to \infty$.

(b) Now suppose that payoffs are stochastic. Let $x < \underline{\pi}$ be such that if $a_t \in (x, \underline{\pi}]$, then for any $\pi_t > \underline{\pi}$, $a_{t+1} > \underline{\pi}$. [Such an x must exist because (A5.1) requires that aspirations move at least $\epsilon > 0$ percent of the way to the realized payoff.] Since the deterministic sequence of $a_0, a_0 + \epsilon(\underline{\pi} - a_0), \ldots$ converges to $\underline{\pi}$, a_t must exceed x in finitely many periods with probability 1. Since this sequence is a lower bound for the a_t's, it follows that $a_t > x$ in finitely many periods with probability 1. Hence, a_t will either be in $(x, \underline{\pi}]$ or it will exceed $\underline{\pi}$ and so must be in $(\underline{\pi}, \overline{\pi})$. If the latter, then by part (i) we are done, since then it will stay in $(\underline{\pi}, \overline{\pi})$ thereafter, not even converging to the boundary states in the limit.

If the former, i.e., $a_t \in (x, \overline{\pi}]$, then a_t will stay there forever if and only if there is an infinite run of $\underline{\pi}$'s without interruption. But that occurs with probability zero as $t \to \infty$, i.e., the probability that the agent gets at least one $\pi_t > \underline{\pi}$ goes to 1 as $t \to \infty$. Then, in that one jump a_t is in the open interval $(\underline{\pi}, \overline{\pi})$, whence part (i) again takes over. □

Proof of remark 5.2. For $n = 1$, the probability of victory for D in period t is p_{t-1}. Assume without loss of generality that $h_t^D > h_t^R$. If $p_{t-1} < 1$, then there is a nonzero probability that R wins in period t, and so voting is not optimal since the voter would prefer D. If $p_{t-1} = 1$, by (A5.2), (A5.3), and the assumption that $\max\{h_t^D, h_t^R\} < 1$, there is a nonzero probability that $p_t < 1$, and so there is a nonzero probability that R wins in period $t + 1$, proving the claim. □

Proof of remark 5.4. Part (i):[1] In period zero the start is unbiased, so the electoral winner in period 1 is equally likely to be a D or an R. Assume without loss of generality that it is a D; the proof for an R goes through identically. Consider a fictional infinite population with a constant $h_*^D = \frac{1}{2} + \epsilon$, where $\epsilon > 0$ can be arbitrarily small. By (A5.2) and (A5.3), since $h_*^D > \frac{1}{2}$ in our infinite population, h_*^D individuals find their propensities to vote for D increased, and $1 - h_*^D$ find theirs decreased at the end of period 1. As a result, the expected value of the population's propensity distribution is greater than $\frac{1}{2}$ at the end of the period. Since the population is infinite, D must win in period 2. But now since we have the same h_*^D in each period, at the end of period 2 the distribution of propensities in this fictional population must trivially first-order stochastically dominate (FOSD) that at the end of period 1 by proposition 5.2. By the law of total probability this implies that the expected value of the propensity is again more than $\frac{1}{2}$, and D must win again. This is true in every period by induction. Since ϵ can be arbitrarily small, we can always choose one small enough so that $h_t^D > h_*^D$ for all t, as long as $h_t^D > \frac{1}{2}$ remains true as t approaches infinity, which implies by proposition 5.2 that the population distribution of propensities at time t FOSDs the one that would have been observed in the fictional population. This yields our result.

(ii) If D wins first, then the result follows from part (i). If R wins first, then since $h_t^R < \frac{1}{2}$ and the population is infinite, by the logic of the

[1] The relations in parts (i) and (ii) of this fact must hold for the infimum of voters' interests as well: e.g., $\inf(h_t^D) > \frac{1}{2}$.

proof of part (i), the expected value of the population's propensity distribution is less than $\frac{1}{2}$ at the end of period 1, so that D wins in the beginning of period 2. The result then follows from part (i).

(iii) All we need to show here is that whenever the average propensity of the population goes above $\frac{1}{2}$ when a D is the incumbent (or below $\frac{1}{2}$ when an R is the incumbent), it eventually goes below (or above) $\frac{1}{2}$ again. Consider without loss of generality a D incumbent and separate the population at any time into two groups: those with $p_{i,t} = 0$ and those with $p_{i,t} > 0$. The latter group must have its average propensity decrease in every period in which D is in office by equal-adjustment, (A5.3), and stationarity, and this average propensity must pass below 0.5 in finite time because of (A5.3) and stationarity. At the same time, the former group can't have its average propensity increase past 0.5 in any period in which D is in office by equal adjustment. The average of these two groups thus must eventually decrease to at least 0.5, implying that D will eventually lose with probability 1. □

APPENDIX B

The Computational Model

B.1 Overview

HERE WE DESCRIBE the computational model used to derive most results in this book.[1] The presentation here is sparse and focuses on that necessary to use the model; a more complete description can be found in chapter 6. Two variants of the model are provided, each available at http://press.princeton.edu/titles/9352.html. The graphical model described first is best used to provide a visualization of, and to collect data on, a series of elections in which all model parameters are kept fixed. This sequence of elections is called a *run* or a *history*. The batch model described in section B.2 serves to collect data across runs, allowing one to observe variation in outcomes arising from variation in parameters. It has no graphical component.

Both model variants are coded in JAVA, an object-oriented language that lends itself to computational models of multiple types of actors and institutional structures. In our case, the types of actors are voters and parties, and the institutional structure is a plurality-rule election that decides which party will hold office during each electoral period. Plurality-rule elections are implemented exactly as one would expect: the party with the most votes wins, with ties broken by a fair die. The behavior of voters and parties is more complex, and as much as possible we hew closely to the analytical framework developed in chapters 3–5.

Thus, parties attempt to win elections by selecting a policy platform (in either one or two dimensions). Winners satisfice, keeping the same platform as before, while losers search for new policies. We offer several options for this search, described in more detail below.

Voters make two independent decisions in every period: whether or not to turn out, and for whom to vote if they do participate. Both decisions are based on endogenously changing aspirations. Whenever payoffs (described in detail below) exceed aspirations, voters become more likely to turn out and to vote for the incumbent. Aspirations rise after such an event. When aspirations exceed payoffs, voters become less likely to turn out and to vote for the incumbent; in

[1] See http://press.princeton.edu/titles/9352.html for links to simulation results from chapter 3 derived from a specialized computational model.

addition, their aspirations fall. We provide different rates of adjustment of propensities for voting and participating, and of aspiration levels.

The same parameters are variable in both versions of the computational model. Section B.2 discusses each in detail, listing all possible settings of each parameter. As noted earlier in the book, there are many more settings available than we have analyzed, and we hope this tool proves useful as you explore new paths.

B.2 Graphical Model

This variant of the model has a graphical interface that allows one to set parameters directly on the screen and then watch the simulated electoral system unfold. Various electoral outcomes—e.g., the incumbent's party and platform, voters' propensity and aspiration distributions, and the location of voters who turned out and/or voted for the incumbent—are displayed on screen as the model runs in a graphical format. Controls allow the user to start, stop, and pause each run. A run's output is written to a new file after the run is stopped. The model shares its core code with the batch version described below but uses several RePAST 3 packages for graphical output and for data collection and output.[2]

A word of caution. To cut down on parameters, some act in different ways depending on which combination of settings is chosen. The descriptions of the parameters below provide all the necessary detail and will serve as a good reference while using the program. A standalone, up-to-date version of this section of the appendix appears on the same site as the program itself for convenience.

B.2.1 Framework of the Program

Order of Events

1. Election occurs (voter choice and turnout decisions);
2. Payoffs are given;
3. Propensities are adjusted;
4. Aspirations are adjusted;
5. Losing party searches;
6. Data for that period are taken; collection begins at period 1.

---

[2] A helpful tutorial on using the RePAST 3 interface can be found at: http://repast.sourceforge.net/repast_3/tutorials.html.

GENERAL MODEL PARAMETERS

Note: unchecking "In Alpha Order" under the RePAST actions tab will order parameters by category rather than alphabetically.

> *ExtraHist*: Check this box to show histograms of aspirations and payoffs. Default is unchecked.
>
> *Inertia*: The probability that all updating decisions (aspiration, propensity, and turnout decision adjustment, as well as party search) do not occur that period, regardless of payoff outcome. Checked independently at each opportunity for updating.
>
> *ElectionsEnd*: If set to greater than zero, ends the run at this election number. Default is zero (user controlled).

VOTER-SPECIFIC PARAMETERS

N: The number of voters. Default is 1,000.

bliss1mean, bliss1stdev, bliss2mean, bliss2stdev: Used in the following ideal point distributions. Individual voters receive 2-D bliss points $(bliss_1, bliss_2)$.

VoterDistribution: A vector containing different options for the initial distribution of voters' ideal points. In all cases, extra voters that don't fit are placed in the center at $(0, 0)$. Note that payoffs derive only from these; ideal points need not be known to voters. At present, the options are:

- "Evenly placed in 1-D": Range of

$$[-3 * bliss1stdev, 3 * bliss1stdev]$$

  is populated by N evenly spaced voters.

- "Evenly placed in 2-D": Area of

$$[-3 * bliss1stdev, 3 * bliss1stdev] \times [-3 * bliss2stdev, 3 * bliss2stdev]$$

  is populated by N evenly spaced voters.

- "Uniform in 1-D": N voters are randomly distributed according to a uniform distribution over

$$[-3 * bliss1stdev + bliss1mean, 3 * bliss1stdev + bliss1mean].$$

- "Uniform in 2-D": N voters are randomly distributed according to a uniform distribution over

$$[-3 * bliss1stdev + bliss1mean, 3 * bliss1stdev + bliss1mean] \times [-3 * bliss2stdev + bliss2mean, 3 * bliss2stdev + bliss2mean].$$

- "Normal in 1-D, One Maximum": N voters are normally distributed with mean *bliss1mean* and standard deviation *bliss-1stdev*.
- "Normal in 2-D, One Maximum": N voters are normally distributed in 2-D with *bliss1mean*, *bliss1stdev*, *bliss2mean*, and *bliss2stdev*.
- "Normal, 5 Maxima": N voters are split up into five equal groups in two dimensions, each normally distributed with means $(-1,-1)$, $(-1,1)$, $(1,-1)$, $(1,1)$, and $(0,0)$, and standard deviations given by *bliss1stdev* in the x-direction and *bliss2stdev* in the y-direction.
- "Bimodal in 1-D": Half the voters are at $(-1,0)$, the other half are at $(1,0)$.
- "Left, Middle, Right in 1-D": Skewed distribution; *bliss1mean* fraction of the voters are located at (*bliss2stdev*, 0), *bliss2mean* fraction of the voters at $(0,0)$, and the rest at (*bliss1stdev*, 0).
- "Triangle": Skewed distribution in 2-D; *bliss1mean* fraction of the voters are located at $(0,-1)$, *bliss2mean* fraction of the voters at (0, *bliss2stdev*), and the rest at (*bliss1stdev*, 0).

Lambda: Rate of adjustment for both vote and turnout propensities; higher values correspond to faster adjustment to previous successes or failures.

StrategyAdjustment: A vector containing different options for how voters attribute their payoff signals. "Update on Incumbent Performance Only" follows the retrospective (or economic) voting model in chapter 5, in which voters know who the incumbent was and attribute their payoffs to him or her. "Update on Incumbent Performance and Last Vote" implies that they also attribute their payoffs to their own last vote and adjust propensities to vote for both the incumbent and for the party for which they voted last, assuming they are different. "Update on Last Vote Only" implies that all voters attribute payoffs only to their own vote, and they do not adjust based on who is the incumbent. The last option makes sense only in multiparty competition and should not be used in two-party competition. As an example, assume that there are parties A, B, and C and that a voter voted for party B in the previous election. Further assume that the voter was satisfied with party A's performance as the incumbent. A voter can increase her likelihood to vote for party A (first option), A and B (second option), or B (third option). The default is option 1.

VoterUtility: A vector containing different options for the utility functions of voters. The setting "Quadratic Loss" uses a quadratic loss function for the portion of the voter's utility function corresponding to the divergence of the incumbent's policy (Inc_1, Inc_2) from the voter's ideal point:

$$-0.5((Inc_1 - bliss_1)^2 + (Inc_2 - bliss_2)^2).$$

"Piecewise Linear (Abs Value) Loss" uses absolute values rather than squared terms:

$$-0.5(|Inc_1 - bliss_1| + |Inc_2 - bliss_2|).$$

The default is quadratic loss.

PropensityInitDist: A vector containing different options for the way the vote propensities are initially distributed across the population. Accompanying parameters are *Propinitmean* and *Propinitstdev*. To get a neutral start, choose the first option and set *Propinitmean* to 0.5 and *Propinitstdev* to 0.

- "Distributed Normally with given Parameters": For two-party competition, each voter's propensity to vote for a Democrat is drawn from a normal distribution with stated parameters. In multiparty competition, propensities for all parties are drawn from independent normal distributions with the same parameters, and then the vector of propensities is normalized to 1.
- "Distributed Uniformly": Same as in the previous description, save all propensities are drawn from a uniform distribution on [0, 1].
- "All Republican (party 0)": Propensities to vote for R/party 0 are set to 1 for all voters, and propensities to vote for all other parties are set to 0.
- "All Democratic (party 1)": Propensities to vote for D/party 1 are set to 1 for all voters, and propensities to vote for all other parties are set to 0.

PropensityAdjustment: A vector containing different options for the way vote propensities are adjusted. Some options obviate other program settings, rendering them inoperable. For all but the first option, voters vote stochastically via their propensity to vote for a particular party. All ties are decided via a fair die with a number of sides equal to the number of parties tied. If the model is in the two-party competition regime, only the propensity to vote Democratic is saved and updated. (The propensity to vote Republican is kept at 1 minus this number.) Under more than two parties, each voter maintains a propensity to vote for each party; these add up to 1. The propensity corresponding to the incumbent (and/or possibly to the party for whom the voter last voted as well; see *StrategyAdjustment* above) is updated as under two-party competition. The vector of propensities is then renormalized to 1. The options are as follows.

- "No Adjustment—Downsian Voters": Propensities are not adjusted, and no data on them are taken. Voters vote deterministically according to whichever party is closer; any payoffs they receive are ignored, as are aspirations and initial vote propensities. Ties for closeness are broken by a fair die.
- "Symmetric Bush-Mosteller (lambda)":

  $$propensity_{t+1} = (1 - lambda) * propensity_t + lambda$$

  if the voter experienced a success, and

  $$propensity_{t+1} = (1 - lambda) * propensity_t$$

  if the voter experienced a failure.
- "Symmetric Equal Adjustment (lambda)":

  $$propensity_{t+1} = \min(propensity_t + lambda, 1)$$

  if the voter experienced a success, and

  $$propensity_{t+1} = \max(propensity_t - lambda, 0)$$

  if the voter experienced a failure.
- "No Adjustment—Stick with Initial Values": Propensities remain at their initial values forever, but, unlike Downsian voting, these propensities are used in determining the winner of the election.

TurnoutInitDist: A vector containing different options for the way the propensities are initially distributed across the population. Accompanying parameters are *Turninitmean* and *Turninitstdev*. To get equal chances of voting and not voting at the start, choose the first option and set *Turninitmean* to 0.5 and *Turninitstdev* to 0. Some of these options, as well as some of the output measures below, make use of a measure of the "extremism" of voters. This measure is the normalized distance of the voter's bliss point from the mean of the voter distribution. For bounded voter distributions, this distance is normalized to lie in [0, 1] by dividing by the maximum distance attainable in the distribution from the mean of the distribution. For unbounded voter distributions, the maximum distance used in normalization is that corresponding to a bliss point three standard deviations away from the mean in all dimensions. More distant bliss points are set to the maximum distance measure, 1. Values of this measure lying closer to 1 represent voters with more extreme underlying interests, while values closer to 0 represent more moderate voters.

- "Distributed Normally with Given Parameters": The chance of turning out is drawn from a normal distribution with stated parameters.
- "Distributed Uniformly": Same as in the previous description but drawn from a uniform distribution on [0, 1].
- "Everyone Votes": All probabilities of voting are set to 1.
- "No One Votes": All probabilities of voting are set to 0.
- "Extremists Vote More": The chance of voting is set equal to the measure of extremism. Thus, the more extreme the voter's interests, the more she likely begins to turn out.
- "Moderates Vote More": The chance of voting is set equal to 1 minus the measure of extremism. Thus, the more moderate the voter's interests, the more she likely begins to turn out.

TurnoutAdjustment: A vector containing different options for the way the likelihood of turning out is adjusted. Some options obviate other program settings, rendering them inoperable. For all but the first option, voters turn out stochastically via their turnout propensities. The options are as follows (the last three are described above).

- "Full Turnout": Likelihoods of voting do not vary, and no data are taken on them. Everyone votes in every election.
- "Symmetric Bush-Mosteller (*lambda*)"
- "Symmetric Equal Adjustment (*lambda*)"
- "No Adjustment—Stick with Initial Values"

votingCost: The cost incurred for choosing to turn out.

Nu: The rate of aspiration adjustment; higher rates indicate faster adjustment.

shockUniform: When checked, indicates that the shock variable is distributed uniformly in the range $[-3 * shockstdev + shockmean, 3 * shockstdev + shockmean]$. When unchecked (the default) it is distributed normally according to mean *shockmean* and standard deviation *shockstdev*.

AspirationsInitDist: A vector containing different options for the way voters' aspirations are initially distributed across the population. Accompanying parameters are *Aspinitmean* and *Aspinitstdev*. Voters' aspirations are adjusted from these initial values endogenously in response to successes (payoffs exceeding aspirations) and failures (payoffs not meeting aspirations). Aspirations adjust via Cyert and March (1963):

$$aspiration_{t+1} = (1 - nu) * aspiration_t + nu * payoff_t.$$

Payoffs are given by the sum of a spatial payoff, a shock term, and a cost of voting. See the parameters *VoterUtility*, *shockUniform*, and *votingCost* for details of each element in the sum. Some of the options of the initial aspiration distribution make use of the same extremism measure as above.

- "Default (Near Center of Payoff Dist)": Aspirations are set at the average payoff arising from each party in two-party competition, and at that arising from the mean of the party distribution in multiparty competition. Specifically, initial aspirations are the sum of *shockmean*, $-votingCost/2$ if turnout propensities are adjusted, and a spatial loss term dependent on other model choices. For two-party competition and quadratic loss (other spatial loss choices are similar), this term averages the quadratic loss under the bliss points of each party:

  $$-0.25 * [(Dpos_1 - bliss_1)^2 + (Dpos_2 - bliss_2)^2 + (Rpos_1 - bliss_1)^2 + (Rpos_2 - bliss_2)^2].$$

  For citizen candidates and the triangle distribution this term is the loss from the true mean of the voter/party distribution:

  $$-0.5 * [(truebliss1mean - bliss_1)^2 + (truebliss2mean - bliss_2)^2].$$

  (The true mean $(truebliss1mean, truebliss2mean)$ is computed from the voter distribution parameters when these parameters don't mirror the actual mean of the distribution, as in the triangle distribution.) For other cases, this term is the loss from the mean of the party distribution:

  $$-0.5 * [(partyPosition0a - bliss_1)^2 + (partyPosition1a - bliss_2)^2].$$

- "Distributed Normally with Given Parameters": The chance of voting is drawn from a normal distribution with stated parameters.
- "Distributed Uniformly": Same as in the previous description but drawn from a uniform distribution on

  $$[-3 * aspinitstdev + aspinitmean, 3 * aspinitstdev + aspinitmean].$$

- "Very High (100)": All aspirations are set to 100.
- "Very Low (−100)": All aspirations are set to −100.
- "Extremists Higher": Aspirations range from $-3 * aspinitstdev + aspinitmean$ to $3 * aspinitstdev + aspinitmean$, with increasingly extreme voters receiving increasingly high initial aspirations.
- "Moderates Higher": Aspirations range from $-3 * aspinitstdev + aspinitmean$ to $3 * aspinitstdev + aspinitmean$, with increasingly moderate voters receiving increasingly high initial aspirations.

PARTY-SPECIFIC PARAMETERS

NumParties: The number of parties present. Not used if the *PartyDistribution* vector described below is set to "Two-Party Competition."

PartyPosition0a, PartyPosition0b, PartyPosition1a, PartyPosition1b: These parameterize the distribution of parties. Under "Two-Party Competition" they correspond to the x- and y-coordinates of the initial policies of the R and D parties, respectively. Under multiparty competition they are distributional parameters, as detailed below. Note that whenever voters are set to a one-dimensional distribution, the program overrides settings in the second dimension and sets parties to be one-dimensional as well.

PartyDistribution: A vector containing different options for the way parties' initial policy platforms are distributed. Some options obviate other program settings, rendering them inoperable. The options are as follows:

- "Two-Party Competition": There are always two parties, and *NumParties* is ignored. *PartyPosition0a* and *PartyPosition0b* correspond to the Republican's bliss points in the x- and y-directions, respectively, and similarly for *PartyPosition1a* and *PartyPosition1b* and the Democrats. This is the default choice.
- "Evenly Placed in 1-D": Range of $[-3 * PartyPosition0b, 3 * PartyPosition0b]$ is populated by *NumParties* evenly spaced parties.

- "Evenly Placed in 2-D": Area of

$$[-3 * \mathit{PartyPosition0b}, 3 * \mathit{PartyPosition0b}] \times [-3 * \mathit{PartyPosition1b}, 3 * \mathit{PartyPosition1b}]$$

  is populated by *NumParties* evenly spaced parties. Extra parties that don't fit are placed in the center at $(0, 0)$.
- "Uniform in 1-D": *NumParties* parties are uniformly distributed over

$$[-3 * \mathit{PartyPosition0b} + \mathit{PartyPosition0a}, 3 * \mathit{PartyPosition0b} + \mathit{PartyPosition0a}].$$

- "Uniform in 2-D": *NumParties* parties are uniformly distributed over

$$[-3 * \mathit{PartyPosition0b} + \mathit{PartyPosition0a}, 3 * \mathit{PartyPosition0b} + \mathit{PartyPosition0a}] \times [-3 * \mathit{PartyPosition1b} + \mathit{PartyPosition1a}, 3 * \mathit{PartyPosition1b} + \mathit{PartyPosition1a}].$$

- "Normal in 1-D, One Maximum": *NumParties* parties are normally distributed with mean *PartyPosition0a* and standard deviation *PartyPosition0b*.
- "Normal in 2-D, One Maximum": *NumParties* parties are normally distributed in 2-D with mean *PartyPosition0a* and standard deviation *PartyPosition0b* in the x-dimension, and mean *PartyPosition1a* and standard deviation *PartyPosition1b* in the y-dimension.
- "Citizen Candidates": *NumParties* parties have their bliss points chosen to match random citizens' ideal points.
- "Nader, Gore, Bush": Three parties are set up, a far left one at $(-2, -2)$, a left one at $(-1, -1)$, and a right one at $(1, 1)$. All distributional parameters are ignored.
- "Triangle": Three parties are placed at $(0, -1)$, $(0, \mathit{bliss2stdev})$, and $(\mathit{bliss1stdev}, 0)$. Designed for use with the "triangle" voter distribution.

PartySearchMean1, PartySearchStdev1, PartySearchMean2, PartySearchStdev2: Parameters that affect the method of search, described in the party search vector below.

PartySophisticationLevel: This parameter dictates how "sophisticated" a party is. A challenger's new policy will be a linear combination of the policy chosen by the search rule, described below, and the mean of the voter distribution, according to the formulas under *PartySearchRule*. This results in sophisticated parties' choosing positions closer to the mean of the voters' ideal point distribution. (Note that the means of the voter distribution used in the search rule are always the true means for that distribution, not the value of the parameters *bliss1mean*, and so on. This is relevant mostly for 1-D and specialized distributions, where not all parameters translate directly.)

PartySearchRule: A vector containing different options for the way challengers search for new positions. Only challengers search within the model. Some options obviate other program settings, rendering them inoperable. Initial party positions are given as described under *PartyDistribution*. Searches are constrained to keep policy in the region

$$[-3 * \textit{bliss1stdev} + \textit{bliss1mean}, 3 * \textit{bliss1stdev} + \textit{bliss1mean}] \\ \times [-3 * \textit{bliss2stdev} + \textit{bliss2mean}, 3 * \textit{bliss2stdev} + \textit{bliss2mean}].$$

The options are as follows.

- "No Search": Parties do not change positions.
- "Local (Incremental) Uniform Search": Parties search around their present position (polLoc_1 and polLoc_2) in a possibly biased fashion. The effective starting point for search is

  $$\begin{aligned} Z &= (Z_1, Z_2) \\ &= (\text{polLoc}_1 + \textit{PartySearchMean1}, \\ &\qquad \text{polLoc}_2 + \textit{PartySearchMean2}). \end{aligned}$$

  They search uniformly within the range

  $$[-3 * \textit{PartySearchStdev1} + Z_1, 3 * \textit{PartySearchStdev1} + Z_1] \\ \times [-3 * \textit{PartySearchStdev2} + Z_2, 3 * \textit{PartySearchStdev2} + Z_2].$$

  This point (p_1, p_2) is then transformed according to

  $$\begin{aligned} p_1 &= \textit{PartySophisticationLevel} * \textit{bliss1mean} \\ &\qquad + (1 - \textit{PartySophisticationLevel}) * p_1; \\ p_2 &= \textit{PartySophisticationLevel} * \textit{bliss2mean} \\ &\qquad + (1 - \textit{PartySophisticationLevel}) * p_2. \end{aligned}$$

- "Global Uniform Search": Same as Local Uniform Search, but with Z=(*PartySearchMean1*, *PartySearchMean2*).
- "Local (Incremental) Normal Search": Same as Local Uniform Search, but the search around Z is according to a bivariate normal with parameters Z_1, *PartySearchStdev1*, Z_2, and *PartySearchStdev2*.
- "Global Normal Search": Same as Local (Incremental) Normal Search, but using the Z from Global Uniform Search.

B.2.2 Output

CHARTS

The program outputs and updates a number of charts in real time. These may safely be minimized to increase program speed. The charts include the following.

1. Incumbent: Displays (in red) the graph of which party is presently in office and (in blue) the average number of elections up to that point won by D. The latter appears only in two-party competition.
2. D's Vote Share: Displays D's vote share in each period. Appears only in two-party competition.
3. Propensity Descriptors: Displays (in red) the mean across the population of the propensities to vote D, (in blue) the standard deviation of the propensities, (in green) the proportion of individuals who voted "correctly" for the party whose platform was closest to their bliss points, and (in black) the point biserial correlation coefficient of realized correct voting totals (the dichotomous variable) to the extremism measure described earlier, for each period. Appears only in two-party competition if voters are not Downsian.
4. Propensity Distribution: An 11-bin histogram of the propensity to vote for D at a given time. Appears only in two-party competition if voters are not Downsian.
5. Vote Count: Displays the percentage of the voting electorate that goes to each party. Appears only when not in two-party competition.
6. Turnout Descriptors: Displays (in red) the mean of the propensities to vote, (in blue) the standard deviation of the propensities, and (in green) the point biserial correlation coefficient of

realized turnout (the dichotomous variable) to the extremism measure described earlier, for each period. Appears only when not set to Full Turnout.

7. Turnout Distribution: An 11-bin histogram of the probability of turning out at a given time. Appears only if not set to Full Turnout.
8. Payoff Distribution: Displays a histogram of payoffs if *ExtraHist* is checked.
9. Aspiration Distribution: Displays a histogram of aspirations if *ExtraHist* is checked.

Main Display

The main display consists of colored rectangles, larger colored circles, and one small black dot. The progress of the simulation can be observed within the main display, but this too can be minimized to speed up the program. Each rectangle collects voters who have bliss points in that region of policy space. The window covers a range of 6**bliss1stdev* in the x-direction, centered on *bliss1mean*, and the same for the y-direction. More extreme voters are collected with the rectangles on the borders. The colors signify several things. Transparent voters of any color did not vote in the last period. If they have never voted, they show up as light green. The last party for which they voted shows up as red or blue. In two-party competition, red signifies a Republican vote, and blue a Democratic one. In multiparty competition, blue signifies a vote for one of the challengers, and red a vote for the incumbent. Mixtures of red and blue signify more than one voter at that spot, and the proportion of red and blue there signifies how that spot leaned in its last vote.

The circles are parties, and all are shades of green. Transparent parties are out of office; opaque ones are in office. In two-party competition, the darker circle is the Republican; with more than two parties the colors are in order of party number. The circles move with the parties' positions. The small black dot corresponds to the implemented policy and is always attached to one of the circles.

Both rectangles and circles (their centers) may be left-clicked, which brings up a window with all the parameters for all voters in that rectangle. The same is true of the party circles. There is an option under the RePAST options tab that lets one update these probes of voters and parties. If this is checked, then many variables relating to the voter or party under examination will change as the simulation runs. Warning: this may bring up many windows, so click with care.

If you plan on watching individual voters, we advise you to keep the number of voters small for that run.

Simulation Data Collection

The program writes to a file "`ibm_data.csv`" each run. If such a file already exists, it is copied to a backup data file, and the new file writes over the old. Backups are labeled sequentially from 1. Each data file consists of the following data taken at each period:

- "Tick": Election number
- "Number of Voters"
- "*X*- and *Y*-Coordinates": The party locations in order, with Republican first in the case of two-party competition.
- "Incumbent": Who won the election that period.
- "*X*- and *Y*-Position of Incumbent": Position of the incumbent in that period.
- "Percent of Votes Captured by D": D's vote share that period. Only in two-party competition.
- "Percent of Elections Won by D": Running percentage of elections won by D. Only in two-party competition.
- "Vote Share": The vote share for each party. Only when not in two-party competition.
- "Number Times Winner": The number of times each party has won an election to that point. Only when not in two-party competition.
- "Effective Number of Parties": The effective number of parties as per the Laakso and Taagepera (1979) measure.
- "Mean Aspiration Level": Taken across the population.
- "Mean Payoff": Taken across the population.

All of the following appear only if not set to Full Turnout:

- "Mean Turnout Level": Taken across the population.
- "Standard Deviation of Turnout": Taken across the population.
- "Correlation of Turnout with Interests": The point biserial correlation coefficient of realized turnout (the dichotomous variable) to the extremism measure described earlier under *TurnoutInitDist.*
- "0–10%," "10–20%," "20–30%," "30–40%," "40–50%," "50–60%," "60–70%," "70–80%," "80–90%," "90–100%": Number of voters in each decile of turnout.

All of the following appear only if propensities update (i.e., voting is not Downsian) within two-party competition:

- "Mean Propensity": Mean value of the propensity to vote D that period.
- "Standard Deviation of Propensities": Standard deviation of the propensity to vote D that period.
- "Correct Voting Percent": The number of individuals who would have voted correctly in a Downsian sense, i.e., for the party whose platform was closest to their bliss points. Note that this includes all individuals whether or not they voted in the last period. As long as one's last vote was correct, one is considered to have voted correctly, even if one did not vote at all. Those who have never voted are never considered to have voted correctly.
- "Correlation of Correct Voting with Interests": The point biserial correlation coefficient of realized correct voting totals (the dichotomous variable) to the extremism measure described earlier under *TurnoutInitDist*.
- "0–10%," "10–20%," "20–30%," "30–40%," "40–50%," "50–60%," "60–70%," "70–80%," "80–90%," "90–100%": Number of voters in each decile of Democratic vote propensity.

B.3 Batch Model

The batch model uses the same core as the graphical model. The primary difference is that it takes as input a file that determines the settings of all parameters in the model, including the number of runs over which to average outputs. By specifying loops over parameters, one can explore the effect of parameter variation on output variables in a controlled fashion. Because of the overlap between models, we limit the discussion below to new settings present in the batch model. A complete description of the batch model may be found on the same website as the program.

B.3.1 Input File

A sample input file can be found on the same website as the program. Each line in the file, named "`IBMInput.txt`," contains the range of variation for a single parameter of the model. There are

42 such lines, though of course not all can or should be varied at once. The order of lines in the input file must be kept the same, but all numerical values may be changed. The first 15 lines of the file contain one integer each, corresponding to program settings over which the program does not loop. The first 11 of these correspond to vectors described in the previous subsection. These parameters are: *Voter Distribution, Propensity Adjustment, Party Search Rules, Turnout Adjustment, Party Distributions, Initial Distribution of Vote Propensities, Initial Distribution of Turnout Propensities, Initial Distribution of Aspirations, Strategy Adjustment, Uniform Shock,* and *Voter Utility*. All settings for these parameters described above are available in the batch model as well. We assign numbers to all settings for these vectors, allowing the integer used in the input file to correspond to the settings discussed earlier. A list of correspondences may be found on the website in the document that accompanies the batch program.

The next two lines set the number of times each set of parameter values is run to yield average values of the simulation data (line 12), and the number of elections that occur in each run (line 13). The last two lines in this section determine whether or not data on each run are recorded. If line 14 is 0, only the mean and the standard deviations of variables are recorded. If line 14 is 1, then in addition one or more output files containing data on every run will be written. Line 15 determines the frequency in electoral cycles that these per-run data are to be taken. For example, when this parameter is set to 10, then all runs are recorded for every tenth election.

The last 27 lines of the input file are of the following form: initial numerical value WHITESPACE final numerical value WHITESPACE increment to be increased in each step. Thus, each line should have the format: 5 10 1. If the initial and final values are the same, then no loop on that parameter occurs, and the parameter is merely set to the initial numerical value provided. Thus, using 5 5 1 for the parameter N sets N to 5 for all simulations being run. The number of values taken on by each parameter is

$$\frac{\text{final value} - \text{initial value}}{\text{increment}} + 1.$$

One note of caution: the time spent in each loop is multiplicative, so asking the program to do 1,000 runs each of 3 parameters that each take on 100 values equates to 10^9 iterations, each containing a potentially large number of elections. The parameters over which the program can loop are:

> *inertia, N, bliss1mean, bliss1stdev, bliss2mean, bliss2stdev, nu, lambda, votingCost, shockmean, shockstdev, numParties, partyPosition0a, partyPosition0b, partyPosition1a, partyPosition1b, partySearchMean1, partySearchStdev1, partySearchMean2, partySearchStdev2, partySophisticationLevel, propinitmean, propinitstdev, turninitmean, turninitstdev, aspinitmean, aspinitstdev.*

B.3.2 Output File(s)

The batch book model writes by default to the output file "`ibm-batch-out.csv`." If such a file exists, it tries "`ibm-batch-out-1.csv`," and so on, until an open file name is found. (So the newest file will always be the one with the largest number at the end. Note that this differs from the graphical version's file enumeration scheme.) This is a text file with comma-separated values. Lines 1 and 2 of this file are parameter names and associated parameter values, respectively, for the first 15 parameters listed above. After these two lines comes a block containing the names and values of the 27 looped input parameters and the output names and data. Output data provided matches that in the graphical model, and we do not repeat the description of the data here. For most output variables we record both the mean and the standard deviation of that variable across runs. Thus, the batch model aggregates across runs but not across periods (elections) within each run, except as noted under specific output data. Consequently, data files can get quite large when the number of elections and the number of parameter values explored are both high.

If the parameter *dumpAllData* is set to 1, additional files are written. The base filename is "`ibm-batch-out-dump.csv`," and additional files are numbered as above. One file is written for each set of parameter values. The first two lines in each file list the values of all parameters. The rest of the file contains a block of simulation data in the following format. For every election that the parameter *dumpEveryNElections* indicates, the per-run values of each of the variables included in the above description of the main output file are written. Be aware that files can grow very large if many runs and many elections are recorded.

Bibliography

Abramowitz, Alan, and Kyle Saunders. 1998. "Ideological Realignment in the U.S. Electorate." *Journal of Politics* 60(3): 634–652.
Acemoglu, Daron, and James A. Robinson. 2006. *Economic Origins of Dictatorship and Democracy.* Cambridge: Cambridge University Press.
Achen, Christopher. 1992. "Social Psychology, Demographic Variables, and Linear Regression: Breaking the Iron Triangle in Voting Research." *Political Behavior* 14(3): 195–211.
Achen, Christopher, and Larry Bartels. 2002. "Ignorance and Bliss in Democratic Politics: Party Competition with Uninformed Voters." Prepared for presentation at the Annual Meeting of the Midwest Political Science Association, Chicago, IL, April 25–28.
——. 2004. "Blind Retrospection: Electoral Responses to Drought, Flu, and Shark Attacks." Unpublished manuscript, Princeton University.
Alesina, Alberto, and Howard Rosenthal. 1995. *Partisan Politics, Divided Government and the Economy.* New York: Cambridge University Press.
Ali, S. Nageeb, and Navin Kartik. 2008. "Social Learning in Elections." Unpublished manuscript, University of California, San Diego.
Anderson, John. 1995. *Cognitive Psychology and Its Implications.* 4th ed. New York: W. H. Freeman.
Ansolabehere, Stephen, James Snyder, and Charles Stewart. 2001. "Candidate Positioning in U.S. House Elections." *American Journal of Political Science* 45(1): 136–159.
Ansolabehere, Stephen, James Snyder, Aaron Strauss, and Michael M. Ting. 2005. "Voting Weights and Formateur Advantages in the Formation of Coalition Governments." *American Journal of Political Science* 49(3): 550–563.
Austen-Smith, David, and Jeffrey Banks. 1999. *Positive Political Theory I: Collective Preference.* Ann Arbor, MI: University of Michigan Press.
Axelrod, Robert. 1984. *The Evolution of Cooperation.* New York: Basic Books.
Bandura, Albert. 1986. *Social Foundations of Thought and Action.* Englewood Cliffs, NJ: Prentice-Hall.
Barberis, Nicholas, and Richard Thaler. 2003. "A Survey of Behavioral Finance." In George M. Constantinides, Milton Harris, and René M. Stulz (eds.), *Handbook of the Economics of Finance*, Vol. 1. Amsterdam: North-Holland Press, Elsevier Science Publishers, pp. 1053–1128.
Bartels, Larry. 1996. "Uninformed Votes: Information Effects in Presidential Elections." *American Journal of Political Science* 40(1): 194–230.
——. 2002. "Beyond the Running Tally: Partisan Bias in Political Perceptions." *Political Behavior* 24(2): 117–150.
Baumeister, Roy, Ellen Bratslavsky, Catrin Finkenauer, and Kathleen Vohs. 2001. "Bad Is Stronger Than Good." *Review of General Psychology* 5(4): 323–370.

Bendor, Jonathan. 2001. "Bounded Rationality." In Neil Smelser and Paul Baltes (eds.), *International Encyclopedia of the Social and Behavioral Sciences.* Oxford: Elsevier, pp. 1303–1307.

——. 2003. "Herbert A. Simon: Political Scientist." In Nelson Polsby (ed.), *Annual Review of Political Science*, Vol. 6. Palo Alto, CA: Annual Reviews, pp. 433–471.

——. Forthcoming. "Aspiration-Based Models of Politics." In Jon Krosnick (ed.), *New Explorations in Political Psychology.* New York: Taylor and Francis.

Bendor, Jonathan, and John Bullock. 2008. "Lethal Incompetence: Voters, Officials, and Systems." *Critical Review* 20: 1–23.

Bendor, Jonathan, Daniel Diermeier, and Michael Ting. 2001. "A Behavioral Model of Turnout." Unpublished manuscript, Stanford University.

——. 2003a. "A Behavioral Model of Turnout." *American Political Science Review* 97(2): 261–280.

——. 2003b. "Recovering Behavioralism: Adaptively Rational Strategic Behavior with Endogenous Aspirations." In Ken Kollman and Scott Page (eds.), *Computational Political Economy.* Cambridge, MA: MIT Press, pp. 213–274.

——. 2007. "Comment: Adaptive Models in Sociology and the Problem of Empirical Content." *American Journal of Sociology* 112(5): 1534–1545.

Bendor, Jonathan, and Sunil Kumar. 2005. "The Perfect Is the Enemy of the Best: Adaptive Versus Optimal Organizational Reliability." *Journal of Theoretical Politics* 17(1): 5–39.

Bendor, Jonathan, Sunil Kumar, and David A. Siegel. 2007. "Rational Parties and Retrospective Voters." In William Barnett and Melvin J. Hinich (eds.), *Topics in Analytical Political Economy, 17.* Oxford: Elsevier, pp. 1–30.

——. 2009. "Satisficing: A 'Pretty Good' Heuristic." *The Berkeley Electronic Journal of Theoretical Economics* 9(1) (Advances), Article 9.

——. 2010. "Adaptively Rational Retrospective Voting." *Journal of Theoretical Politics* 22(1): 1–38.

Bendor, Jonathan, and Adam Meirowitz. 2004. "Spatial Models of Delegation." *American Political Science Review* 98(2): 293–310.

Bendor, Jonathan, Dilip Mookherjee, and Debraj Ray. 2001. "Aspiration-Based Reinforcement Learning in Repeated Games." *International Game Theory Review* 3: 159–174.

——. 2006. "Satisficing and Selection in Electoral Competition." *Quarterly Journal of Political Science* 1(2): 171–200.

Berry, Donald A., and Bert Fristedt. 1985. *Bandit Problems: Sequential Allocation of Experiments.* London: Chapman and Hall.

Besley, Timothy, and Stephen Coate. 1997. "An Economic Model of Representative Democracy." *Quarterly Journal of Economics* 112(1): 85–114.

Bettman, James, Mary Frances Luce, and John Payne. 1998. "Constructive Consumer Choice Processes." *Journal of Consumer Research* 25(December): 187–217.

Bikhchandani, Sushil, David Hirshleifer, and Ivo Welch. 1992. "A Theory of Fads, Fashion, Custom, and Cultural Change as Informational Cascades." *Journal of Political Economy* 100(5): 992–1026.

Bikhchandani, Sushil, David Hirshleifer, and Ivo Welch. 1998. "Learning from the Behavior of Others: Conformity, Fads, and Informational Cascades." *Journal of Economic Perspectives* 12(3): 151–170.

Billman, Dorrit. 1999. "Representation." In William Bechtel and George Graham (eds.), *A Companion to Cognitive Science.* Oxford: Blackwell, pp. 649–659.

Bower, Gordon. 1994. "A Turning Point in Mathematical Learning Theory." *Psychological Review* 101(2): 290–300.

Braybrooke, David. 2004. *Utilitarianism: Restorations, Repairs, Renovations.* Toronto: University of Toronto Press.

Brown, Donald. 1991. *Human Universals.* New York: McGraw-Hill.

Bush, Robert, and Frederick Mosteller. 1955. *Stochastic Models of Learning.* New York: Wiley.

Calvert, Randall L. 1985. "Robustness of the Multidimensional Voting Model: Candidate Motivations, Uncertainty, and Convergence." *American Journal of Political Science* 29(1): 69–95.

Camerer, Colin. 2003. *Behavioral Game Theory.* Princeton, NJ: Princeton University Press.

Camerer, Colin, George Loewenstein, and Matthew Rabin (eds.). 2004. *Advances in Behavioral Economics.* Princeton, NJ: Princeton University Press.

Campbell, Angus, Philip Converse, Warren Miller, and Donald Stokes. 1960. *The American Voter.* New York: Wiley.

Carlsson, Hans, and Eric van Damme. 1993. "Global Games and Equilibrium Selection." *Econometrica* 61(5): 989–1018.

Chappell, Henry, and William Keech. 1986. "Policy Motivation and Party Differences in a Dynamic Spatial Model of Party Competition." *American Political Science Review* 80(3): 881–899.

Chhibber, Pradeep, and Ken Kollman. 1998. "Party Aggregation and the Number of Parties in India and the United States." *American Political Science Review* 92(2): 329–342.

Chiappori, Pierre-Andre, Steve Levitt, and Tim Groseclose. 2002. "Testing Mixed-Strategy Equilibria When Players Are Heterogeneous: The Case of Penalty Kicks in Soccer." *American Economic Review* 92(4): 1138–1151.

Clark, Peter, and James Q. Wilson. 1961. "Incentive Systems: A Theory of Organizations." *Administrative Science Quarterly* 6(2): 129–166.

Coate, Stephen, and Michael Conlin. 2004. "A Group Rule-Utilitarian Approach to Voter Turnout: Theory and Evidence." *American Economic Review* 94(5): 1476–1504.

Collins, Nathan A. 2008. "Why Do We Pay Attention to Candidate Race, Gender, and Party? A Theory of the Development of Political Categorization Schemes." Unpublished manuscript, Stanford University.

Conlisk, John. 1996. "Why Bounded Rationality?" *Journal of Economic Literature* 34(2): 669–700.

Converse, Philip E. 1965. "Electoral Myth and Reality: The 1964 Election." *American Political Science Review* 59(2): 321–336.

Converse, Philip E. 1990. "Popular Representation and the Distribution of Information." In John Ferejohn and James Kukinski (eds.), *Information and Democratic Processes.* Urbana, IL: University of Illinois Press, pp. 369–388.

——. 2000. "Assessing the Capacity of Mass Electorates." *Annual Review of Political Science*, Vol. 3: 331–353.

Cowan, Nelson. 2000. "The Magical Number 4 in Short-Term Memory: A Reconsideration of Mental Storage Capacity." *Behavioral and Brain Sciences* 24(1): 87–185.

Cox, Gary. 1987a. "Electoral Equilibrium under Alternative Voting Institutions." *American Journal of Political Science* 31(1): 82–108.

——. 1987b. "The Uncovered Set and the Core." *American Journal of Political Science* 31(2): 408–422.

——. 1987c. "Duverger's Law and Strategic Voting." Unpublished manuscript, University of California, San Diego.

——. 1994. "Strategic Voting Equilibria Under the Single Non-Tranferable Vote." *American Political Science Review* 88(3): 608–621.

——. 1997. *Making Votes Count.* Cambridge: Cambridge University Press.

Cox, Gary, and Jonathan Katz. 2002. *Elbridge Gerry's Salamander: The Electoral Consequences of the Reapportionment Revolution.* Cambridge: Cambridge University Press.

Cremer, Jacques. 1986. "Cooperation in Ongoing Organizations." *Quarterly Journal of Economics* 101(1): 33–50.

Cross, John. 1983. *A Theory of Adaptive Economic Behavior.* Cambridge: Cambridge University Press.

Cyert, Richard, and James March. 1963. *A Behavioral Theory of the Firm.* Englewood Cliffs, NJ: Prentice-Hall.

Dal Bó, Ernesto, Pedro Dal Bó and Rafael Di Tella. 2006. "Plata o Plomo?: Bribe and Punishment in a Theory of Political Influence." *American Political Science Review* 100(1): 41–53.

Dalton, Russell, and Hans-Dieter Klinemann. 2007. "Citizens and Political Behavior." In Dalton, Russell, and Hans-Dieter Klinemann (eds.), *The Oxford Handbook of Political Behavior.* Oxford: Oxford University Press, pp. 3–26.

Deaton, Angus. 2008. "Income, Health, and Well-Being around the World: Evidence from the Gallup World Poll." *Journal of Economic Perspectives* 22(2): 53–72.

Deci, Edward, Richard Koestner, and Richard Ryan. 1999. "A Meta-Analytic Review of Experiments Examining the Effects of Extrinsic Rewards on Intrinsic Motivation." *Psychological Bulletin* 125(6): 627–668.

Delli Carpini, Michael, and Scott Keeter. 1996. *What Americans Know about Politics and Why It Matters.* New Haven, CT: Yale University Press.

Diener, Ed, and Eunkook Suh. 1999. "National Differences in Subjective Well-Being." In D. Kahneman, E. Diener, and N. Schwarz (eds.), *Well-Being: The Foundations of Hedonic Psychology.* New York: Russell Sage Foundation, pp. 434–450.

Diermeier, Daniel, Hulya Eraslan, and Antonio Merlo. 2003. "A Structural Model of Government Formation." *Econometrica* 71(1): 27–70.

Diermeier, Daniel, and Keith Krehbiel. 2003. "Institutionalism as a Methodology." *Journal of Theoretical Politics* 15(2): 123–144.

Downs, Anthony. 1957. *An Economic Theory of Democracy.* New York: Harper & Row.

Dranove, David, Daniel Kessler, Mark McClellan, and Mark Satterthwaite. 2003. "Is More Information Better? The Effects of 'Report Cards' on Health Care Providers." *Journal of Political Economy* 111(3): 555–588.

Duverger, Maurice. 1954. *Political Parties: Their Organization and Activity in the Modern State.* New York: Wiley.

Easterlin, Richard A. 2001. "Income and Happiness: Towards a Unified Theory." *Economic Journal* 111(July): 465–484.

Eldersveld, Samuel. 1982. *Political Parties in American Society.* New York: Basic Books.

Enelow, James, and Melvin Hinich. 1984. *The Spatial Theory of Voting.* Boston, MA: Cambridge University Press.

Epstein, David. 1998. "Uncovering Some Subtleties of the Uncovered Set: Social Choice Theory and Distributive Politics." *Social Choice and Welfare* 15(1): 81–93.

Epstein, David, and Sharyn O'Halloran. 2005. "Higher-Dimension Markov Models." Paper prepared for presentation at the Political Methodology Summer Meetings. Tallahassee, FL, July 21–23.

Erev, Ido, and Alvin Roth. 1999. "On the Role of Reinforcement Learning in Experimental Games: the Cognitive Game-Theoretic Approach." In David Budescu, Ido Erev, and Rami Zwick (eds.), *Games and Human Behavior: Essays in Honor of Amnon Rapoport.* Mahwah, NJ: Lawrence Erlbaum, pp. 53–77.

Ericsson, K. Anders. 1999. "Creative Expertise as Superior Reproducible Performance: Innovative and Flexible Aspects of Expert Performance." *Psychological Inquiry* 10(4): 329–333.

Ericsson, K. Anders, and A. C. Lehmann. 1996. "Expert and Exceptional Performance: Evidence of Maximal Adaptation to Task Constraints." *Annual Review of Psychology*, Vol. 47: 273–305.

Evans, Jonathan. 2008. "Dual-Processing Accounts of Reasoning, Judgment, and Social Cognition." *Annual Review of Psychology*, Vol. 59: 255–278.

Feddersen, Timothy. 1992. "A Voting Model Implying Duverger's Law and Positive Turnout." *American Journal of Political Science* 36(4): 938–962.

——. 2004. "Rational Choice Theory and the Paradox of Not Voting." *Journal of Economic Perspectives* 18(1): 99–112.

Feddersen, Timothy J., and Wolfgang Pesendorfer. 1996. "The Swing Voter's Curse." *American Economic Review* 86(3): 408–424.

——. 1997. "Voting Behavior and Information Aggregation in Elections with Private Information." *Econometrica* 65(5): 1029–1058.

Feddersen, Timothy J., and Alvaro Sandroni. 2006. "A Theory of Participation in Elections." *American Economic Review* 96(4): 1271–1282.

Feinberg, Yossi. 2004. "Learning to Optimize While Optimizing Learning." Unpublished manuscript, Graduate School of Business, Stanford University.

Feller, William. 1950. *An Introduction to Probability Theory and Its Applications.* New York: Wiley.

Feng, Lei, and Mark Seasholes. 2005. "Do Investor Sophistication and Trading Experience Eliminate Behavioral Biases in Financial Markets?" *Review of Finance* 9(3): 305–351.

Ferejohn, John. 1995. "The Development of the Spatial Theory of Elections." In J. Farr and J. Dryzek (eds.), *Political Science and History.* Cambridge: Cambridge University Press, pp. 253–275.

Ferejohn, John, and Morris Fiorina. 1974. "The Paradox of Not Voting." *American Political Science Review* 68(2): 525–536.

Ferejohn, John, Morris Fiorina, and Edward Packel. 1980. "Nonequilibrium Solutions for Legislative Systems." *Behavioral Science* 25(2): 140–148.

Ferejohn, John, Richard McKelvey, and Edward Packel. 1984. "Limiting Distributions for Continuous State Markov Voting Models." *Social Choice and Welfare* 1(1): 45–67.

Fey, Mark. 1997. "Stability and Coordination in Duverger's Law: A Formal Model of Pre-election Polls and Strategic Voting." *American Political Science Review* 91(1): 135–147.

Fiorina, Morris. 1981. *Retrospective Voting in American National Elections.* New Haven, CT: Yale University Press.

——. 1990. "Information and Rationality in Elections." In John Ferejohn and James Kuklinski (eds.), *Information and Democratic Processes.* Urbana, IL: University of Illinois Press, pp. 329–342.

Fiorina, Morris P., Samuel J. Abrams, and Jeremy C. Pope. 2005. *Culture War? The Myth of a Polarized America.* New York: Pearson Longman.

Flaherty, Charles. 1996. *Incentive Relativity.* Cambridge: Cambridge University Press.

Forsythe, Robert, Roger Myerson, Thomas Rietz, and Robert Weber. 1993. "An Experiment on Coordination in Multi-Candidate Elections: The Importance of Polls and Election Histories." *Social Choice and Welfare* 10(3): 223–247.

Fowler, James. 2006. "Habitual Voting and Behavioral Turnout." *Journal of Politics* 68(2): 335–344.

Friedman, Daniel, and Dominic Massaro. 1998. "Understanding Variability in Binary and Continuous Choice." *Psychonomic Bulletin & Review* 5(3): 370–389.

Friedman, Jeffrey (ed.). 1996. *The Rational Choice Controversy.* New Haven, CT: Yale University Press.

Friedman, Milton. 1953. "The Methodology of Positive Economics." In *Essays in Positive Economics.* Chicago, IL: University of Chicago Press, 3–43.

Gigerenzer, Gerd. 2004. "Fast and Frugal Heuristics: The Tools of Bounded Rationality." In D. Koehler and N. Harvey (eds.), *Handbook of Judgment and Decision Making.* Oxford: Blackwell, pp. 62–88.

Gigerenzer, Gerd, and Daniel Goldstein. 1996. "Reasoning the Fast and Frugal Way: Models of Bounded Rationality." *Psychological Review* 103(4): 650–669.

Gigerenzer, Gerd, and Reinhard Selten. 2001. *Bounded Rationality: The Adaptive Toolbox.* Boston, MA: MIT Press.

Gilovich, Thomas, and Dale Griffin. 2002. "Introduction—Heuristics and Biases: Then and Now." In T. Gilovich, D. Griffin, and D. Kahneman (eds.), *Heuristics and Biases: The Psychology of Intuitive Judgment.* New York: Cambridge University Press.

Gilovich, Thomas, Dale Griffin, and Daniel Kahneman. 2002. *Heuristics and Biases: The Psychology of Intuitive Judgment.* Cambridge: Cambridge University Press.

Gode, Dhananjay, and Shyam Sunder. 1993. "Allocative Efficiency of Markets with Zero-Intelligence Traders." *Journal of Political Economy* 101(1): 119–137.

Goldstone, Robert, and Ji Yun Son. 2005. "Similarity." In Keith Holyoak and Robert Morrison (eds.), *The Cambridge Handbook of Thinking and Reasoning.* Cambridge: Cambridge University Press, pp. 13–36.

Green, Donald, and Ian Shapiro. 1994. *Pathologies of Rational Choice Theory.* New Haven, CT: Yale University Press.

Greene, Joshua, Sylvia Morelli, Kelly Lowenberg, Leigh Nystrom, and Jonathan Cohen. 2008. "Cognitive Load Selectively Interferes with Utilitarian Moral Judgment." *Cognition* 107(3): 1144–1154.

Griffin, Dale, and Daniel Kahneman. 2003. "Judgmental Heuristics: Human Strengths or Human Weaknesses." In L. Aspinwall and U. Staudinger (eds.), *Blackwell Handbook of Social Psychology: Intraindividual Processes.* Malden, MA: Blackwell.

Grossman, Gene M., and Elhanan Helpman. 1994. "Protection for Sale." *American Economic Review* 84(4): 833–850.

Hajcak, Greg, Jason S. Moser, Clay B. Holroyd, and Robert F. Simons. 2006. "The Feedback-Related Negativity Reflects the Binary Evaluation of Good Versus Bad Outcomes." *Biological Psychology* 71(2): 148–154.

Hansen, Steven, Thomas Palfrey, and Howard Rosenthal. 1987. "The Relationship Between Constituency Size and Turnout: Using Game Theory to Estimate the Cost of Voting." *Public Choice* 52(1): 15–33.

Hausman, Daniel M. 1992. *The Inexact and Separate Science of Economics.* Cambridge: Cambridge University Press.

Heath, Anthony, Roger Jowell, John K. Curtice, and Pippa Norris. "British General Election Cross-Section Survey," 1997 (computer file). 2nd ICPSR version. London, England: Social and Community Planning Research (producer), 1998. Colchester, England: The Data Archive/Ann Arbor, MI: Inter-University Consortium for Political and Social Research (distributors), 2000.

Helson, Harry. 1964. *Adaptation-Level Theory.* New York: Harper and Row.

Herrera, Helios, and Cesar Martinelli. 2006. "Group Formation and Voter Participation." *Theoretical Economics* 1(4): 461–487.

Hilgard, Ernest R., and Gordon H. Bower. 1966. *Theories of Learning.* New York: Appleton-Century-Crofts.

Hinich, Melvin J., and Michael C. Munger. 1994. *Ideology and the Theory of Political Choice.* Ann Arbor, MI: University of Michigan Press.

Hogarth, Robin. 1987. *Judgement and Choice.* New York: Wiley.

——. 2001. *Educating Intuition.* Chicago, IL: University of Chicago Press.

Hsee, Christopher, George Loewenstein, Sally Blount, and Max Bazerman. 1999. "Preference Reversals Between Joint and Separate Evaluations of Options: A Review and Theoretical Analysis." *Psychological Bulletin* 125(5): 576–590.

Huber, John D., and Charles R. Shipan. 2002. *Deliberate Discretion? The Institutional Foundations of Bureaucratic Autonomy.* New York: Cambridge University Press.

Jackson, John. 1975. "Issues, Party Choices, and Presidential Votes." *American Journal of Political Science* 19(2): 161–185.

Jennings, Kent, and Gregory Markus. 1984. "Partisan Orientations over the Long Haul." *American Political Science Review* 78(4): 1000–1018.

Kahneman, Daniel. 2002. "Maps of Bounded Rationality: A Perspective on Intuitive Judgment and Choice." Nobel Prize Lecture.

Kahneman, Daniel, Ed Diener, and Norbert Schwarz (eds.). 1999. *Well-Being: The Foundations of Hedonic Psychology.* New York: Russell Sage Foundation.

Kahneman, Daniel, and Shane Frederick. 2002. "Representativeness Revisited: Attribute Substitution in Intuitive Judgment." In T. Gilovich, D. Griffin, and D. Kahneman (eds.), *Heuristics and Biases: The Psychology of Intuitive Judgment.* New York: Cambridge University Press, pp. 49–81.

Kahneman, Daniel, Jack L. Knetsch, and Richard H. Thaler. 1991. "Anomalies: The Endowment Effect, Loss Aversion, and Status Quo Bias." *Journal of Economic Perspectives* 5(1): 193–206.

Kahneman, Daniel, and Amos Tversky. 1979. "Prospect Theory: An Analysis of Decision under Risk." *Econometrica* 47(2): 263–291.

——. 2000. *Choices, Values, and Frames.* Cambridge: Cambridge University Press.

Kanazawa, Satoshi. 1998. "A Possible Solution to the Paradox of Voter Turnout." *Journal of Politics* 60(4): 974–995.

Karandikar, Rajeeva, Dilip Mookherjee, Debraj Ray, and Fernando Vega-Redondo. 1998. "Evolving Aspirations and Cooperation." *Journal of Economic Theory* 80(2): 292–331.

Karlin, Samuel, and Howard M. Taylor. 1975. *A First Course in Stochastic Processes.* New York: Academic Press.

——. 1998. *An Introduction to Stochastic Modeling.* San Diego, CA: Academic Press.

Kemeny, John, and J. Laurie Snell. 1960. *Finite Markov Chains.* Princeton, NJ: Van Nostrand.

Key, V. O. 1964. *Politics, Parties, and Pressure Groups,* 5th ed. New York: Thomas Crowell.

——. 1966. *The Responsible Electorate: Rationality in Presidential Voting 1936–1960.* Cambridge, MA: Belknap Press.

Key, V. O. 1984. *Southern Politics in State and Nation.* Knoxville, TN: University of Tennessee Press.

Kiefer, J., and J. Wolfowitz. 1952. "Stochastic Approximation of a Regression Function." *Annals of Mathematical Statistics* 23(3): 462–466.

Kinder, Donald. 1998. "Opinion and Action in the Realm of Politics." In D. Gilbert, S. Fiske and G. Lindzey (eds.), *The Handbook of Social Psychology*, 4th ed. Boston, MA: McGraw-Hill, pp. 778–867.

Kingdon, John. 1984. *Agendas, Alternatives and Public Choice.* Boston, MA: Little, Brown.

Kollman, Ken, John Miller, and Scott Page. 1992. "Adaptive Parties in Spatial Elections." *American Political Science Review* 86(4): 929–937.

——. 1998. "Political Parties and Electoral Landscapes." *British Journal of Political Science* 28(1): 139–158.

Kollman, Ken, and Scott Page. 2006. "Computational Methods and Models of Politics." In Leigh Tesfatsion and Kenneth L. Judd (eds.), *Handbook of Computational Economics*, Vol. 2. Amsterdam: North-Holland/Elsevier, pp. 1433–1463.

Kramer, Gerald. 1977. "A Dynamical Model of Political Equilibrium." *Journal of Economic Theory* 16(2): 310–334.

Krehbiel, Keith. 1991. *Information and Legislative Organization.* Ann Arbor, MI: University of Michigan Press.

Kreps, David. 1990. *Game Theory and Economic Modelling.* Oxford: Clarendon Press.

Laasko, Markku, and Rein Taagepera. 1979. "Effective Number of Parties: A Measure with Application to West Europe." *Comparative Political Studies* 12(1): 3–27.

Lakatos, Imre. 1970. "Falsification and the Methodology of Scientific Research Programs." In I. Lakatos and A. Musgrave (eds.), *Criticism and the Growth of Knowledge.* London: Cambridge University Press, pp. 91–196.

Lau, Richard, David Andersen, and David Redlawsk. 2008. "An Exploration of Correct Voting in Recent U.S. Presidential Elections." *American Journal of Political Science* 52(2): 395–411.

Lau, Richard, and David Redlawsk. 1997. "Voting Correctly." *American Political Science Review* 91(3): 585–598.

——. 2006. *How Voters Decide: Information Processing During Election Campaigns.* New York: Cambridge University Press.

Laudan, Larry. 1977. *Progress and Its Problems.* Berkeley, CA: University of California Press.

Lavie, Nilli. 1995. "Perceptual Load as a Necessary Condition for Selective Attention." *Journal of Experimental Psychology: Human Perception and Performance* 21(3): 451–468.

Layard, Richard. 2006. "Happiness and Public Policy: A Challenge to the Profession." *Economic Journal* 116: C24–C33.

Ledyard, John O. 1984. "The Pure Theory of Large Two Candidate Elections." *Public Choice* 44(1): 7–41.

Levendusky, Matthew. 2009. *The Partisan Sort: How Liberals Become Democrats and Conservatives Become Republicans.* Chicago, IL: University of Chicago Press.

Levine, David K., and Thomas R. Palfrey. 2007. "The Paradox of Voter Participation? A Laboratory Study." *American Political Science Review* 101(1): 143–158.

Levitt, Steven. 1996. "How Do Senators Vote? Disentangling the Role of Voter Preferences, Party Affiliation, and Senator Ideology." *American Economic Review* 86(3): 425–441.

Lewin, Kurt, Tamara Dembo, Leon Festinger, and Pauline Sears. 1944. "Level of Aspiration." In J. McV. Hunt (ed.), *Personality and the Behavior Disorder*, Vol. 1. New York: Ronald Press, pp. 333–378.

Lucas, Richard, Andrew Clark, Yannis Georgellis, and Ed Diener. 2004. "Unemployment Alters the Set Point for Life Satisfaction." *Psychological Science* 15(1): 8–13.

Luskin, Robert. 2002. "From Denial to Extenuation (and Finally Beyond): Political Sophistication and Citizen Performance." In J. Kuklinski (ed.), *Thinking about Political Psychology*. New York: Cambridge University Press, pp. 281–305.

Macy, Michael, and Andreas Flache. 2002. "Learning Dynamics in Social Dilemmas." *Proceedings of the National Academy of Sciences* 99(10): 7229–7236.

March, James. 1966. "The Power of Power." In David Easton (ed.), *Varieties of Political Theory*. Englewood Cliffs, NJ: Prentice-Hall, pp. 39–70.

——. 1991. "Exploration and Exploitation in Organizational Learning." *Organization Science* 2(1): 71–87.

——. 1994. *A Primer on Decision Making: How Decisions Happen*. New York: Free Press.

Markman, Arthur. 1999. *Knowledge Representation*. Mahwah, NJ: Erlbaum.

Markman, Arthur, and Eric Dietrich. 2000. "In Defense of Representation." *Cognitive Psychology* 40(2): 138–171.

McKelvey, Richard. 1976. "Intransitivities in Multidimensional Voting Models and Some Implications for Agenda Control." *Journal of Economic Theory* 12(3): 472–482.

——. 1986. "Covering, Dominance, and Institution-free Properties of Social Choice." *American Journal of Political Science* 30(2): 283–314.

Merrill, Samuel, III, and Bernard Grofman. 1999. *A Unified Theory of Voting: Directional and Proximity Spatial Models*. Cambridge: Cambridge University Press.

Merton, Robert K., and Alice S. Rossi. 1950. "Contributions to the Theory of Reference Group Behavior." In R. K. Merton and P. Lazarsfeld (eds.), *Continuities in Social Research: Studies in the Scope and Method of "The American Soldier."* New York: Free Press, 40–105.

Miller, George. 1956. "The Magical Number Seven, Plus or Minus Two: Some Limits on Our Capacity for Processing Information." *Psychological Review* 63(2): 81–97.

Miller, Nicholas. 1980. "A New Solution Set for Tournaments and Majority Voting." *American Journal of Political Science* 24(1): 68–96.

Miller, Nicholas. 1986. "Information, Electorates, and Democracy: Some Extensions and Interpretations of the Condorcet Jury Theorem." In Bernard Grofman and Guillermo Owen (eds.), *Information Pooling and Group Decision Making.* Greenwich, CT: JAI Press. pp. 173–192.

Milyo, Jeffrey. 2001. "What Do Candidates Maximize (and Why Should Anyone Care)?" *Public Choice* 109(1–2): 119–139.

Morton, Rebecca B. 1991. "Groups in Rational Turnout Models." *American Journal of Political Science* 35(3): 758–776.

Moshman, David. 2000. "Diversity in Reasoning and Rationality: Metacognitive and Developmental Considerations." *Behavioral and Brain Sciences* 23(5): 689–690.

Mullainathan, Sendhil, and Richard Thaler. 2000. "Behavioral Economics." MIT, Department of Economics Working Paper No. 00-27.

Munro, Alistair, and Robert Sugden. 2003. "On the Theory of Reference-Dependent Preferences." *Journal of Economic Behavior and Organization* 50(4): 407–428.

Myatt, David P. 2007. "On the Theory of Strategic Voting." *Review of Economic Studies* 74(1): 255–281.

Myatt, David P., and Stephen D. Fisher. 2002a. "Tactical Coordination in Plurality Electoral Systems." *Oxford Review of Economic Policy* 18(4): 504–522.

——. 2002b. "Everything Is Uncertain and Uncertainty Is Everything: Strategic Voting in Simple Plurality Elections." University of Oxford, Department of Economics, Discussion Paper Series.

Myerson, Roger. 1998. "Population Uncertainty and Poisson Games." *International Journal of Game Theory* 27(3): 375–392.

——. 2002. "Comparison of Scoring Rules in Poisson Voting Games." *Journal of Economic Theory* 103(1): 219–251.

Myerson, Roger, and Robert Weber. 1993. "A Theory of Voting Equilibria." *American Political Science Review* 87(1): 102–114.

Nadeau, Richard, and Michael Lewis-Beck. 2001. "National Economic Voting in U.S. Presidential Elections." *Journal of Politics* 63(1): 159–181.

Newell, Allen. 1969. "Heuristic Programming: Ill-Structured Problems." In Julius Aronofsky (ed.), *Progress in Operations Research: The Relationship Between OR and the Computer,* Vol. 3. New York: Wiley, pp. 360–414.

Newell, Allen, and Herbert A. Simon. 1972. *Human Problem Solving.* Englewood Cliffs, NJ: Prentice-Hall.

North, Douglas, and Barry Weingast. 1989. "Constitutions and Commitment: The Evolution of Institutions Governing Public Choice in 17th Century England." *Journal of Economic History* 49(4): 803–832.

Novick, Laura, and Miriam Bassok. 2005. "Problem Solving." In Keith Holyoak and Robert Morrison (eds.), *The Cambridge Handbook of Thinking and Reasoning.* New York: Cambridge University Press, pp. 321–349.

Osborne, Martin, and Al Slivinski. 1996. "A Model of Political Competition with Citizen Candidates." *Quarterly Journal of Economics* 111(1): 65–96.

Page, Scott. 2006. "Path Dependence." *Quarterly Journal of Political Science* 1(1): 87–113.

Palfrey, Thomas. 1989. "A Mathematical Proof of Duverger's Law." In Peter Ordershook (ed.), *Models of Strategic Choice in Politics.* Ann Arbor, MI: University of Michigan Press, pp. 239–268.

Palfrey, Thomas, and Howard Rosenthal. 1983. "A Strategic Calculus of Voting." *Public Choice* 41(1): 7–53.

——. 1985. "Voter Participation and Strategic Uncertainty." *American Political Science Review* 79(1): 62–78.

Patty, John W., James M. Snyder, and Michael M. Ting. 2009. "Two's Company, Three's an Equilibrium: Strategic Voting and Multicandidate Elections." *Quarterly Journal of Political Science* 4(3): 251–278.

Persson, Torsten, and Guido Tabellini. 2003. *The Economic Effects of Constitutions.* Cambridge, MA: MIT Press.

Plott, Charles R. 1967. "A Notion of Equilibrium and Its Possibility under Majority Rule." *American Economic Review* 57(4): 787–806.

Pólya, George. 1945. *How to Solve It.* Princeton, NJ: Princeton University Press.

Pomper, Gerald. 1972. "From Confusion to Clarity: Issues and American Voters, 1956–1968." *American Political Science Review* 66(2): 415–428.

Powell, Robert. 2004. "The Inefficient Use of Power: Costly Conflict with Complete Information." *American Political Science Review* 98(2): 231–241.

Rabin, Matthew. 1998. "Psychology and Economics." *Journal of Economic Literature* 36(1): 11–46.

Reed, Steven. 1990. "Structure and Behaviour: Extending Duverger's Law to the Japanese Case." *British Journal of Political Science* 20(3): 335–356.

Richerson, Peter, and Robert Boyd. 2005. *Not by Genes Alone: How Culture Transformed Human Evolution.* Chicago, IL: University of Chicago Press.

Riker, William H. 1982. "The Two-Party System and Duverger's Law: An Essay on the History of Political Science." *American Political Science Review* 76(4): 753–766.

Riker, William, and Peter Ordeshook. 1968. "A Theory of the Calculus of Voting." *American Political Science Review* 62(1): 25–42.

Roemer, John. 2001. *Political Competition: Theory and Applications.* Cambridge, MA: Harvard University Press.

Rosenthal, Robert, Jason Shachat, and Mark Walker. 2003. "Hide and Seek in Arizona." *International Journal of Game Theory* 32(2): 273–293.

Ross, Lee. 1977. "The Intuitive Psychologist and His Shortcomings: Distortion in the Attribution Process." In Leonard Berkowitz (ed.), *Advances in Experimental Social Psychology*, Vol. 10. New York: Academic Press, pp. 173–220.

Rubinstein, Ariel. 1998. *Modeling Bounded Rationality.* Cambridge, MA: MIT Press.

Samuels, Richard, Stephen Stich, and Michael Bishop. 2002. "Ending the Rationality Wars: How to Make Disputes about Human Rationality Disappear." In R. Elio (ed.), *Common Sense, Reasoning and Rationality*, Vancouver Studies in Cognitive Science, Vol. 11. New York: Oxford University Press, pp. 236–268.

Samuels, Richard, Stephen Stich, and Luc Faucher. 2004. "Reason and Rationality." In I. Niiniluoto, M. Sintonen, and J. Wolenski (eds.), *Handbook of Epistemology*. Dordrecht: Kluwer, pp. 131–179.

Satz, Debra, and John Ferejohn. 1994. "Rational Choice and Social Theory." *Journal of Philosophy* 91(2): 71–87.

Schofield, Norman. 1977. "Transitivity of Preferences on a Smooth Manifold." *Journal of Economic Theory* 14(1): 149–171.

Schuessler, Alexander. 2000. *A Logic of Expressive Choice*. Princeton, NJ: Princeton University Press.

Shachar, Ron, and Barry Nalebuff. 1999. "Follow the Leader: Theory and Evidence on Political Participation." *American Economic Review* 89(3): 525–547.

Shanks, David, Richard Tunney, and John McCarthy. 2002. "A Re-examination of Probability Matching and Rational Choice." *Journal of Behavioral Decision Making* 15(3): 233–250.

Shepard, Roger, and Jacqueline Metzler. 1971. "Mental Rotation of Three-Dimensional Objects." *Science* 171: 701–703.

Shepsle, Kenneth. 1996. "Statistical Political Philosophy and Positive Political Theory." In Jeffrey Friedman (ed.), *The Rational Choice Controversy*. New Haven, CT: Yale University Press, pp. 213–222.

Siegel, David A. 2009. "Social Networks and Collective Action." *American Journal of Political Science* 53(1): 122–138.

Silver, E. A. 2004. "An Overview of Heuristic Solution Methods." *Journal of the Operational Research Society* 55(9): 936–956.

Simon, Herbert A. 1954. "Bandwagon and Underdog Effects and the Possibility of Election Predictions." *Public Opinion Quarterly* 18(3): 245–253.

——. 1955. "A Behavioral Model of Rational Choice." *Quarterly Journal of Economics* 69(1): 99–118.

——. 1956. "Rational Choice and the Structure of the Environment." *Psychological Review* 63(2): 129–138.

——. 1957. *Models of Man: Social and Rational*. New York: Wiley.

——. 1964. "The Concept of Organizational Goal." *Administrative Sciences Quarterly* 9(1): 1–22.

——. 1976. "From Substantive to Procedural Rationality." In S. Latsis (ed.), *Method and Appraisal in Economics*. Cambridge: Cambridge University Press, pp. 129–148.

——. 1979a. "Rational Decision Making in Business Organizations." *American Economic Review* 69(4): 493–513.

——. 1979b. *Models of Thought*, Vols. 1 and 2. New Haven, CT: Yale University Press.

——. 1990. "Invariants of Human Behavior." In M. Rosenzweig and L. Porter (eds.), *Annual Review of Psychology*, Vol. 41. Palo Alto, CA: Annual Reviews, pp. 1–19.

——. 1996. *The Sciences of the Artificial*, 3rd ed. Cambridge, MA: MIT Press.

——. 1999. "Problem Solving." In Robert Wilson and Frank Keil (eds.), *The MIT Encyclopedia of the Cognitive Sciences*. Cambridge, MA: MIT Press, pp. 674–676.

Simon, Herbert A. 2001. “Complex Systems: The Interplay of Organizations and Markets in Contemporary Society.” *Computational and Mathematical Organization Theory* 7(2): 79–85.

Simon, Herbert, and Jonathan Schaeffer. 1992. “The Game of Chess.” In Robert J. Aumann and Sergiu Hart (eds.), *Handbook of Game Theory with Economic Applications*, Vol. 1. Amsterdam: North-Holland Press, Elsevier Science Publishers.

Slovic, Paul. 1995. “The Construction of Preference.” *American Psychologist* 50(5): 364–371.

Slovic, Paul, and Sarah Lichtenstein. 1983. “Preference Reversals: A Broader Perspective.” *American Economic Review* 73(4): 596–605.

Sniderman, Paul. 2000. “Taking Sides: A Fixed Choice Theory of Political Reasoning.” In Arthur Lupia, Mathew McCubbins, and Samuel Popkin (eds.), *Elements of Reason: Cognition, Choice, and the Bounds of Rationality.* Cambridge: Cambridge University Press, pp. 67–84.

Sniderman, Paul M., and John Bullock. 2004. “A Consistency Theory of Public Opinion and Political Choice: The Hypothesis of Menu Dependence.” In Willem E. Saris and Paul M. Sniderman (eds.), *Studies in Public Opinion.* Princeton, NJ: Princeton University Press, pp. 337–357.

Stalnaker, Robert. 1999. “Logical Omniscience, Problem of.” In Robert Wilson and Frank Keil (eds.), *The MIT Encyclopedia of the Cognitive Sciences.* Cambridge, MA: MIT Press, pp. 489–490.

Stanovich, Keith, and Richard West. 2000. “Individual Differences in Reasoning: Implications for the Rationality Debate?” *Behavioral and Brain Sciences* 23(5): 645–665.

Stevenson, Betsey, and Justin Wolfers. 2008. “Economic Growth and Subjective Well-Being: Reassessing the Easterlin Paradox.” *Brookings Papers on Economic Activity*, Spring 2008: 1–87.

Stokes, Donald. 1963. “Spatial Models of Party Competition.” *American Political Science Review* 57(2): 368–377.

Stokes, Susan. 1999. “Political Parties and Democracy.” In Nelson Polsby (ed.), *Annual Review of Political Science*, Vol. 2. Palo Alto, CA: Annual Reviews, pp. 243–267.

Stufflebeam, Robert. 1999. “Representation and Computation.” In William Bechtel and George Graham (eds.), *A Companion Guide to Cognitive Science.* Oxford: Blackwell, pp. 636–648.

Taylor, Howard, and Samuel Karlin. 1998. *An Introduction to Stochastic Modeling*, 3rd ed. New York: Academic Press.

Thorndike, Edward L. 1898. “Animal Intelligence: An Experimental Study of the Associative Processes in Animals.” *Psychological Review* (Monograph Supplement) 2(8).

Tversky, Amos, and Daniel Kahneman. 1983. “Extensional Versus Intuitive Reasoning: The Conjunction Fallacy in Probability Judgment.” *Psychological Review* 90(4): 293–315.

——. 1986. “Rational Choice and the Framing of Decisions.” *Journal of Business* 59(4): S251–S278.

Tversky, Barbara. 2005. "Visuospatial Reasoning." In Keith Holyoak and Robert Morrison (eds.), *The Cambridge Handbook of Thinking and Reasoning.* Cambridge, MA: Cambridge University Press, pp. 209–240.

Vulkan, Nir. 2000. "An Economist's Perspective on Probability Matching." *Journal of Economic Surveys* 14(1): 101–118.

Weber, Elke, and Eric Johnson. 2009. "Mindful Judgment and Decision Making." *Annual Review of Psychology*, Vol. 60. Palo Alto, CA: Annual Reviews, pp. 53–85.

West, Richard, and Keith Stanovich. 2003. "Is Probability Matching Smart? Associations Between Probabilistic Choices and Cognitive Ability." *Memory and Cognition* 31(2): 243–251.

Whittle, Peter. 1983. *Optimization over Time: Dynamic Programming and Stochastic Control.* New York: Wiley.

Wittman, Donald. 1983. "Candidate Motivation: A Synthesis of Alternative Theories." *American Political Science Review* 77(1): 142–157.

Wrong, Dennis. 1961. "The Oversocialized Conception of Man in Modern Sociology." *American Sociological Review* 26(2): 183–193.

Index